Part 7 Types of Speeches 155

22. Informative Speaking 156
23. Principles of Persuasive Speaking 167
24. Constructing the Persuasive Speech 174
25. Speaking on Special Occasions 192

Part 8 Online, Group, and Business Contexts 203

26. Preparing Online Presentations 204
27. Communicating in Groups 210
28. Delivering Group Presentations 214
29. Business and Professional Presentations 218

Part 9 Speaking in Other College Courses 225

30. Presentations Assigned across the Curriculum 226
31. Science and Mathematics Courses 231
32. Technical Courses 235
33. Social Science Courses 238
34. Arts and Humanities Courses 240
35. Education Courses 243
36. Nursing and Allied Health Courses 245

Appendices 249

A. Citation Guidelines 250
B. Question-and-Answer Sessions 263
C. Preparing for Mediated Communication 264
D. Tips for Non-Native Speakers of English 266

Glossary 270

Index 305

Macmillan Education
LaunchPadSolo

macmillanhighered.com/pocketspeak5e

A Pocket Guide to Public Speaking

FIFTH EDITION

Dan O'Hair
University of Kentucky

Hannah Rubenstein

Rob Stewart
Texas Tech University

Bedford/St.Martin's
A Macmillan Education Imprint

Boston • New York

For Bedford/St. Martin's

Vice President, Editorial, Macmillan Higher Education Humanities: Edwin Hill

Publisher for Communication: Erika Gutierrez

Development Manager: Susan McLaughlin

Senior Developmental Editor: Lorraina Morrison

Senior Media Editor: Tom Kane

Editorial Assistant: Will Stonefield

Senior Production Editor: Pamela Lawson

Production Supervisors: Dennis Conroy, Victoria Anzalone

Marketing Manager: Thomas Digiano

Copy Editor: Denise P. Quirk

Director of Rights and Permissions: Hilary Newman

Senior Art Director: Anna Palchik

Text Design: Kall Design

Cover Design: John Callahan

Composition: Jouve

Printing and Binding: RR Donnelley and Sons

0   9   8
f   e

For information, write: Bedford/St. Martin's, 75 Arlington Street, Boston, MA 02116   (617-399-4000)

ISBN 978-1-4576-7040-4   Manufactured in China.
ISBN 978-1-319-01977-8   Manufactured in the U.S.

Acknowledgments

Joe Ayres and Tim S. Hopf. "Visualization: Is It More than Extra-Attention?" From Communication Education, Volume 38 (1989), pp. 1–5. Reprinted by permission of Taylor & Francis Ltd. **www .informaworld.com**.

At the time of publication all Internet URLs published in this text were found to accurately link to their intended website. If you do find a broken link, please forward the information to Will.Stonefield@macmillan.com so that it can be corrected for the next printing.

How to Use the Book and Digital Resources ●●●●

A Pocket Guide to Public Speaking, Fifth Edition, is designed to provide quick, clear answers to your questions about public speaking—whether you're in a public speaking class, in a course in your major, on the job, or in your community. Here you will find the tools you need to help you prepare and deliver a wide range of speeches and presentations.

In Parts 1 through 5 you will find chapters that cover all the steps necessary to create a speech—from planning, research, and development to organization, practice, and delivery. Part 6 includes three chapters about presentation aids and how to use them effectively. Chapters in Part 7 contain guidelines for creating three of the most commonly assigned speeches in public speaking classes: *informative, persuasive,* and *special occasion.* For specific guidelines on preparing online presentations, communicating and speaking in small groups, and speaking on the job, see Part 8. Part 9 contains advice on speaking in other college courses, from science and math to engineering, education, and nursing and allied health.

◉ Finding What You Need

TABLES OF CONTENTS. Browsing through the brief table of contents inside the front cover will usually guide you to the information you need. If not, consult the more detailed table of contents included inside the back cover.

INDEX. If you can't locate what you need in either set of contents, consult the index at the back of the book, beginning on page 305. This can be especially useful if you're looking for something specific and you know the term for it. For example, if you need to prepare a sales proposal for a business course, you could simply look under "sales proposal" in the index and then go to the designated pages.

LISTS OF FEATURES. On pages 317–21 (just before the end of the book), you'll find a quick guide to some of the most consulted parts of this book: the *Checklists, Quick Tips, Visual Guides* (illustrated explanations of key points), and full-length model speeches.

SPEAKING BEYOND THE SPEECH CLASSROOM. In Part 8, "Online, Group, and Business Contexts," you'll find useful information on preparing online presentations, communicating and speaking in groups, and interacting in the workplace. In Part 9, "Speaking in Other College Courses," you'll find detailed directions for speaking in a range of college classes including courses in the social sciences, arts and humanities, education, science and mathematics, engineering and architecture, and nursing and allied health.

GLOSSARY. For definitions of key terms highlighted in the book, see pages 270–90.

Quick Speech Preparation

If you have to prepare a speech quickly (for example, giving a first speech early in the semester), consult Chapters 1–3 in *A Pocket Guide:*

- Chapter 1, "Becoming a Public Speaker," provides a brief discussion of public speaking basics.
- Chapter 2, "From A to Z: Overview of a Speech," offers quick guidance on each step in the speechmaking process, from selecting a topic to delivery.
- Chapter 3, "Managing Speech Anxiety," provides techniques that will help you overcome any fears of public speaking you may have.

For more on specific types of speeches, consult Chapters 22–25 in Part 7 on informative, persuasive, and special occasion speeches, or the appropriate chapter in Part 8 or Part 9.

Other Useful Tools

CITATION GUIDELINES. Appendix A (pp. 250–62) contains guidelines for documenting sources in the following styles: *Chicago*, American Psychological Association (APA), Modern Language Association (MLA), Council of Science Editors (CSE), and Institute of Electrical and Electronics Engineers (IEEE).

TIPS FOR NON-NATIVE SPEAKERS OF ENGLISH. Appendix D (pp. 266–69) addresses the most common ESL challenges, including pronunciation of certain words and challenges in being understood.

macmillanhighered.com/pocketspeak5e

LaunchPad Solo is a new, easy-to-use platform that offers digital tools to support the speechmaking process. It contains high-quality multimedia content and ready-made assessment options, including LearningCurve adaptive quizzing that will give you a leg up on learning the concepts. Your book may have come with an access card to LaunchPad Solo at your instructor's request. If not, access can be purchased online from the URL listed above.

✓ LearningCurve

LearningCurve is an online learning tool that adapts to what you already know and helps you learn the topics that you need to practice. LearningCurve ensures that you receive as much targeted practice as you need in order to master the material.

▶ Video

LaunchPad Solo for *A Pocket Guide to Public Speaking* provides access to more than two hundred fifty video clips. The functionality of VideoTools aids in the review of student speech videos by enabling instructors to create video assignments. Students can easily upload their own speech videos for review and evaluation. Both instructors and students can add video from the LaunchPad Library, YouTube, or their own collection, use time-based comments to discuss the video, and then evaluate video using rubrics.

Video icons appear near sample speeches to encourage students to watch the related video in LaunchPad Solo.

e E-readings

E-readings offer additional and useful online content, including a complete tutorial on how to create presentation aids using Microsoft PowerPoint, Prezi, and Apple Keynote.

E-readings icons are included in the chapters and highlighted when additional reference materials are available in LaunchPad Solo.

Preface ● ●●

The Fifth Edition of *A Pocket Guide to Public Speaking* reflects our continuing mission to provide students with a truly effective speech resource that is comprehensive yet brief, affordable, and student friendly, based on solid scholarship and the rhetorical tradition. We designed this guide to be useful in the widest possible range of situations, from the traditional speech classroom and courses across the curriculum, to the workplace, and in the community.

Our primary goal in writing *A Pocket Guide* has always been to meet the needs of speech instructors who find mainstream, full-size introductory speech texts either too overwhelming or too prescriptive for their classes. In addition, we hope to satisfy instructors in other disciplines who want an easy and affordable tool for teaching presentation skills. We also aim to adapt to the changing realities of technology in the discipline by providing helpful guidance on online research and online presentations as well as digital options for reading and studying with *A Pocket Guide* that students can access easily on a number of devices.

A Pocket Guide to Public Speaking has been a popular choice for instructors and students since the first edition was published in 2003. More than 280,000 instructors and students across the academic spectrum—from courses in speech and the humanities to education, engineering, and business—have embraced the book, making it the most successful pocket-size speech text available. We have used their helpful feedback to create this fifth edition.

◉ Features

A Pocket Guide to Public Speaking addresses all of the topics and skills typically covered in an introductory speech text. And because the book is meant to be used throughout students' academic careers and in a wide variety of classroom settings and beyond, examples are drawn from a broad range of speech situations and disciplines. Speech excerpts, sample outlines, and full-length visually annotated sample speeches provide useful models that help students see how speech fundamentals can be applied effectively.

Throughout the text, users will find many tools to help them focus on key public speaking concepts: charts and tables that summarize salient points; *Checklists* that reinforce critical content; insightful *Quick Tips* that offer succinct and practical advice; *Visual Guides* that illustrate the steps for accomplishing challenging speech tasks; and *Appendices* that offer citation guidelines, help with question-and-answer sessions and mediated communication, and support for non-native speakers of English.

◉ **New to This Edition**

As with previous editions, we received feedback from hundreds of instructors about the challenges of teaching and learning public and presentational speaking. The new edition is designed to help students master basic skills while also addressing the new challenges that digital technology brings to public speaking:

- **An all-new, four-color design makes it even easier for students to find the advice that they need.** Vibrant color now directs students to the text's rich pedagogical features including *Quick Tips, Checklists, Visual Guides,* graphs, and tables. New yellow "sticky notes" visually annotate sample speeches instantly and highlight speech commentary.

- **Two new informative speeches and two new persuasive speeches,** accompanied by questions in LaunchPad Solo, show how speakers can polish their organization and delivery. These all-new, professionally shot speech videos include high-interest topics such as "freeganism" and social media. The LaunchPad Solo features "Needs Improvement" clips to help students recognize and avoid common pitfalls in their own speeches. Full-text versions of one informative and one persuasive speech appear in the book, along with electronic transcripts and closed captioning online. Also new to this edition is a sample special occasion speech: President Obama's moving eulogy for Nelson Mandela.

- **Comprehensive video collection in LaunchPad Solo containing more than 250 clips and full-length speeches,** including professional speeches, model student speeches, and "Needs Improvement" clips that highlight typical issues.

- **A wealth of new research.** The fifth edition of *A Pocket Guide* reflects research gleaned from a record 113 new peer-reviewed studies, in chapters ranging from listening (12 new studies), ethics (12), and audience analysis (17), to persuasion (15) and many others.

- **Even better coverage of the basic principles of speechmaking.** Thoroughly revised core chapters on listening, audience analysis, ethics, topic, and purpose succinctly address core principles while incorporating the most recent scholarship.

- **More comprehensive coverage of persuasive speaking.** Expanded coverage in two chapters includes an overview of classical and contemporary approaches (Chapter 23, "Principles of Persuasive Speaking"), and the building blocks of argument and tools of reasoning (Chapter 24,

"Constructing the Persuasive Speech"). New sections on counterargument and a call to action show students how to use these techniques to make the most effective appeals in their speeches.

- **New chapter on researching the speech reflects contemporary realities of how students locate sources.** Chapter 9, "Finding Credible Sources in Print and Online," offers a practical and ethical approach to searching for supporting materials aligned with the way that students do their research today.

- **New coverage of creating presentation aids and delivering virtual presentations.** Revised Chapters 19–21 show students how to create and deliver effective presentations while avoiding technical glitches. Chapter 21 provides an overview of using presentation software; a LaunchPad–only tutorial offers in-depth coverage of Microsoft PowerPoint, Prezi, and Apple Keynote. An updated chapter on online presentations (Chapter 26) provides students with more detailed techniques and a new video of an online speech in LaunchPad Solo.

- **New coverage of speaking in other college courses backed by professionals from each field.** We received detailed comments from professors who teach public speaking in the social sciences, sciences, and humanities, and incorporated this feedback into the revision. New guidelines and reenvisioned chapter content give today's students the tools and templates they need to prepare presentations in other disciplines. Chapters 30–36 offer guidance on *23 types of specialized presentations*, from scientific talks, to literature reviews, service learning presentations, reports and proposals in business and technical courses, presentations in nursing and allied health, and much more.

Digital and Print Formats

- For more information on formats and packaging options, please visit the online catalog at **macmillanhighered .com/pocketspeak/catalog**

- LaunchPad Solo for *A Pocket Guide to Public Speaking* is available as a print text. To get the most out of the book, package the print book with LaunchPad Solo for *A Pocket Guide to Public Speaking*, a dynamic platform that dramatically enhances teaching and learning. LaunchPad Solo includes LearningCurve adaptive quizzing; VideoTools, with over 250 sample speech videos, which enables instructors to create video assignments; and a tutorial on creating presentations using Microsoft PowerPoint, Apple Keynote, and Prezi. It is available packaged at a significant discount with the text. Use ISBN: 978-1-4576-7040-4.

- **E-books.** *A Pocket Guide to Public Speaking* is available in PDF e-book formats for use on computers, tablets, and e-readers. See **macmillanhighered.com/ebooks** to learn more.

- **Customize *A Pocket Guide to Public Speaking*.** Add your own content or more of ours to make the book your own. Qualified adopters will have the ability to create a version of *A Pocket Guide to Public Speaking* that exactly matches your specific needs. Learn more about custom options at **macmillanhighered.com/catalog /page/custom-solutions**.

Resources for Students and Instructors

For more information on student resources or to learn about package options, please visit the Macmillan online catalog at **macmillanhighered.com/pocketspeak/catalog**.

Print Resources for Students

- ***The Essential Guides.*** These brief yet comprehensive and affordable print booklets focus on a range of topics and are designed to supplement a main text in a public speaking course. These guides are available to be packaged with *A Pocket Guide to Public Speaking* for a very low price. Versions include *The Essential Guide to Rhetoric* by William M. Keith and Christian O. Lundberg; *The Essential Guide to Presentation Software*, Second Edition, by Allison Joy Bailey and Rob Patterson; *The Essential Guide to Intercultural Communication* by Jennifer Willis-Rivera; *The Essential Guide to Interpersonal Communication*, Second Edition, by Dan O'Hair and Mary O. Wiemann; and *The Essential Guide to Group Communication*, Second Edition, by Dan O'Hair and Mary O. Wiemann.

Instructor Resources

For more information or to download the instructor resources, please visit the online catalog at **macmillanhighered.com /pocketspeak/catalog**. These instructor resources are also available with LaunchPad Solo for *A Pocket Guide to Public Speaking*.

- ***Instructor's Resource Manual.*** The online instructor's manual is prepared by Karin Becker, *University of North Dakota*; Paula Baldwin, *George Mason University*; Elaine Wittenberg-Lyles, *University of North Texas*; and Melinda M. Villagran, *George Mason University*. This comprehensive manual offers useful guidance for new and experienced instructors, and outlines and activities for every chapter in the main text. The *Instructor's Resource Manual for A Pocket Guide to Public Speaking*, Fifth Edition, offers new guidance on online instruction and using video from LaunchPad Solo, advice about civility in the classroom, suggestions for preparing mediated presentations, and updated guidelines on presentations across the curriculum.

- **Computerized Test Bank.** The Computerized Test Bank is prepared by Diana Rehling, *St. Cloud State University*; Paula K. Baldwin, *George Mason University*; Elaine Wittenberg-Lyles, *University of North Texas*; and Merry Buchanan, *University of Central Oklahoma*. The Computerized Test Bank contains more than fifteen hundred true/false, multiple-choice, fill-in-the-blank, and essay/ short answer questions that have been carefully crafted to test students' specific knowledge of the text. The questions appear in easy-to-use software that allows instructors to add, edit, resequence, and print questions and answers. Instructors can also export the questions into a variety of course management systems. The Computerized Test Bank can be downloaded from the Instructor Resources tab of the book's catalog page, and the content is loaded into LaunchPad Solo.

- **ESL Students in the Public Speaking Classroom: A Guide for Instructors, Second Edition.** Robbin D. Crabtree, *Loyola Marymount University*; and David Alan Sapp, *Fairfield University*. This guide addresses specific challenges ESL students may experience in the public speaking course and offers instructors valuable advice for helping students overcome obstacles.

◉ Acknowledgments

We would like to thank all our colleagues at Bedford/St. Martin's: Vice President of Editorial for the Humanities Edwin Hill, Publisher Erika Gutierrez, Development Manager Susan McLaughlin, Marketing Manager Tom Digiano, Managing Editor Elise Kaiser, hardworking and careful Senior Project Editor Pamela Lawson, Senior Production Supervisor Dennis Conroy, lightning-quick and helpful Editorial Assistant Will Stonefield, Editor Alexis Smith, and Senior New Media Editor Tom Kane—we are truly grateful for your knowledge, creativity, expertise, and hard work throughout this process. We are especially grateful to freelance development editor Angela Kao for her thoughtful and patient editing and Senior Editor Lorraina Morrison for her supervisory developmental editing and tireless stewarding of this text through every stage of this revision and to market.

Thanks to all the instructors who participated in reviews for the fifth edition: Marlene Atkins, *The Illinois Institute of Art-Shaumburg;* Karin Becker, *University of North Dakota;* Kathy Berggren, *Cornell University;* Ayanna Bridges, *Metropolitan Community College–Maple Woods;* Sharee Broussard, *Spring Hill College;* Carolyn Clark, *Salt Lake Community College;* Elaine Vander Clute, *Wor-Wic Community College;* Donna Craine, *Front Range Community College;* Judith Ferrand, *Wor-Wic Community College;* Natalie Gerber, *State University of New York at Fredonia;* Cheryl Golemo, *William Rainey Harper College;* Nicholas Greco IV, *Columbia College of Missouri–Lake County Campus;* Kim Higgs, *University of North Dakota;* Bruce Holmes, *Stratford University;* Lynn Ingram, *University of North Carolina Wilmington;* Nancy Jennings, *Cuyamaca College;* Amanda Martinez, *Davidson College;* William Maze, *Northwest Mississippi Community College;* Renae Myszkowski, *University of North Dakota;* Mary Haslerud Opp, *University of North Dakota;* Diana Rehling, *St. Cloud State University;* Anne Scarlett, *Columbia College;* Brian Simmons, *University of Portland;* Amy M. Smith, *Salem State University;* Ron Vanderveer, *Eastern Florida State College;* Kerri Williams, *Lourdes University;* Calvin Young, *Fullerton College.*

part

Getting Started

● ● ● ● ● ● ● ● ● ● ● ● ●

1. Becoming a Public Speaker   2

2. From A to Z: Overview of a Speech   8

3. Managing Speech Anxiety   13

4. Ethical Public Speaking   20

5. Listeners and Speakers   27

CHAPTER 1

Becoming a Public Speaker

Whether in the classroom, workplace, or community, the ability to speak confidently and convincingly before an audience is empowering. This pocket guide offers the tools you need to create and deliver effective speeches, from presentations to fellow students to speeches delivered in virtually any setting—including those delivered online. Here you will find the basic building blocks of any good speech and acquire the skills to deliver presentations in a variety of specialized contexts—from the college classroom to the civic, business, and professional arenas. You'll also find proven techniques to build your confidence by overcoming the anxiety associated with public speaking.

◎ Gain a Vital Life Skill

Skill in public speaking will give you an unmistakable edge Now, more than ever, public speaking has become both a vital life skill and a potent weapon in career development. Business magnate Warren Buffet passionately extols the role that public speaking has played in his success:

> Be sure to do it, whether you like it or not . . . do it until you get comfortable with it. . . . Public speaking is an asset that will last you 50 or 60 years, and it's a necessary skill; and if you don't like doing it, that will also last you 50 or 60 years. . . . Once you tackle the fear and master the skill, you can run the world. You can walk into rooms, command people, and get them to listen to you and your great ideas.[1]

SKILLS EMPLOYERS SEEK

1. Leadership ability
2. Ability to work in a team
3. Skill in written communication
4. Problem-solving skills
5. Strong work ethic
6. Analytic/quantitative and technical skills
7. **Skill in verbal communication**
8. Initiative
9. Computer skills
10. Flexibility/adaptability

Source: National Association of Colleges and Employers, *Job Outlook 2015*, **www.naceweb.org**.

Skill in public speaking will give you an unmistakable edge professionally. Recruiters of recent graduates report that what distinguishes the most sought-after candidates is not the "hard" knowledge of their majors, which employers take for granted, but the "soft" skills of superior communication, which fewer candidates display.[2] Similarly, dozens of surveys of managers and executives reveal that ability in oral and written communication is among the most important skills they look for in new hires. For example, oral communication skills consistently rank in the top spots among such critical areas as leadership, teamwork, problem-solving, analytic and technical skills, and work ethic. Survey after survey confirm the value of verbal and written communication skills to employers across the board, making the public speaking course potentially the most valuable one you can take during your undergraduate career.

Enhance Your Career as a Student

Preparing speeches calls upon numerous skills that you can apply in other college courses. As in the speech class, many courses also require that you research and write about topics, analyze audiences, outline and organize ideas, and support claims. These and other skill sets covered in this pocket guide, such as working with presentation media and controlling voice and body during delivery, are valuable in any course that includes an oral-presentation component, from English composition to engineering.

Find New Opportunities for Civic Engagement

Public speaking also offers you ways to enter the public conversation about social concerns and become a more engaged citizen. Public speaking gives you a voice that can be heard and can be counted.

Climate change, energy, government debt, immigration reform — such large civic issues require our considered judgment and action. Yet today too many of us leave it up to politicians, journalists, and other "experts" to make decisions about critical issues such as these. Not including presidential elections, only about 35 percent of people in the United States regularly vote. Of these, only 22 percent are 18 to 29 years old.[3] When we as citizens speak up in sufficient numbers, democracy functions better and change that truly reflects the will of the people occurs.

As you study public speaking, you will have the opportunity to research topics that are meaningful to you, consider alternate viewpoints, and choose a course of action.[4] You will learn to distinguish between argument that advances constructive goals and uncivil speech that serves merely to inflame and demean others. You will learn, in short, the "rules of engagement" for effective public discourse.[5] As you do, you will gain confidence in your ability to join your voice with others in pursuit of issues you care about.

◉ The Classical Roots of Public Speaking

Originally, the practice of giving speeches was known as **rhetoric** or **oratory**. Rhetoric flourished in the Greek city-state of Athens in the fifth century B.C.E. and referred to making effective speeches, particularly those of a persuasive nature.

Athens was the site of the world's first direct democracy, and public speaking was the vehicle that allowed it to succeed. Meeting in a public square called the **agora**, Athenians routinely spoke with great skill on the issues of public policy; and their belief that citizenship demands active participation in public affairs endures in modern democracies to this day.

Greek, and later Roman, teachers divided the process of preparing a speech into five parts—*invention, arrangement, style, memory,* and *delivery*—called the **canons of rhetoric**. These parts correspond to the order in which these teachers believed a speech should be put together.

- *Invention* refers to discovering the types of evidence and arguments you will use to make your case.
- *Arrangement* is organizing the speech in ways best suited to the topic and audience.
- *Style* is the way the speaker uses language to express the speech ideas.
- *Memory* is the practice of the speech until it can be delivered artfully.
- *Delivery* is the vocal and nonverbal behavior you use when speaking.

Although founding scholars such as the great Greek rhetorician Aristotle (384–322 B.C.E.) and the Roman statesman and orator Cicero (106–43 B.C.E.) surely did not anticipate the omnipresent Prezi slide show that accompanies contemporary speeches, the speechmaking structure they bequeathed to us as the canon of rhetoric remains remarkably intact. Often identified by terms other than the original, these canons nonetheless continue to be taught in current books on public speaking, including this pocket guide.

◉ Learning to Speak in Public

None of us is born knowing how to deliver a successful speech. Instead, public speaking is an acquired skill that improves with practice. It is also a skill that shares much in common with other familiar activities, such as conversing and writing, and

QUICK TIP

Voice Your Ideas in a Public Forum

The Greeks called it the *agora*; the Romans the *forum*. Today, the term **public forum** denotes a variety of venues for the discussion of issues of public interest, including traditional physical spaces such as town halls as well as virtual forums streamed to listeners online. Participation in any of these forums offers an excellent opportunity to pose questions and deliver brief comments, thereby providing exposure to an audience and building confidence. To find a forum in your area, check with your school or local town government, or check online at sites such as the National Issues Forum (**www.nifi.org**).

it can be much less daunting when you realize that you can draw on expertise you already have.

Draw on Conversational Skills

In several respects, planning and delivering a speech resembles engaging in a particularly important conversation. When speaking with a friend, you automatically check to make certain you are understood and adjust your meaning accordingly. You also tend to discuss issues that are appropriate to the circumstances. When a relative stranger is involved, however, you try to get to know his or her interests and attitudes before revealing any strong opinions. These instinctive adjustments to your audience, topic, and occasion represent critical steps in creating a speech. Although public speaking requires more planning, both the conversationalist and the public speaker try to uncover the audience's interests and needs before speaking.

Draw on Skills in Composition

Preparing a speech also has much in common with writing. Both depend on having a focused sense of who the audience is.[6] Both speaking and writing often require that you research a topic, offer credible evidence, employ effective transitions, and devise persuasive appeals. The principles of organizing a speech parallel those of organizing an essay, including offering a compelling introduction, a clear thesis statement, supporting ideas, and a thoughtful conclusion.

Develop an Effective Oral Style

Although public speaking has much in common with everyday conversation and with writing, a speech is a unique form of communication characterized by an oral style of language.

Spoken language is simpler, more rhythmic, more repetitious, and more interactive than either conversation or writing.[7] Effective speakers use familiar words and easy-to-follow sentences. *Repetition* in even the briefest speeches is key, and speakers routinely repeat key words and phrases to emphasize ideas and help listeners follow along.

Spoken language also is often more *interactive* and *inclusive* of the audience than written language. Audience members want to know what the speaker thinks and feels and that he or she recognizes them and relates the message to them. Speakers accomplish this by making specific references to themselves and to the audience. Yet in contrast to conversation, in order to develop an effective oral style you must practice the words you will say and the way you will say them.

Effective public speakers, engaging conversationalists, and compelling writers share an important quality: They keep their focus on offering something of value for the audience.

Demonstrate Respect for Difference

Every audience member wants to feel that the speaker has his or her particular needs and interests at heart, and to feel recognized and included in the message. To create this sense of inclusion, a public speaker must be able to address diverse audiences with sensitivity, demonstrating respect for differences in culture and identity. Striving for inclusion and adopting an audience-centered perspective will bring you closer to the goal of every public speaker—establishing a genuine connection with the audience.

◉ Public Speaking as a Form of Communication

Public speaking is one of four categories of human communication: dyadic, small group, mass, and public speaking.

- **Dyadic communication** happens between two people, as in a conversation.
- **Small group communication** involves a small number of people who can see and speak directly with one another.
- **Mass communication** occurs between a speaker and a large audience of unknown people who usually are not present with the speaker, or who are part of such an immense crowd that there can be little or no interaction between speaker and listener. In **public speaking**, a speaker delivers a message with a specific purpose to an audience of people who are present during the delivery of the speech.

Public speaking always includes a speaker who has a reason for speaking, an audience that gives the speaker its attention, and a message that is meant to accomplish a specific purpose. Public speakers address audiences largely without interruption and take responsibility for the words and ideas being expressed.

◉ Public Speaking as an Interactive Communication Process

In any communication event, several elements are present. These include the source, the receiver, the message, the channel, and shared meaning (see Figure 1.1).

The **source**, or sender, creates a message. Creating, organizing, and producing the message is called **encoding**—the process of converting thoughts into words.

The recipient of the source's message is the **receiver**, or audience; interpreting the message is called **decoding**. Audience members decode the meaning of the message selectively, based on their own experiences and attitudes. **Feedback**, the audience's response to a message, can be conveyed both verbally and nonverbally.

The **message** is the content of the communication process: thoughts and ideas put into meaningful expressions, expressed verbally and nonverbally.

The medium through which the speaker sends a message is the **channel**. If a speaker delivers a message in front of a live audience, the channel is the air through which sound waves travel. Other channels include telephone, television, and the Internet.

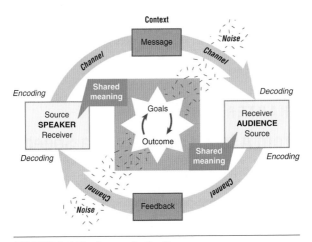

FIGURE 1.1 The Communication Process

Noise is any interference with the message. Noise can disrupt the communication process through physical sounds such as cell phones ringing and people talking or texting, through psychological distractions such as heated emotions, or through environmental interference such as a frigid room or the presence of unexpected people.

Shared meaning is the mutual understanding of a message between speaker and audience. The lowest level of shared meaning exists when the speaker has merely caught the audience's attention. As the message develops, a higher degree of shared meaning is possible. Thus listener and speaker together truly make a speech a speech—they "co-create" its meaning.

Two other factors are critical to consider when preparing and delivering a speech—context and goals. *Context* includes anything that influences the speaker, the audience, the occasion—and thus, ultimately, the speech. In classroom speeches, the context would include (among other things) recent events on campus or in the outside world, the physical setting, the order and timing of speeches, and the cultural orientations of audience members. Successful communication can never be divorced from the concerns and expectations of others.

Part of the context of any speech is the situation that created the need for it in the first place. All speeches are delivered in response to a specific **rhetorical situation**, or a circumstance calling for a public response.[8] Bearing the rhetorical situation in mind ensures that you maintain an **audience-centered perspective**—that is, that you keep the needs, values, attitudes, and wants of your listeners firmly in focus.

A clearly defined *speech purpose* or goal—what you want the audience to learn or do as a result of the speech—is a final prerequisite for an effective speech. Establishing a speech purpose early on will help you proceed through speech preparation and delivery with a clear focus in mind.

CHAPTER 2 ●●●●

From A to Z: Overview of a Speech

Public speaking is an applied art, and every speaking opportunity, including that provided by the classroom, offers you valuable hands-on experience. To help you get started as quickly as possible, this chapter previews the steps involved in putting together any speech or presentation. Subsequent chapters expand on these steps.

◉ Analyze the Audience

Figure 2.1 illustrates the process of preparing for a speech. The first step is to consider the audience—how their interests, needs, and opinions will influence their responses toward a given topic, speaker, and occasion. *Audience analysis* is a process of learning about audience members' attributes and motivations through techniques such as interviews and questionnaires (see Chapter 6). For a brief first speech, however, gather what information you can about the audience in the time allotted. Consider some *demographic characteristics:* ratio of males to females, age ranges, cultural background, and socioeconomic status. Take into account these characteristics as you select your topic and draft the speech, focusing on ways you can relate it meaningfully to your audience.

◉ Select a Topic

Unless the topic is assigned, the next step is to decide what you want to speak about. First, consider the speech occasion and reason for speaking. What topics will be suitable to your audience's needs and wants in these circumstances? Within these parameters, use your own interests and expertise to guide you in selecting something to speak about (see Chapter 7 for a discussion on finding topics).

◉ Determine the Speech Purpose

Decide what you want to accomplish with your speech. For any given topic, you should direct your speech toward one of three *general speech purposes*—to *inform*, to *persuade*, or to *mark a special occasion.* Thus you need to decide whether your goal is simply to give your audience information about the topic, to convince them to accept one position to the exclusion of other positions, or to mark a special occasion such as a wedding, a funeral, or an awards event.

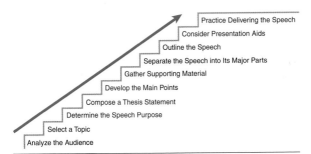

FIGURE 2.1 **Steps in the Speechmaking Process**

Your speech should also have a *specific speech purpose*—what you want the audience to learn or do as a result of your speech. For example, if your general purpose is to inform, your specific purpose might be "to inform my audience about recent changes in federal college student loan programs." If your general purpose is to persuade, the specific purpose might be "to convince my audience that they should support improving government aid to college students."

◉ Compose a Thesis Statement

Next, compose a thesis statement that clearly expresses the central idea of your speech. While the specific purpose focuses your attention on the outcome you want to achieve with the speech, the *thesis statement* concisely identifies to your audience, in a single sentence, what the speech is about:

General Purpose:	To inform
Specific Purpose:	To inform my audience about three critical steps we can take to combat identity theft and maintain identity security.
Thesis Statement:	The best ways to combat identity theft and keep yourself secure are to review your monthly financial statements, periodically check your credit report, and secure your personal information in both digital and print form.

From this point forward in the development of your speech, refer to the thesis statement often to make sure that you are on track to illustrate or prove it.

QUICK TIP

Speak with Purpose

To ensure that the audience learns or does what you want them to as a result of your speech, keep your thesis and speech goals in sight. Write your thesis statement and general and specific speech purposes on a sticky note and place it on the edge of your computer screen. It will be an important guide in developing your speech.

◉ Develop the Main Points

Organize your speech around two or three *main points*. These are the primary pieces of knowledge (in an informative speech) or the key claims (in a persuasive speech). If you create a clear thesis for your speech, the main points will be easily identifiable, if not explicit:

Thesis: The best ways to combat identity theft and keep yourself secure are to review your monthly financial statements, periodically check your credit report, and secure your personal information in both digital and print form.

    I. Review your monthly bank statements, credit card bills, and similar financial records to be certain that you are aware of all transactions.

    II. Check your consumer credit report at least twice a year.

    III. Keep your personal identifying digital and print information secure.

◉ Gather Supporting Materials

Illustrate the main points with supporting material that clarifies, elaborates, and verifies your ideas. Supporting material potentially includes the entire world of information available to you—from personal experiences to every conceivable kind of external source. Plan to research your topic to provide evidence for your assertions and lend credibility to your message (see Chapter 9).

◉ Separate the Speech into Its Major Parts

Every speech will have an *introduction*, a *body*, and a *conclusion.* Develop each part separately, then bring them together using transition statements (see Chapter 11). The *introduction* serves to gain the audience's attention and interest by introducing the topic and speaker and alerting the audience to your thesis (see Chapter 14). The speech *body* contains the speech's main points and subpoints, arranged to support the speech's thesis. The *conclusion* restates the speech thesis and reiterates how the main points confirm it (see Chapter 14).

◉ Outline the Speech

An outline is a plan for arranging the elements of your speech in support of your thesis. Outlines are based on the principle of *coordination and subordination*—the logical placement of ideas relative to their importance to one another. *Coordinate points* are of equal importance and are indicated by their parallel alignment. *Subordinate points* are given less weight than

---

DEVELOPING SPEECH PARTS

Introduction

- Pique the audience's interest with a quotation, a short story, an example, or other means of gaining their attention described in Chapter 14.
- Introduce yourself and your topic.
- Preview the thesis and main points.

(Use a transition statement to signal the start of the speech body.)

Body

- Develop the main points and illustrate each one with relevant supporting material.
- Organize your ideas and evidence in a structure that suits the topic, audience, and occasion.

(Use transitions to move between main points and to the conclusion.)

Conclusion

- Review the thesis and reiterate how the main points confirm it.
- Leave the audience with something to think about.

---

the main points they support and are placed to the right of the points they support. (For a full discussion of outlining, see Chapter 13.)

Coordinate Points	**I.** Main Point 1
	II. Main Point 2
	A. Subpoint 1
	B. Subpoint 2
Subordinate Points	**I.** Main Point 1
	A. First level of subordination
	1. Second level of subordination
	2. Second level of subordination
	a. Third level of subordination
	b. Third level of subordination

As your speeches become more detailed, you will need to select an appropriate *organizational pattern* (see Chapters 12 and 24). You will also need to familiarize yourself with developing both working and speaking outlines (see Chapter 13). To allow for the full development of your ideas, *working outlines* generally contain points stated in close-to-complete sentences. *Speaking outlines* are far briefer and use either short phrases or key words.

◖ Consider Presentation Aids

As you prepare your speech, consider whether using visual, audio, or a combination of different *presentation aids* will help the audience understand points. (See Chapters 19–21.)

◖ Practice Delivering the Speech

Preparation and practice are necessary for the success of even your first speech in class. You will want to feel and appear "natural" to your listeners, an effect best achieved by rehearsing both the verbal and nonverbal **delivery** of your speech (see Chapters 17 and 18). So practice your speech often. It has been suggested that a good speech is practiced at least six times. For a four- to six-minute speech, that's only about one-half hour (figuring in restarts and pauses) of actual practice time.

QUICK TIP

Be Aware of Your Nonverbal Delivery

Audiences are highly attuned to a speaker's facial expressions, gestures, and general body movement. As you rehearse, practice smiling and otherwise animating your face in ways that feel natural to you. Audiences want to feel that you care about what you are saying, so avoid a deadpan, or blank, expression. Make eye contact with your practice audience. Doing so will make audience members feel that you recognize and respect them. Practice gestures that feel natural to you, steering clear of exaggerated movements.

CHAPTER 3 ●●●●

Managing Speech Anxiety

Contrary to what most of us think, feeling nervous about giving a speech is not only normal but desirable. Channeled properly, nervousness can actually boost performance. The difference between seasoned public speakers and the rest of us is that the seasoned speakers know how to make their nervousness work *for* rather than *against* them. They use specific anxiety-reducing techniques, described in this chapter, to help them cope with and minimize their tension.

I focus on the information rather than being graded. I also practice my speech a ton to really make sure I do not speak too quickly. I time myself so that I can develop an average time. This makes me more confident [in dealing] with time requirements. And, because I know that I am well prepared, I really try to just relax.

—Kristen Obracay, student

◎ Identify What Makes You Anxious

Anxiety is a state of uneasiness brought on by fear. Lacking positive public-speaking experience, feeling different from members of the audience, or feeling uneasy about being the center of attention—each of these factors can lead to the onset of **public-speaking anxiety** (PSA)—a situation-specific social anxiety that arises from anticipating giving an oral presentation.[1] Fortunately, the great majority of us can learn techniques to tame this anxiety in each of these situations and make it work for us.

Lack of Positive Experience

If you are new to public speaking or have had unpleasant experiences, anxiety about what to expect is only natural. And without positive experience to draw on, it's hard to put this anxiety into perspective. It's a bit of a vicious circle. Some people react by deciding to avoid speeches altogether, yet gaining more experience is key to overcoming speech anxiety.

Feeling Different

The prospect of getting up in front of an audience makes many of us extrasensitive to our personal idiosyncrasies, such as a less-than-perfect haircut or an accent. We may believe that no one could possibly be interested in anything we have to say.

As inexperienced speakers, we assume that being different somehow means being inferior, which leads to anxiety. Actually, everyone is different from everyone else in many ways. However, nearly everyone experiences nervousness about giving a speech.

I control my anxiety by mentally viewing myself as being 100 percent equal to my classmates.

—Lee Morris, student

Being the Center of Attention

Certain audience behaviors—such as chatting with a neighbor or checking text messages during a presentation—can cause us as speakers to think we lost the audience's attention by doing something wrong; we wonder about our mistakes and whether others noticed these supposed flaws. Left unchecked, this kind of thinking can distract us from the speech itself, with all our attention now focused on "me." Our self-consciousness makes us feel even more conspicuous and sensitive to even the smallest faults, which increases our anxiety! Actually, an audience rarely notices anything about us that we don't want to reveal.

◎ Pinpoint the Onset of Anxiety

Different people become anxious at different times during the speechmaking process. Depending on when it strikes, the consequences of public-speaking anxiety can include everything from procrastination to poor speech performance. But by pinpointing the onset of speech anxiety, you can manage it promptly with specific anxiety-reducing techniques.

Pre-Preparation Anxiety

Some people feel anxious the minute they know they will be giving a speech. **Pre-preparation anxiety** can be a problem when we delay planning for the speech, or when it so preoccupies us that we miss vital information necessary to fulfill the speech assignment. If this form of anxiety affects you, start very early using the stress-reducing techniques described later in this chapter.

Preparation Anxiety

For a few people, anxiety arises only when they actually begin to prepare for the speech.[2] These individuals might feel overwhelmed by the time and planning required or hit a roadblock that puts them behind schedule. Preparation pressures produce a cycle of stress, procrastination, and outright avoidance, all of which contribute to **preparation anxiety**. If you find yourself feeling anxious during this stage, immerse yourself in the speech's preparation but calm your nerves by taking short, relaxing breaks to regain your confidence and focus.

Pre-performance Anxiety

Some people experience anxiety as they rehearse their speech. This is when the reality of the situation sets in: they worry that the audience will be watching and listening only to them, feel that their ideas aren't expressed as well as they should be, or sense that preparation time is short. If this **pre-performance anxiety** is strong enough, some may even decide to stop rehearsing. If you experience heightened anxiety at this point, consider using the **anxiety stop-time technique**: Allow your anxiety to present itself for up to a few minutes until you declare time for confidence to step in so you can proceed to complete your practice.[3]

> I experience anxiety before, during, and after the speech. My "before speech" anxiety begins the night before my speech, but then I begin to look over my notecards, and I start to realize that I am ready for this speech. I practice one more time and I tell myself I am going to be fine.
>
> —*Paige Mease, student*

Performance Anxiety

For most people, anxiety is highest just as a speech begins.[4] **Performance anxiety** usually is most pronounced during the introduction of the speech when we are most aware of the audience's attention. Audiences we perceive as negative usually cause us to feel more anxious than those we sense are positive or neutral.[5] But experienced speakers agree that by controlling their nervousness during the introduction, the rest of the speech goes quite smoothly.

Regardless of when anxiety about a speech strikes, the important thing to remember is that you can manage the anxiety and not let it manage you—by harming your motivation, or by causing you to avoid investing the time and energy required to deliver a successful speech.

◉ Use Proven Strategies to Build Your Confidence

A number of proven strategies exist to help you rein in your fears about public speaking, from *meditation* and *visualization* to other forms of relaxation techniques. The first step in taming speech anxiety is to have a thorough plan for each presentation.

Prepare and Practice

If you know your material and have adequately rehearsed your delivery, you're far more likely to feel confident. Once you have prepared the speech, be sure to rehearse it several times.

Modify Thoughts and Attitudes

Negative thoughts about speechmaking increase speech anxiety.[6] A positive attitude, on the other hand, actually results in lowered heart rate and reduced anxiety during the delivery of the speech.[7] As you prepare for and deliver your speech, envision it as a valuable, worthwhile, and challenging activity. Think positively about public speaking, and focus on it as an opportunity toward, not a threat to, personal growth.

QUICK TIP

Envision Your Speech as a Conversation

Rather than thinking of your speech as a formal performance where you will be judged and critiqued, try thinking of it as a kind of ordinary conversation. In this way, you will feel less threatened and more relaxed about the process.

Just before a speech those feelings of anxiety undoubtedly try to sneak in. The way I keep them from taking over is to not let my mind become negative. As long as I keep positive thoughts of confidence in my head, anxiety doesn't stand a chance!

—*Morgan Verdery, student*

Visualize Success

Visualization—the practice of summoning feelings and actions consistent with successful performance[8]—is a highly effective method of reducing speech anxiety.[9] The following is a script for visualizing success on a public-speaking occasion. It requires you, the speaker, to close your eyes and visualize a series of positive feelings and actions that will occur on the day of your speech.

Close your eyes and allow your body to get comfortable in the chair in which you are sitting. Take a deep, comfortable breath and hold it . . . now slowly release it through your nose. Now take another deep breath and make certain that you are breathing from the diaphragm . . . hold it . . . now slowly release it and note how you feel while doing this. Now one more deep breath . . . hold it . . . and release it slowly . . . and begin your normal breathing pattern.

Now begin to visualize the beginning of a day in which you are going to give an informative speech. See yourself getting up in the morning, full of energy, full of confidence, looking forward to the day's challenges. As you dress, think about how the clothes you choose make you look and feel good about yourself. As you are drive, ride, or walk to the speech setting, note how clear and confident you feel. You feel thoroughly prepared for the topic you will be presenting today.

Now you see yourself standing or sitting in the room where you will present your speech, talking very comfortably and confidently with others in the room. The people to whom you will be presenting your speech appear to be quite friendly and are very cordial in their greetings and conversations prior to the presentation. You feel absolutely sure of your material and of your ability to present the information in a forceful, convincing, positive manner.

Now you see yourself approaching the area from which you will present. You are feeling very good about this presentation and see yourself move eagerly forward. All of your audiovisual materials are well organized, well planned, and clearly aid your presentation.[10]

◉ Activate the Relaxation Response

Before, during, and sometimes after a speech you may experience rapid heart rate and breathing, dry mouth, faintness, freezing-up, or other uncomfortable sensations. These physiological reactions result from the **"fight-or-flight" response**—the body's automatic response to threatening or fear-inducing events. Research shows that you can counteract these sensations by activating a relaxation response[11] using techniques such as meditation and controlled breathing.

Briefly Meditate

You can calm yourself considerably before a presentation with this brief meditation exercise:

1. Sit comfortably in a quiet space.
2. Relax your muscles, moving from neck to shoulders to arms to back to legs.
3. Choose a word, phrase, or prayer (e.g.,"Namaste," "Om," "Hail Mary, Full of Grace"). Breathe slowly and say it until you become calm (about ten to twenty minutes).

QUICK TIP

Stretch Away Stress

You can significantly lessen pre-speech jitters by stretching. A half-hour to one-hour session of whole body stretches and yoga poses, combined with deep breathing, will help discharge nervous energy.

Use Stress-Control Breathing

When you feel stressed, the center of your breathing tends to move from the abdomen to the upper chest, leaving you with a reduced supply of air. The chest and shoulders rise, and you feel out of breath. *Stress-control breathing*[12] gives you more movement in the stomach than in the chest. Try it in two stages.

STAGE ONE Inhale air and let your abdomen go out. Exhale air and let your abdomen go in. Do this for a while until you get into the rhythm of it.

STAGE TWO As you inhale, use a soothing word such as "calm" or "relax," or use a personal mantra like this: "Inhale calm, abdomen out, exhale calm, abdomen in." Go slowly, taking about three to five seconds with each inhalation and exhalation.

Begin stress-control breathing *several days* before a speech. Then, once the occasion arrives, perform it while awaiting your turn at the podium and just before you start your speech.

> I have two ways to cope with my nervousness before I'm about to speak. I take a couple of deep breaths from my stomach; I breathe in through my nose and out through my mouth. This allows more oxygen to the brain so you can think clearly. I also calm myself down by saying, "Everything will be okay, and the world is not going to crumble before me if I mess up."
>
> *Jenna Sanford, student*

 LaunchPadSolo Go to LaunchPad Solo to listen to the Relaxation Audio download at macmillanhighered.com /pocketspeak5e

◎ Use Movement to Minimize Anxiety

During delivery, you can use controlled movements with your hands and body to release nervousness. Practice natural gestures, such as holding up your index finger when stating your first main point. Think about what you want to say as you do this, instead of thinking about how you look or feel. (See Chapter 18 for tips on practicing natural gestures.) You don't have to stand perfectly still behind the podium when you deliver a speech. Walk around as you make some of your points. Movement relieves tension and helps hold the audience's attention.

QUICK TIP

Enjoy the Occasion

Most people ultimately find that giving speeches can indeed be fun. It's satisfying and empowering to influence people, and a good speech is a sure way to do this. Think of giving a speech in this way, and chances are you will find much pleasure in it.

◎ Learn from Feedback

Speech evaluations help to identify ways to improve what you do. You can learn a lot through self-evaluation, but self-perceptions can be distorted,[13] so objective evaluations by

> ✓ **CHECKLIST**
>
> **Steps in Gaining Confidence**
>
> ❑ Prepare and practice, early on and often.
> ❑ Modify thoughts and attitudes—think positively.
> ❑ Visualize success.
> ❑ Use stress-control breathing, meditation, and other relaxation techniques.
> ❑ Incorporate natural, controlled movements.
> ❑ Learn from the experience of public speaking and enjoy it.

others often are more helpful. Ultimately, all speakers rely on audience feedback to evaluate the effectiveness of their speeches.

CHAPTER 4 ●●●●

Ethical Public Speaking

When we have an audience's attention, we are in the unusual position of being able to influence or persuade listeners and, at times, to move them to act—for better or worse. With this power to affect the minds and hearts of others comes *responsibility*—"a charge, trust, or duty for which one is accountable."[1] Taking responsibility for your words lies at the heart of being an ethical speaker.

Ethics is the study of moral conduct. Applied to public speaking, it addresses our responsibilities when seeking influence over other people and for which there are positive and negative, or "right" and "wrong," choices of action.[2] For example, should you show a gory photograph without warning to convince audience members not to text and drive? Should you bother to check the credibility of a suspect source before offering it to the audience? Is it ethical to present only one side of an argument?

◎ Demonstrate Competence and Character

Ethics is derived from the Greek word **ethos**, meaning "character." As Aristotle first noted, audiences listen to and trust speakers if they demonstrate *positive ethos*, or good character. Speakers in ancient Greece were regarded positively if they were well prepared, honest, and respectful toward their audience. Today, surprisingly little has changed. Modern research on **source credibility** reveals that people place their greatest trust in speakers who:

- Have a solid grasp of the subject,
- Display sound reasoning skills,
- Are honest and straightforward,
- Are genuinely interested in the welfare of their listeners.[3]

◉ Respect Your Listeners' Values

Our ethical conduct is a reflection of our **values**—our most enduring judgments or standards of what's good and bad in life, of what's important to us. Values shape our worldview[4] and form the basis on which we judge the actions of others. Conflicting values lie at the heart of many controversies that today's public speakers might address, making it difficult to speak about certain topics without challenging cherished beliefs. The United States is a country of immigrants, for example, but half of the population with only a high school education believe that immigrants threaten traditional U.S. values, while only a quarter of college-educated Americans agree.[5]

Consideration of audience members' values is an important aspect of preparing an ethical speech. As you prepare speeches on controversial topics, anticipate that audience members will hold a range of values that will differ not only from your own, but from each other's. Audience analysis is key to discovering and planning for these differences (see Chapter 6).

◉ Contribute to Positive Public Discourse

An important measure of ethical speaking is whether it contributes something positive to **public discourse**—speech involving issues of importance to the larger community, such as whether to decriminalize marijuana or engage in a military conflict.

Perhaps the most important contribution you can make to public debates of this nature is the *advancement of constructive goals*. An ethical speech appeals to the greater good rather than narrow self-interest. It steers clear of **invective**, verbal attacks, designed to discredit and belittle those with whom you disagree. Ethical speakers avoid arguments that target a person instead of the issue at hand (ad hominem attack) or that are built upon other fallacies of reasoning (see Chapter 23).

◎ Use Your Rights of Free Speech Responsibly

The United States vigorously protects **free speech**—defined as the right to be free from unreasonable constraints on expression[6]—thereby assuring protection both to speakers who treat the truth with respect and to those whose words are inflammatory and offensive.

Though often legally protected under the **First Amendment** (which guarantees freedoms concerning religion, expression of ideas, and rights of assembly and petition), racist, sexist, or ageist slurs, gay-bashing, and other forms of negative or hate speech clearly are unethical. **Hate speech** is any offensive communication—verbal or nonverbal—directed against people's race, ethnicity, national origin, gender, religion, sexual orientation, disability, and the like.

Be aware that even under the First Amendment, certain types of speech are not only unethical but actually illegal:

- Speech that provokes people to violence (termed "incitement" or **"fighting words"**)
- Speech that can be proved to be defamatory (termed **slander**) or potentially harmful to an individual's reputation at work or in the community
- Speech that invades a person's privacy, such as disclosing personal information about an individual that is not in the public record

How can you tell if your speech contains defamatory language? If you are talking about public figures or matters of public concern, you will not be legally liable unless it can be shown that you spoke with a **reckless disregard for the truth**—that is, if you knew that what you were saying was false but said it anyway. If your comments refer to private persons, it will be easier for them to assert a claim for defamation. You will have the burden of proving that what you said was true.

QUICK TIP

Beware the Heckler's Veto

Drowning out a speaker's message with which you disagree—called a **heckler's veto**—demonstrates disrespect both to the speaker and to fellow listeners. It robs audience members of the ability to make up their own minds about an issue and silences the free expression of ideas. Tolerance for opposing viewpoints is a necessary ingredient of an ethical—and democratic—society.

✓ CHECKLIST

An Ethical Inventory

❏ Have you distorted any information to make your point?

❏ Have you acknowledged each of your sources?

❏ Does your speech focus on issues rather than on personalities?

❏ Have you tried to foster a sense of inclusion?

❏ Does your topic add something positive to public discourse?

❏ Have you checked your arguments for *ad hominen* attacks or other fallacies of reasoning? (See pp. 182–83.)

❏ Is the content of your message supported by sound evidence and reasoning?

❏ Do you avoid speech that demeans those with whom you disagree?

◉ Observe Ethical Ground Rules

Ethical speech rests on a foundation of dignity and integrity. **Dignity** refers to bearing and conduct that is respectful to self and others. **Integrity** signals the speaker's incorruptibility—that he or she will avoid compromising the truth for the sake of personal expediency.[7] Speaking ethically also requires that we adhere to certain moral ground rules, or "pillars of character," including being *trustworthy, respectful, responsible, fair,* and *civic-minded.*[8]

- **Trustworthiness** is a combination of honesty and dependability. Trustworthy speakers support their points truthfully and don't offer misleading or false information.

- We demonstrate **respect** by treating audience members with civility and courtesy.[9] Respectful speakers address listeners as unique human beings, refrain from any form of personal attack, and focus on issues rather than on personalities.

- **Responsibility** means being accountable for what you say. For example, will learning about your topic in some way benefit listeners? Do you use sound evidence and reasoning? Do you offer emotional appeals because they are appropriate rather than to shore up otherwise weak arguments?

- **Fairness** refers to making a genuine effort to see all sides of an issue and acknowledging the information listeners need in order to make informed decisions.[10] Few subjects are black and white; rarely is there only one right or wrong way to view a topic.

- Being **civic-minded** means caring about your community, in word and deed. It means recognizing that things don't get better unless people volunteer their efforts to improve things. At the broadest level, being civic-minded is essential to the democratic process because democracy depends on our participation in it.

◉ Avoid Plagiarism

Crediting sources is a crucial aspect of any speech. **Plagiarism**—the use of other people's ideas or words without acknowledging the source—is unethical. You are obviously plagiarizing when you simply "cut and paste" material from sources into your speech and represent it as your own. But it is also plagiarism to copy material into your speech draft from a source (such as a magazine article or website) and then change and rearrange words and sentence structure here and there to make it appear as if it were your own.[11]

Orally Acknowledge Your Sources

The rule for avoiding plagiarism as a public speaker is straightforward: *Any source that requires credit in written form should be acknowledged in oral form.* These sources include direct quotations, as well as paraphrased and summarized information—any facts and statistics, ideas, opinions, or theories gathered and reported by others. For each source that requires citation, you need to include the *type of source* (magazine, book, personal interview, website, etc.), the *author or origin of the source*, the *title or a description of the source,* and the *date of the source*.

Oral presentations need not include the full bibliographic reference (i.e., full names, dates, titles, volume, and page numbers). However, you should include complete references in a bibliography or at the end of the speech outline. (For more on creating a written bibliography for speeches, see Appendix A.) Rules for avoiding plagiarism apply equally to print and online sources. For specific guidelines on how to record and cite sources found on websites, see "From Source to Speech" on pp. 68–69.

One exception to sources needing citation is the use of **common knowledge**—information that is likely to be known by many people (though such information must *truly* be widely disseminated). For example, it is common knowledge that in March 2011 a massive earthquake in Japan triggered a tsunami. It is not common knowledge that the last earthquake of similar magnitude to hit Japan happened 1,200 years ago. This fact requires acknowledgment of a source—in this case, a compilation of facts published by Francie Diep in *Scientific American*.[12]

Citing Quotations, Paraphrases, and Summaries

When citing other people's ideas, you can present them in one of three ways:

- **Direct quotations** are verbatim—or word for word—presentations of statements made by someone else. Direct quotes should always be acknowledged in a speech.
- A **paraphrase** is a restatement of someone else's ideas, opinions, or theories in the speaker's own words. Because paraphrases alter the *form* but not the *substance* of another person's ideas, you must acknowledge the original source.
- A **summary** is a brief overview of someone else's ideas, opinions, or theories. While a paraphrase contains approximately the same number of words as the original source material stated in the speaker's own words, a summary condenses the same material, distilling only its essence.

Note how a speaker could paraphrase and summarize, *with credit*, the following excerpt from an article published in the *New Yorker* titled "Strange Fruit: The Rise and Fall of Açai," by John Calapinto.

> **Original Version:** Açai was virtually unknown outside Brazil until 10 years ago, when Ryan and Jeremy Black, two brothers from Southern California, and their friend Edmund Nichols began exporting it to the United States. Since then, the fruit has followed a cycle of popularity befitting a teenage pop singer: a Miley Cyrus–like trajectory from obscurity to hype, critical backlash, and eventual ubiquity. Embraced as a "superfruit"—a potent combination of cholesterol-reducing fats and anti-aging antioxidants—açai became one of the fastest-growing foods in history. . . ."

Compare the original version of the excerpt to how it could be properly quoted, paraphrased, or summarized in a speech. Oral citation language is bolded for easy identification.

Direct Quotation:	**As John Calapinto states in an article titled "Strange Fruit: The Rise and Fall of Açai," published in the May 30, 2011, issue of the *New Yorker*,** "The fruit has followed a cycle of popularity befitting a teenage pop singer: a Miley Cyrus–like trajectory from obscurity to hype, critical backlash, and eventual ubiquity."
Oral Paraphrase:	**In an article titled "Strange Fruit: The Rise and Fall of Açai," published in the May 30, 2011, issue of the *New Yorker*, John Calapinto explains that** until two brothers from Southern California named Ryan and Jeremy Black, along with their friend Edmund Nichols, began exporting açai to the United States ten years ago, it was unknown here. Now, says Calapinto, açai is seen as a "superfruit" that can help with everything from lowering cholesterol to fighting aging through its antioxidant properties.
Oral Summary:	**In an article titled "Strange Fruit: The Rise and Fall of Açai," published in the May 30, 2011, issue of the *New Yorker*, John Calapinto says that** açai, a fruit grown in Brazil that was unknown in this country until ten years ago, is now marketed as a "superfruit" that has powerful health benefits.

For detailed directions on crediting sources in your speech, see Chapter 10, "Citing Sources in Your Speech."

✓ CHECKLIST

Correctly Quote, Paraphrase, and Summarize Information

- ❏ If *directly quoting* a source, repeat the source word for word and acknowledge whose words you are using.
- ❏ If *paraphrasing* someone else's ideas, restate the ideas in your own words and acknowledge the source.
- ❏ If *summarizing* someone else's ideas, briefly describe their essence and acknowledge the source.

◉ Fair Use, Copyright, and Ethical Speaking

Copyright is a legal protection afforded the creators of original literary and artistic works.[13] When including copyrighted materials in your speeches, you must determine when and if you need permission to use such works.

When a work is copyrighted, you may not reproduce, distribute, or display it without the permission of the copyright holder. For any work created from 1978 to the present, a copyright is good during the author's lifetime, plus seventy years. After that, unless extended, the work falls into the *public domain*, which means anyone may reproduce it. Not subject to copyright are federal (but *not* state or local) government publications, common knowledge, and select other categories.

An exception to the prohibitions of copyright is the doctrine of **fair use**, which permits the limited use of copyrighted works without permission for the purposes of scholarship, criticism, comment, news reporting, teaching, or research.[14] This means that when preparing speeches for the classroom, you have much more latitude to use other people's creative work without seeking permission, but *with* credit in all cases, including display of the copyright symbol (©) on any copyrighted handouts or visual aids you include in your speech. Different rules apply to the professional speaker, whose use of copyrighted materials is considered part of a for-profit "performance." (For more information, see **www.copyright.gov**.)

Creative Commons is an organization that allows creators of works to decide how they want other people to use their copyrighted works. It offers creators six types of licenses, three of which are perhaps most relevant to students in the classroom: *attribution* (lets you use the work if you give credit the way the author requests); *noncommercial* (lets you use the work for *noncommercial purposes* only); and *no derivative works* (lets you use only verbatim—exact—versions of the work).

The rules of fair use apply equally to works licensed under Creative Commons and the laws of copyright. Student speakers may search the Creative Commons Web site for suitable materials for their speech at **creativecommons.org**.

CHAPTER 5 ●●●●

Listeners and Speakers

Imagine giving a speech that no one heard. Merely considering such a circumstance points to the central role of the listener in a speech. In fact, all successful communication is two-way, including that of public speaking. It is speaker and listener together who truly make a speech possible.

Connecting with a speaker takes focus. While **hearing** is the physiological, largely passive process of perceiving sound, **listening** is the conscious act of *receiving*, constructing meaning from, and responding to spoken and nonverbal messages.[1] We can decide to tune out the speaker and ignore the message, uncritically accept or hypercritically reject whatever is said, or bring our full attention and critical faculties to bear.

QUICK TIP

Get Ahead by Listening

College students in the United States spend more time listening (about 24 percent) than they do on any other communication activity, such as speaking (20 percent), using the Internet (13 percent), writing (9 percent), or reading (8 percent).[2] Listening is also the number one activity employees do during the work day.[3] Managers overwhelmingly associate listening skills with competence, efficiency, and leadership potential, promoting employees who display them and hiring new entrants who possess them.[4] In both college and work arenas, skill in listening leads to success.

◎ Recognize That We Listen Selectively

In any given situation, no two audience members will process the information in exactly the same way. The reason lies in **selective perception**—people's perceptions are subject to their own biases and expectations, leading them to pay attention selectively to certain messages while ignoring others.[5] Several factors influence what we listen to and what we ignore:

- We pay attention to what we hold to be important.
- We pay attention to information that touches our experiences and backgrounds.
- We sort and filter new information on the basis of what we already know (e.g., we learn by analogy).

The principle of selective perception suggests key steps you can take in your dual roles as listener and speaker:

- As a *listener*, examine your own expectations and motivations to hear things in a certain way. Ask yourself whether you are really hearing what the speaker is saying.
- As a *speaker*, demonstrate why your topic is relevant to the audience's interest and needs. Use analogies to help the audience learn new ideas.

◎ Anticipate Obstacles to Listening

Active listening—listening that is focused and purposeful—isn't possible under conditions that distract us. In any listening situation, including that of listening to speeches, try to identify and overcome common obstacles.

Refrain from Multitasking

You cannot actively listen well while multitasking. Activities such as checking a cell phone or calendar, finishing an assignment, or responding to a text divert our attention from the message and reduce our ability to interpret it accurately.

Work to Overcome Cultural Barriers

Differences in dialects or accents, nonverbal cues, word choices, and even physical appearance can serve as barriers to listening, but they need not if you keep your focus on the message rather than the messenger. Refrain from judging a speaker on the basis of his or her accent, appearance, or demeanor; focus instead on what is actually being said. Whenever possible, reveal your needs to him or her by asking questions.

QUICK TIP

Listening Styles and Cultural Differences

Research suggests a link between our listening styles and a culture's predominate communication style.[6] A study of young adults in the United States, Germany, and Israel[7] found distinct listening style preferences that mirrored key value preferences, or preferred states of being, of each culture. Germans tended toward action-oriented listening, Israelis displayed a content-oriented style, and Americans exhibited both people- and time-oriented styles. While preliminary in nature, and not valid as a means of stereotyping a given culture's group behavior, these findings confirm the cultural component of all forms of communication, including listening. They also point to the need to focus on intercultural understanding as you learn about your audience.

Minimize External and Internal Distractions

A *listening distraction* is anything that competes for the attention we are trying to give to something else. External distractions can originate outside of us, in the environment, while internal distractions occur with our own thoughts and feelings.

✔ CHECKLIST

Dealing with Distractions While Delivering a Speech

❏ *Problem:* Passing distractions (chatting, entry of latecomers)
   Solution: Pause until distraction recedes
❏ *Problem:* Ongoing noise (construction)
   Solution: Raise speaking volume
❏ *Problem:* Sudden distraction (collapsing chair, falling object)
   Solution: Minimize response and proceed
❏ *Problem:* Audience interruption (raised hand, prolonged comment)
   Solution: Acknowledge audience reaction and either follow up or defer response to conclusion of speech.

External listening distractions, such as the din of jackhammers or competing conversations, can significantly interfere with our ability to listen, so try to anticipate and plan for them. If you struggle to see or hear over noise or at a distance, arrive early and sit in the front. To reduce *internal listening distractions*, avoid daydreaming, be well rested, monitor yourself for lapses in attention, and consciously focus on listening.

Guard against Scriptwriting and Defensive Listening

When we, as listeners, engage in *scriptwriting*, we focus on what we, rather than the speaker, will say next.[8] Similarly, people who engage in **defensive listening** decide either that they won't like what the speaker is going to say or that they know better. Remind yourself that effective listening precedes effective rebuttal. Try waiting for the speaker to finish before devising your own arguments.

Beware of Lazy and Overconfident Listening

Laziness and overconfidence can manifest themselves in several ways: We may expect too little from speakers, ignore important information, or display an arrogant attitude. Later, we discover we missed important information.

◎ Practice Active Listening

Setting listening goals, listening for main ideas, and watching for nonverbal cues are practical steps you can take to become more adept at listening actively.

Set Listening Goals

Determine ahead of time what you need and expect from the listening situation:

1. **Identify your listening needs:** "I must know my classmate's thesis, purpose, main points, and type of organization in order to complete and hand in a written evaluation."

2. **Identify why listening will help you:** "I will get a better grade on the evaluation if I am able to identify and evaluate the major components of Sara's speech."

3. **Make an action statement (goal):** "I will minimize distractions, take notes, and practice the active listening steps during the speech, asking questions about anything I do not understand."

4. **Assess goal achievement:** "I did identify the components of the speech I decided to focus upon and wrote about them in class."

Listen for Main Ideas

Try these strategies to ensure that you identify and retain the speaker's main points:

- Listen for a preview of important ideas in the introduction and reiteration of them in the conclusion.
- Take notes of main points, for example, "Bipolar disorder is actually a spectrum of disorders."
- Indent supporting points under main points to indicate subordination of ideas.

QUICK TIP

Listen Responsibly

As listeners, we are ethically bound to refrain from disruptive and intimidating tactics—such as heckling, name-calling, or interrupting—that are meant to silence those with whom we disagree. If we find the arguments of others morally offensive, we are equally bound to speak up appropriately in refutation.

Evaluate Evidence and Reasoning

The ability to think critically—to evaluate claims on the basis of well-supported reasons—goes hand in hand with active listening. As you listen to speeches, use your critical faculties to do the following:

- *Evaluate the speaker's evidence.* Is it accurate? Are the sources credible?

- *Analyze the speaker's assumptions and biases.* What lies behind the speaker's assertions? Does the evidence support or contradict these assertions?
- *Assess the speaker's reasoning.* Does it betray faulty logic? Does it rely on fallacies in reasoning? (See pp 183–84.)
- *Consider multiple perspectives.* Is there another way to view the argument? How do other perspectives compare with the speaker's?
- *Summarize and assess the relevant facts and evidence.* How will you think or act on the basis of the evidence?

◉ Strive for the Open and Respectful Exchange of Ideas

In contrast to *monologue,* in which we try merely to impose what we think on another person or group of people, **dialogic communication** is the open sharing of ideas in an atmosphere of respect.[9] True dialogue encourages both listener and speaker to reach conclusions together. For listeners, this means maintaining an open mind and listening with empathy.[10] For the speaker, this means approaching a speech not as an argument that must be "won," but as an opportunity to achieve understanding with audience members.

◉ Offer Constructive and Compassionate Feedback

Follow these guidelines when evaluating the speeches of others:

- *Be honest and fair in your evaluation of the speech.* Assess the speech as a whole and remain open to ideas and beliefs that differ from your own.
- *Adjust to the speaker's style.* Each of us has a unique communication style, a way of presenting ourselves through a mix of verbal and nonverbal signals. Don't judge the content of a speaker's message by his or her style.
- *Be compassionate in your criticism.* Always start by saying something positive, and focus on the speech, not the speaker.
- *Be selective in your criticism.* Make specific rather than global statements. Rather than statements such as, "I just couldn't get into your topic," give the speaker something he or she can learn from: "I wanted more on why the housing market is falling. . . ."

part

Development

6. **Analyzing the Audience** 34

7. **Selecting a Topic and Purpose** 44

8. **Developing Supporting Material** 54

9. **Finding Credible Sources in Print and Online** 60

10. **Citing Sources in Your Speech** 70

CHAPTER 6

Analyzing the Audience

Advertisers are shrewd analysts of people's needs and wants, extensively researching our buying habits and lifestyle choices to identify what motivates us. To engage your listeners and encourage their involvement in your message, you too must investigate your audience. **Audience analysis** is the process of gathering and analyzing information about audience members' attributes and motivations with the *explicit aim of preparing your speech in ways that will be meaningful to them*. This is the single most critical aspect of preparing for any speech.

Assuming an **audience-centered perspective** throughout the speech preparation process—from selection and treatment of the speech topic to making decisions about how you will organize, word, and deliver it—will help you prepare a presentation that your audience will want to hear.

◉ Adapt to Audience Psychology: Who Are Your Listeners?

Audience analysis involves investigating the audience's attitudes, beliefs, and values—their *feelings and opinions*—toward the topic, toward you as the speaker, and toward the speech occasion.

Taking the measure of the audience is critical because audience members tend to evaluate information in terms of their own point of view rather than the speaker's—at least until they are convinced to take a second look.[1] You may want your audience to support a cause, but unless you know something about their perspectives on the topic, you won't be able to appeal to them effectively.

Attitudes, beliefs, and values, while intertwined, reflect distinct mental states that reveal a great deal about us. **Attitudes** are our general evaluations of people, ideas, objects, or events.[2] To evaluate something is to judge it as relatively good or bad, desirable or undesirable. People generally act in accordance with their attitudes (although the degree to which they do so depends on many factors).[3]

Attitudes are based on **beliefs**—the ways in which people perceive reality.[4] Beliefs are our feelings about what is true or real. The less faith listeners have in the existence of something—UFOs, for instance—the less open they are to hearing about it.

Both attitudes and beliefs are shaped by **values**—our most enduring judgments about what's good in life, as shaped by our culture and our unique experiences within it. We feel our values strongly and strive to realize them.

As a rule, audience members are more interested in and pay greater attention to topics toward which they have positive attitudes and that are in keeping with their values and beliefs. The less we know about something, the more indifferent we tend to be. It is easier (though not simple) to spark interest in an indifferent audience than it is to turn negative attitudes around.

"If the Value Fits, Use It"

Evoking some combination of the audience's attitudes, beliefs, and values in the speeches you deliver will make them more personally relevant and motivating. For example, the Biodiversity Project, an organization that helps environmental groups raise public awareness, counsels speakers to appeal directly to the three foremost values their audience members hold about the environment (discovered in nationally representative surveys commissioned by the Project), offering the following as an example:

> You care about your family's health (value #1 as identified in survey) and you feel a responsibility to protect your loved ones' quality of life (value #2). The local wetland provides a sanctuary to many plants and animals. It helps clean our air and water and provides a space of beauty and serenity (value #3). All of this is about to be destroyed by irresponsible development.[5]

Gauge Listeners' Feelings toward the Topic

Consideration of the audience's attitudes (and beliefs and values) about a topic is key to offering a speech that will resonate with them (see Chapter 7). Is your topic one with which the audience is familiar, or is it new to them? Do your listeners hold positive, negative, or neutral attitudes toward the topic? Once you have this information (using tools such as interviews and questionnaires, see p. 42), adjust the speech accordingly (see also the table in Chapter 24 for specific persuasive strategies for appealing to different audiences).

If the topic is *new* to listeners,

- Start by showing why the topic is relevant to them.
- Relate the topic to familiar issues and ideas about which they already hold positive attitudes.

If listeners know *relatively little* about the topic,

- Stick to the basics and include background information.
- Steer clear of jargon, and define unclear terms.
- Repeat important points, summarizing information often.

If listeners are *negatively disposed* toward the topic,

- Focus on establishing rapport and credibility.
- Don't directly challenge listeners' attitudes; instead begin with areas of agreement.
- Discover why they have a negative bias in order to tactfully introduce the other side of the argument.
- Offer solid evidence from sources they are likely to accept.
- Give good reasons for developing a positive attitude toward the topic.[6]

If listeners hold *positive attitudes* toward the topic,

- Stimulate the audience to feel even more strongly by emphasizing the side of the argument with which they already agree.
- Tell stories with vivid language that reinforce listeners' attitudes.[7]

If listeners are a *captive audience*,

- Motivate listeners to pay attention by stressing what is most relevant to them.
- Pay close attention to the length of your speech.

Gauge Listeners' Feelings toward You as the Speaker

How audience members feel about you will also have significant bearing on their responsiveness to the message. A speaker who is well liked can gain an initial hearing even when listeners are unsure what to expect from the message itself.

To create positive audience attitudes toward you, first display the characteristics of speaker credibility (ethos) described in Chapter 4. Listeners have a natural desire to identify with

---

✅ CHECKLIST

Appeal to Audience Attitudes, Beliefs, and Values

Have you . . .

- ❏ Investigated audience members' attitudes, beliefs, and values toward your topic?
- ❏ Assessed the audience's level of knowledge about the topic?
- ❏ Considered strategies to address positive, negative, and neutral responses to your speech topic?
- ❏ Considered appealing directly to audience members' attitudes and values in your speech?

the speaker and to feel that he or she shares their perceptions,[8] so establish a feeling of commonality, or **identification**, with them. Use eye contact and body movements to
include the audience in your message. Sharing a personal
story, emphasizing a shared role, and otherwise stressing
mutual bonds all help to create identification. So, too, does
the strategic use of inclusive language such as *we*, *you*, *I*, and
me (see p. 118).

Gauge Listeners' Feelings toward the Occasion

Depending on the circumstances calling for the speech,
people will bring different sets of expectations and emotions
to it. Members of a **captive audience**, who are required to
hear the speaker, may be less positively disposed to the occasion than those of a **voluntary audience** who attend of their
own free will. Whether planning a wedding toast or a business presentation, failure to anticipate and adjust for the
audience's expectations risks alienating them.

◉ Adapt Your Message to Audience Demographics

Demographics are the statistical characteristics of a given
population. At least eight characteristics are typically considered when analyzing speech audiences: *age, ethnic and
cultural background, socioeconomic status* (including *income,
occupation,* and *education*), *religious and political affiliations,
gender,* and *group affiliations.* Any number of other traits — for
example, disability, sexual orientation, and place of residence — may be important to investigate as well.

Knowing where audience members fall in relation to
audience demographics will help you identify your **target
audience** — those individuals within the broader audience
whom you are most likely to influence in the direction you
seek. You may not be able to please everyone, but you should
be able to establish a connection with your target audience.

Age

Each age group has its own concerns, psychological drives,
and motivations. People of the same generation often share
a familiarity with significant individuals, local and world
events, noteworthy popular culture, and so forth. Thus being
aware of the **generational identity** of your audience, such as
the Baby Boomers (those born between 1946 and 1964), millennials (those born between 1980 and 1999), or Generation Z (those born since 2000), allows you to develop points
that are relevant to the experiences and interests of the
widest possible cross section of your listeners. The table,

Generational Identity and Today's Generations	
Generation	Characteristics
Traditional 1925–1945	Respect for authority and duty, disciplined, strong sense of right and wrong
Baby Boomer 1946–1964	Idealistic, devoted to career, self-actualizing, values health and wellness
Generation X 1965–1979	Seeks work-life balance, entrepreneurial, technically savvy, flexible, questions authority figures, skeptical
Generation Y/ Millennials 1980–1999	Technically savvy, optimistic, self-confident, educated, appreciative of diversity, entrepreneurial, respectful of elders, short attention spans
Generation Z 2000–	Comfortable with the highest level of technical connectivity, naturally inclined to collaborate online, boundless faith in power of technology to make things possible[9]

Generational Identity and Today's Generations, lists some of the prominent characteristics and values of today's generations.

Ethnic or Cultural Background

An understanding of and sensitivity to the ethnic and cultural composition of your listeners are key factors in delivering a successful (and ethical) speech. Some audience members may have a great deal in common with you. Others may be fluent in a language other than yours and must struggle to understand you. Some members of the audience may belong to a distinct **co-culture**, or social community whose perspectives and style of communicating differ significantly from yours. All will want to feel recognized by the speaker. (See pp. 40–42.)

Socioeconomic Status

Socioeconomic status (SES) includes income, occupation, and education. Knowing roughly where an audience falls in terms of these key variables can be critical in effectively targeting your message.

INCOME   *Income* determines people's experiences on many levels. It directly affects how they are housed, clothed, and fed, and determines what they can afford. Beyond this, income has a ripple effect, influencing many other aspects of life. For example, depending on income, home ownership is either a taken-for-granted budget item or an out-of-reach dream. The same is true for any activity dependent on income. Given how pervasively income affects people's life experiences, insight into this aspect of an audience's makeup can be quite important.

OCCUPATION   In most speech situations, the *occupation* of audience members is an important and easily identifiable demographic characteristic. Occupational interests often are tied to other areas of social concern, such as politics, the economy, education, and social reform. Personal attitudes, beliefs, and goals are also closely tied to occupational standing.

EDUCATION   Level of *education* strongly influences people's perspectives and range of abilities. Higher levels of education often lead to increased lifetime earnings, better health out-comes, and greater civic engagement.[10] Depending upon audience members' level of education, your speech may treat topics at a higher or lower level of sophistication, with fewer or more examples and illustrations.

Religion

Social and political views can be tied to religious traditions, making *religion* another key demographic variable. At least a dozen major religious traditions coexist in the United States.[11] Not all members of the same religious tradition will agree on all issues. Catholics disagree on birth control and divorce, Jews disagree on whether to recognize same-sex unions, and so forth. Awareness of an audience's general *religious orientation* can be critical when your speech touches on a topic as potentially controversial as religion itself. Capital punishment, same-sex marriage, and teaching about the origins of humankind—all are rife with religious implications.

Political Affiliation

As with religion, beware of making unwarranted assumptions about an audience's *political values and beliefs*. Some people avoid anything that smacks of politics while others enjoy a lively debate. Conservative individuals hold certain views that liberals dispute, and the chasm between far right and far left is great indeed. Unless you have prior information about the audience's political values and beliefs, you won't know where your listeners stand.

Gender

Gender is another important factor in audience analysis, if only as a reminder to avoid *gender stereotyping*. Distinct from the fixed physical characteristics of biological sex, **gender** is our social and psychological sense of ourselves as males or females.[12] Making assumptions about the preferences, abilities, and behaviors of your audience members based on their presumed gender can seriously undermine their receptivity to your message. Beyond ensuring that you treat issues of gender evenly, try to anticipate the audience members' attitudes with respect to gender and plan accordingly.

Group Affiliations

The various groups to which audience members belong—whether social, civic, work-related, or religiously or politically affiliated—reflect their interests and values and so provide insight into what they care about. Investigating the audience members' group affiliations will help you craft a message that will appeal to them.

QUICK TIP

Be Sensitive to Disability When Analyzing an Audience

One out of every five people in the United States has some sort of physical or mental disability; 14 percent of those enrolled in college and graduate school are counted as disabled.[13] Problems range from sight and hearing impairments to constraints on physical mobility and employment. Thus disability is another demographic variable to consider when analyzing an audience. Keep *persons with disabilities (PWD)* in mind when you speak, and use language and examples that afford them respect and dignity.

◉ Adapt to Diverse Audiences

In the United States, one-third of the population, or nearly 105 million people, belong to a racial or an ethnic minority group, and 38 million people, or 13 percent, are foreign born. Nationwide, nearly 20 percent of the population speaks a language other than English in the home; two-thirds of these speak Spanish.[14] These figures suggest that audience members will hold different cultural perspectives and employ different styles of communicating that may or may not mesh with your own.

How might you prepare to speak in front of an ethnically and culturally diverse audience, including that of your classroom? In any speaking situation, your foremost concern should be to treat your listeners with dignity and to act with integrity. Since values are central to who we are, identifying those of your listeners with respect to your topic can help you to avoid ethnocentrism (see p. 20) and deliver your message in a culturally sensitive manner.

Consider Cross-Cultural Values

People in every culture possess **cultural values** related to their personal relationships, religion, occupation, and so forth. Understanding these values can help you deliver your message sensitively. While dominant cultural values in U.S. society include *achievement and success, equal opportunity, material comfort,* and *democracy,* surveys of several Asian societies reveal such values as a *spirit of harmony, humility toward one's superiors, awe of nature,* and a *desire for prosperity.* In Mexico, *group loyalty, cyclical time,* and *fatalism,* among others, as cultural values.[15] Becoming familiar with differences, as well as points of sameness, in values will help you to anticipate and appeal to the values of your audience members.

Individual audience analysis is always the first step when seeking to learn about an audience. But public speakers will also benefit by sensitizing themselves to broader national differences in cultural values. Geert Hofstede's wide-ranging research reveals five major "value dimensions," or "broad

---

✅ CHECKLIST

Reviewing Your Speech in the Light of Audience Demographics

❏ Does your speech acknowledge potential differences in values and beliefs and address them sensitively?

❏ Have you reviewed your topic in light of the age range and generational identity of your listeners? Do you use examples they will recognize and find relevant?

❏ Have you tried to create a sense of identification between yourself and audience members?

❏ Are your explanations and examples at a level appropriate to the audience's sophistication and education?

❏ Do you make any unwarranted assumptions about the audience's political or religious values and beliefs?

❏ Does your topic carry religious or political overtones that are likely to stir your listeners' emotions in a negative way?

preferences for one state of affairs over another," as being significant across all cultures, but in widely varying degrees. To see variations in values among fifty nations, see **geert -hofstede.com**.

Several other global surveys can also be extremely useful for learning about cultural values, including the *Pew Global Attitudes Project* (**pewglobal.org**), *Gallup World View* (**worldview .gallup.com**), and the World Values Survey (**www.worldvalues survey.org**).

Focus on Universal Values

As much as possible, try to determine the attitudes, beliefs, and values of audience members. At the same time, you can focus on certain values that, if not universally shared, are probably universally aspired to in the human heart. These include love, truthfulness, fairness, freedom, unity, tolerance, responsibility, and respect for life.[16]

◎ Interview and Survey Audience Members

You can discover information about your audience through personal interviews, telephone or in-person surveys, and published sources. Often, it takes just a few questions to get some idea of where audience members stand psychologically and demographically.

Conduct Interviews

Interviews, even brief ones, can reveal a lot about the audience's interests and needs. You can conduct interviews one-on-one or in a group, in person or by telephone or online. Consider interviewing a sampling of the audience, or even just one knowledgeable representative of the group that you will address. As with questionnaires (see "Survey the Audience," which follows), interviews usually consist of a mix of open- and closed-ended questions. (See Chapter 9, pp. 67–69, for more on conducting interviews.)

Survey the Audience

Surveys can be as informal as a poll of several audience members or as formal as the pre-speech distribution of a written survey, or *questionnaire*—a series of open- and closed-ended questions. **Closed-ended questions** (also called *structured questions*) elicit a small range of specific answers:

"Do you smoke cigarettes?"

Yes _____ No _____ I quit, but I smoked for _____ years.

Closed-ended questions may be either fixed-alternative or scale questions. **Fixed-alternative questions** contain a limited choice of answers, such as "Yes," "No," or "For *x* years" (as in the preceding example). **Scale questions**—also called *attitude scales*—measure the respondent's level of agreement or disagreement with specific issues:

> "Flag burning should be outlawed."
>
> 1) Strongly Agree   2) Agree   3) Undecided   4) Disagree
> 5) Strongly Disagree

Scale questions can be used to measure how important listeners judge something to be and how frequently they engage in a particular behavior:

> "How important is religion in your life?"
>
> 1) Very Important   2) Important   3) Moderately Important
> 4) Of Minor Importance   5) Unimportant

Open-ended questions (also called *unstructured questions*) begin with a "how," "what," "when," "where," or "why," and they are particularly useful for probing beliefs and opinions. This style of question allows respondents to elaborate as much as they wish:

> "How do you feel about using the results of DNA testing to prove innocence or guilt in criminal proceedings?"

Often, it takes just a few fixed-alternative and scale questions to draw a fairly clear picture of audience members' backgrounds and attitudes and where they fall in demographic categories. You may wish to use Web-based survey software, such as SurveyMonkey or QuestionPro, to generate surveys electronically using premade templates and distribute them online.

Consult Published Sources

Organizations of all kinds publish information describing their missions, operations, and achievements. Sources include websites and related online articles, brochures, newspaper and magazine articles, and annual reports.

Although *published opinion polls* won't specifically reflect your particular listeners' responses, they too can provide valuable insight into how a representative state, national, or international sample feels about the issue in question. Consider consulting these and other polling organizations:

- Pew Research Center for the People & the Press: **people press.org**
- National Opinion Research Center (NORC): **www.norc .uchicago.edu**

- Roper Center for Public Opinion Research: **ropercenter .uconn.edu**
- Gallup: **www.gallup.com**

◉ Analyze the Speech Setting and Context

As important as analyzing the audience is assessing (and then preparing for) the setting in which you will give your speech—size of audience; location; time; length of speech; and rhetorical situation:

1. What is the physical setting of the speech—auditorium, banquet hall, classroom?
2. How will you need to position yourself and adjust your voice, with or without a microphone?
3. What is the time of event and length of the speech?
4. How many people will attend?
5. How will any equipment I plan to use in my speech, such as an LCD projector, function in the space?
6. Where will I stand or sit in relation to the audience?
7. Will I be able to interact with the listeners?
8. Who else will be speaking?
9. Are there special events or circumstances of concern to my audience that I should acknowledge?

CHAPTER 7 ● ● ●●

Selecting a Topic and Purpose

One of the first tasks in preparing a speech is to select a topic and purpose for speaking that are appropriate to the audience and occasion. Unless you can clearly identify *what* you want to say and *why* you want to say it—your topic and purpose—prior to delivering a speech, you won't be able to give one that works.

◉ Exploring Topics for Your Speech

As you explore topics, consider each one's potential appeal to the audience and its appropriateness to the rhetorical situation. Even when the topic is assigned, as often happens in the classroom and workplace, you must still decide which aspects of it best match your unique audience and speech circumstance. The "From Source to Speech: Narrowing Your

Topic to Fit the Audience" later in this chapter demonstrates how you can do this.

Identify Personal Interests

Personal interests run the gamut from favorite activities and hobbies to deeply held goals and values. You can translate personal experiences into powerful topics, especially if sharing them in some way benefits the audience (see the table, Identifying Topics.) "What it's like" stories also yield captivating topics. For example, what is it like to go hang gliding in the Rocky Mountains or to be part of a medical mission team working in Uganda?

Consider Current Events and Controversial Issues

Think about events and issues that are most important to you and your audience, and consider whether you can make a difference. Be aware, however, that people rarely respond to perspectives opposed to their core values, so plan speeches on such topics carefully using audience analysis (see Chapter 6).

QUICK TIP

Explore Topics on *CQ Researcher*

Librarians often refer students to two related publications — *CQ Researcher* (published weekly) and *CQ Global Researcher* (published monthly) — for trustworthy background information on pressing social, political, environmental, and regional issues. Available online as part of your library's electronic holdings, for each topic they include an overview and assessment of the current situation, pro/con statements from representatives of opposing positions, and bibliographies of key sources.

Survey Grassroots Issues: Engage the Community

Audience members respond with interest to local issues that may affect them directly. College students want to know why their loan rates have increased; residents want to know about local environmental issues. People are also interested in what other people in their communities are doing. Review your community's newspapers and news blogs for the local headlines.

Steer Clear of Overused and Trivial Topics

To avoid boring your classmates and instructor, stay away from tired issues, such as drunk driving and the health risks of cigarettes, as well as trite topics such as "how to change a tire." People want to hear new information and different perspectives. For ideas, consult your favorite print or online publications. Consider, too, how you can apply relevant secondary research to personal experience to form a compelling topic (see Chapter 9).

Identifying Topics	
Favorite Activities	**Personal Experiences**
• Playing sports • Building computers • Fixing cars • Designing clothes • Reading poetry • Playing video games • Playing music • Travel • Cooking	• Travel to international destinations • Service in the armed forces • Volunteer work in the U.S. or abroad • Emigrating to the U.S. • Surviving a life-threatening disease • Surviving disaster • Growing up in a non-traditional family
Values	**Goals**
• Building a greater sense of community • Spirituality • Philanthropy • Political activism • Living a sustainable life	• Becoming a high-tech entrepreneur • Attending graduate or professional school • Starting a family • Staying fit • Learning more about one's religion
Specific Subject Interests	**Social Problems**
• Local history • Genealogy • U.S. or global politics • Photography and art • Religion • Science	• Road rage • Bullying in schools • Gun violence • Unemployment • Racism • Lack of affordable child care

Health and Nutrition	Current Events
• Diets • Exercise regimens • Autism spectrum disorder • Mental health benefits • Insomnia • Eating organic or gluten-free	• Pending legislation • Political races • Climate and biodiversity • National security • Same-sex marriage
Grassroots Issues	**New or Unusual Angles**
• Student loan relief options • Safer schools • Caring for the homeless • Drought and water conservation	• Unsolved crimes • Unexplained disappearances • Scandals • Conspiracy theories • Life hacks for living a more efficient life
Issues of Controversy	
• Corporate personhood • Medical marijuana • Concealed handguns • Veterans Affairs • Immunizations	

Try Brainstorming to Generate Ideas

Brainstorming is a method of spontaneously generating ideas through word association, topic mapping, or Internet browsing using search engines and directories. Brainstorming works—it is a structured and effective way to identify topic ideas in a relatively brief period of time.

To brainstorm by **word association**, write down *one* topic that might interest you and your listeners. Then jot down the first thing that comes to mind related to it. Repeat the process until you have fifteen to twenty items. Narrow the list to two or three, and then select a final topic:

cars → maintenance → engines → advantages of diesel fuels

Topic (mind) mapping is a brainstorming technique in which you lay out words in diagram form to show categorical

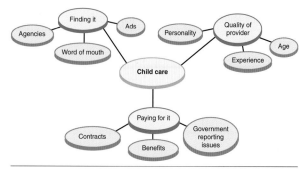

FIGURE 7.1 A Topic Map

relationships among them. Put a potential topic in the middle of a piece of paper. As related ideas come to you, write them down, as shown in Figure 7.1.

Utilize Internet Tools

Excellent online tools for finding (and narrowing) a topic are the databases available on a library's portal, or its home page (see also p. 61). Consult general databases such as Academic OneFile (for browsing and starting the search process) and subject-specific databases such as Ethnic NewsWatch (for in-depth research on a topic). Popular Internet search engines such as Google and Bing also offer a wealth of resources to discover and narrow topics. Each search engine offers options for specialized searches within books, news, blogs, finance, images, and other sources. You can further narrow topics by limiting searches to within a range of dates (e.g., 1900–1950), to a geographic region (e.g., Europe), or to a particular language.

◉ Identify the General Purpose of Your Speech

Once you have an idea for a topic, you'll need to refine and adapt it to your general speech purpose. The **general speech purpose** for any speech answers the question, "What is my objective in speaking on this topic to this audience on this occasion?" Public speakers typically accomplish one of three general purposes: to inform, to persuade, or to mark a special occasion.

- Do you aim primarily to educate or inform listeners about your topic? The general purpose of an **informative speech** is *to increase the audience's awareness and understanding of a topic by defining, describing, explaining, or demonstrating knowledge of the subject.*

- Is your goal to influence listeners to accept your position on a topic and perhaps to take action (e.g., "only eat wild salmon")? The general purpose of the **persuasive speech** is *to effect some degree of change in the attitudes, beliefs, values, and behaviors of audience members.*
- Are you there to mark a special occasion, such as an awards ceremony? The **special occasion speech** serves the general purpose *of entertaining, celebrating, commemorating, inspiring, or setting a social agenda*, and includes speeches of introduction, acceptance, and presentation; roasts and toasts; eulogies; and after-dinner speeches, among others.

The speech occasion itself often suggests an appropriate general speech purpose. A town activist, invited to address a civic group about installing solar panels in town buildings, may choose a *persuasive purpose* to encourage the group to get behind the effort. If invited to describe the initiative to the town finance committee, the activist may choose an *informative purpose*, in which the main goal is to help the committee understand project costs. If asked to speak at an event celebrating the project's completion, the speaker will choose a *special occasion purpose*. Addressing the same topic, the speaker selects a different general speech purpose to suit the audience and occasion.

◉ Refine the Topic and Purpose

Once you have an idea for a topic and have established a general speech purpose, you'll need to narrow your focus to align with the nature of the occasion, audience expectations, and time constraints.

Narrow Your Topic

Just as brainstorming can be used to discover a topic, it can also be helpful in narrowing one. Using topic mapping, you can brainstorm by category (e.g., subtopic). Say your general topic is video games. Some related categories are platform (handheld, arcade), type (racing, role playing), and operating system (Linux, Macintosh, Windows).

Form a Specific Speech Purpose

Once you've narrowed the topic, you need to refine your speech goal. You know you want to give either an informative or persuasive speech (your general purpose), but you also need to decide more specifically what you want to accomplish. The **specific speech purpose** lays out precisely what you want the audience to take away from your presentation.

✓ CHECKLIST

Narrowing Your Topic

- ❏ What is my audience most likely to know about the subject?
- ❏ What do my listeners most likely want to learn?
- ❏ What aspects of the topic are most relevant to the occasion?
- ❏ Can I develop the topic using just two or three main points?
- ❏ How much can I competently research and report on in the time I am given to speak?

Ask yourself: What do you want the audience to learn/do/reconsider/agree with? Be specific about your aim, and then state it in action form, as in the following, written for an informative speech:

General Topic: Consolidating Student Loans

Narrowed Topic: Understanding when and why consolidating student loans makes sense

General Purpose: To inform

Specific Speech Purpose: To inform my audience about the factors to consider when deciding whether or not to consolidate student loans

Although the specific purpose statement need not be articulated in the actual speech, it is important to know and to keep in mind exactly what you want to accomplish.

Compose a Thesis Statement

The **thesis statement** (also called *central idea*) is the theme of the speech stated as a single, declarative sentence. It concisely expresses what the speech will attempt to demonstrate or prove. The main points, the supporting material, and the conclusion all serve to flesh out the thesis.

Both thesis and specific purpose statements describe the speech topic, but in different forms. *The specific purpose describes in action form what you want to achieve with the speech; the thesis statement concisely identifies, in a single idea, what the speech is about.* By clearly stating your speech thesis (what it's about), you set in your mind exactly what outcome you want to accomplish (the specific purpose).

The difference between the thesis and specific purpose can be clearly seen in the following examples.

EXAMPLE 1

Speech Topic:	Blogs
General Speech Purpose:	To inform
Specific Speech Purpose:	To inform my audience of three benefits of keeping a blog
Thesis Statement:	Maintaining a blog provides the opportunity to practice writing, a means of networking with others who share similar interests, and the chance to develop basic website management skills.

EXAMPLE 2

Speech Topic:	Service learning courses
General Speech Purpose:	To persuade
Specific Speech Purpose:	To persuade my audience that service learning courses are beneficial for gaining employment after schooling.
Thesis Statement:	To prepare for a difficult job market and enhance your résumé while making a significant difference for other people, you should take one or more service learning courses.

✓ CHECKLIST

Identifying the Speech Topic, Purpose, and Thesis

- ❏ Is the topic appropriate to the occasion?
- ❏ Will the topic appeal to my listeners' interests and needs?
- ❏ Will I be able to offer a fresh perspective on the topic?
- ❏ Have I identified the *general speech purpose*—to inform, persuade, or mark a special occasion?
- ❏ Have I identified what I want the audience to gain from the speech—the specific speech purpose?
- ❏ Have I considered how much I can competently research and then report on in the time I am given to speak?
- ❏ Does my thesis statement sum up in a single sentence what my speech is about?
- ❏ Does my thesis statement make the claim I intend to make about my topic?

FROM SOURCE TO SPEECH

Narrowing Your Topic to Fit Your Audience

How do you narrow a topic to fit the audience and the speech occasion? Consider the following case study.

A Case Study

Jenny is a member of the campus animal rights club and a student in a public speaking class. She is giving two persuasive speeches this semester: one to her public speaking class and one to the student council, as a representative of her club. For both presentations, Jenny plans to speak on the broad topic of animal rights. But she must narrow this topic considerably to fit each audience and speech occasion.

First, Jenny draws a topic map to generate ideas.

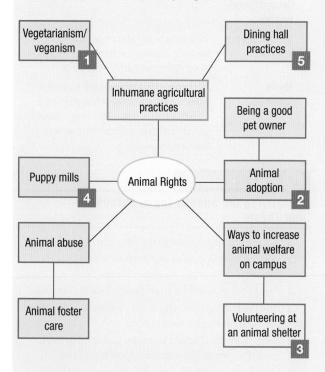

For each presentation, Jenny narrows her topic after considering her audience and the speech occasion.

Public Speaking Class (25–30 people):

- Mixed ages, races, and ethnicities, and an even mix of males and females
- Busy with classes, jobs, sports, and clubs
- Half live in campus housing, where pets are not allowed

Anderson Ross/Digital Vision/Getty Images

1 Jenny eliminates vegetarianism because she will be unlikely to change listeners' minds in a six-minute speech.

2 She eliminates animal adoption because it may not be feasible for many students.

3 Volunteering at an animal shelter is an option for all animal lovers, even those who are not allowed to have pets on campus. Jenny argues that students should donate an hour a week to a nearby shelter, so that busy students can still participate.

Student Council (8–10 people):

- Mixed demographic characteristics
- Similar interests: government, maintaining a rich campus life, an investment in ethics and the honor code, and an interest in keeping student affairs within budget

Manfred Rutz/The Image Bank/ Getty Images

4 Jenny eliminates puppy mills—though the student council may agree that the mills are harmful, they are not in a position to directly address the problem.

5 Jenny zeroes in on dining hall practices, which are directly tied to campus life. Her club's proposed resolution to use free-range eggs in the campus dining hall benefits all students and requires the support of the council—an ideal topic for this audience.

In an informative speech, the thesis conveys the scope of the topic, the steps associated with the topic, or the underlying elements of it. It describes what the audience will learn.

In a persuasive speech, the thesis represents what you are going to prove in the address. Notice, too, that in both examples, after you read the thesis you find yourself asking "Why?" or thinking "Prove it!" This will be accomplished by the evidence you give in the speech points (see Chapter 11).

CHAPTER 8 ●●●●

Developing Supporting Material

Good speeches contain relevant, motivating, and audience-centered **supporting material** in the form of examples, stories, testimony, facts, and statistics. Supporting material, such as you might discover in a magazine or journal article, illustrates and elaborates upon your ideas, provides the audience with evidence for your arguments, and engages them in the topic.

◉ Offer Examples

An **example** is a typical instance of something. Without examples to illustrate the points a speaker wants to convey, listeners would get lost in a sea of abstract statements. Examples can be *brief* or *extended* and may be either *factual* or *hypothetical*.

Brief examples offer a single illustration of a point. In a speech titled "The Coming Golden Age of Medicine," Richard F. Corlin offers the following brief example to illustrate what American medicine can do:

> We often hear about the problems of the American health care delivery system, but just think what it can do. My 88-year-old father who needed a hip replacement got it— the week it was discovered that he needed it. That couldn't happen in any other country in the world.[1]

Sometimes it takes more than a brief example to effectively illustrate a point. **Extended examples** offer multifaceted illustrations of the idea, item, or event being described, thereby allowing the speaker to create a more detailed picture for the audience.

Here, TED speaker Jonathan Drori uses an extended example to illustrate how pollen (the fertilizing element of plants) can link criminals to their crimes:

[Pollen forensics] is being used now to track where counterfeit drugs have been made, where banknotes have come from. . . . And murder suspects have been tracked using their clothing. . . . Some of the people were brought to trial [for war crimes in Bosnia] because of the evidence of pollen, which showed that bodies had been buried, exhumed, and then reburied somewhere else.[2]

In some speeches, you may need to make a point about something that could happen in the future if certain events were to occur. Since it hasn't happened yet, you'll need a **hypothetical example** of what you believe the outcome might be. Republican Representative Vernon Ehlers of Michigan offered the following hypothetical example at a congressional hearing on human cloning:

What if in the cloning process you produce someone with two heads and three arms? Are you simply going to euthanize and dispose of that person? The answer is no. We're talking about human life.[3]

◎ Share Stories

One of the most powerful means of conveying a message and connecting with an audience is through a **story** or **narrative**. Stories help us make sense of our experiences;[4] they tell tales, both real and imaginary, relating personal experiences, folk wisdom, parables, myths, and so forth. Common to all stories are the essential elements of a plot, characters, setting, and some sort of time line.

Stories can be relatively short and simple descriptions of incidents worked into the speech, or longer accounts that constitute most of the presentation and even serve as the organizing framework for it (see narrative pattern of organization, p. 94). In either case, a successful story will strike an emotional connection between speaker and audience members.

In a speech on helping college students finish their degrees, Melinda French Gates offered the following brief story to illustrate the hardships many must overcome:

Last year, we met a young man named Cornell at Central Piedmont Community College in Charlotte, North Carolina. We asked him to describe his typical day. He clocks into work at 11 P.M. When he gets off at 7 the next morning, he sleeps for an hour. In his car. Then he goes to class until 2 o'clock. "After that," Cornell said, "I just crash."[5]

Many speakers liberally sprinkle their speeches with **anecdotes**—brief stories of interesting and often humorous incidents based on real life. The most important part of an anecdote is the *moral*—the lesson the speaker wishes to convey.[6] For example, in a speech to students at Maharishi University, comedian Jim Carrey talked about how his father's fear of being impractical led him to become an accountant instead of the comedian he wanted to be. This spurred Carrey to take another path:

> So many of us choose our path out of fear disguised as practicality. . . . I learned many great lessons from my father, not the least of which was that you can fail at what you don't want, so you might as well take a chance on doing what you love.[7]

Draw on Testimony

Consider quoting or paraphrasing people who have an intimate knowledge of your topic. **Testimony** is firsthand findings, eyewitness accounts, and people's opinions; **expert testimony** includes findings, eyewitness accounts, or opinions from professionals trained to evaluate a given topic. **Lay testimony**, or testimony by nonexperts such as eyewitnesses, can reveal compelling firsthand information that may be unavailable to others.

Credibility plays a key role in the effectiveness of testimony, so establish the qualifications of the person whose testimony you use, and inform listeners when and where the testimony was offered:

> In testimony before the U.S. House Subcommittee on Human Rights and Wellness last week, Derek Ellerman (co-executive director of the Polaris Project) said, "Many people have little understanding of the enormity and the brutality of the sex trafficking industry in the United States. . . ."[8]

QUICK TIP

Use a Variety of Supporting Materials

Listeners respond most favorably to a variety of supporting materials derived from multiple sources to illustrate each main point.[9] Alternating among different types of supporting material—moving from a story to a statistic, for example—will make the presentation more interesting and credible while simultaneously appealing to your audience members' different learning styles.

Provide Facts and Statistics

Most people (especially in Western society) require some type of evidence, usually in the form of facts and statistics, before they will accept someone else's claims or position.[10]

Facts represent documented occurrences, including actual events, dates, times, people, and places. Listeners are not likely to accept your statements as factual unless you back them up with credible sources.

Use Statistics Accurately

Statistics are quantified evidence that summarizes, compares, and predicts things.

Statistics add precision to speech claims, *if* you know what the numbers actually mean and use terms that describe them accurately. Following are some basic statistical terms commonly used in speeches that include statistics.

USE FREQUENCIES TO INDICATE COUNTS   A **frequency** is simply a count of the number of times something occurs:

> On the midterm exam there were 8 A's, 15 B's, 7 C's, 2 D's, and 1 F.

Frequencies can indicate size, describe trends, or help listeners understand comparisons between two or more categories:

- Inside the cabin, the Airbus A380 has room for at least 525 passengers—and as many as 853.[11] *(shows size)*
- According to the Centers for Disease Control (CDC), while cigarette use has declined 33 percent since 2000, the use of large cigars has increased 233 percent over this period.[12] *(describes a trend)*
- According to 2012 estimates from the U.S. Census Bureau, the total population of the state of Colorado comprised nearly 2,700,000 males and 2,600,000 females.[13] *(compares two categories)*

USE PERCENTAGES TO EXPRESS PROPORTION   As informative as frequencies can be, the similarity or difference in magnitude between things may be more meaningfully indicated in a **percentage**—the quantified portion of a whole. Percentages help audience members easily grasp comparisons between things, such as the unemployment rate in several states:

> In May 2013, Nevada had the highest rate of unemployment, at 9.5 percent. At 3.8 percent, Nebraska had the lowest rate.[14]

Because audience members cannot take the time to pause and reflect on the figures as they would with written text, consider how you can help listeners interpret the numbers you offer them, as in this example:

> As you can see, Nevada's unemployment rate is two and one-half times greater than that of Nebraska.

> ## QUICK TIP
>
> ### Use Statistics Selectively—and Memorably
> Rather than overwhelm the audience with numbers, put a few figures into context, to make your message more compelling. For example, instead of citing the actual number of persons belonging to Facebook worldwide (over 1.5 billion and counting), use a simple ratio to drive home the company's enormous reach: "Today, at least 38 percent of people in the world has a Facebook account, roughly the population of China."[15]

USE TYPES OF AVERAGES ACCURATELY   An **average** describes information according to its typical characteristics. Usually we think of the average as the sum of the scores divided by the number of scores. This is the *mean,* the computed average. But there are two other kinds of averages—the *median* and the *mode.* As a matter of accuracy, in your speeches you should distinguish among these three kinds of averages.

Consider a teacher whose nine students scored 5, 19, 22, 23, 24, 26, 28, 28, and 30, with 30 points being the highest possible grade. The following illustrates how she would calculate the three types of averages:

- The **mean** score is 22.8, the *arithmetic average*, the sum of the scores divided by 9.
- The **median** score is 24, *the center-most score in a distribution* or the point above and below which 50 percent of the nine scores fall.
- The **mode** score is 28, the *most frequently occurring score* in the distribution.

The following speaker, claiming that a policy institute misrepresented the "average" tax rate for American families, illustrates how the inaccurate use of averages can deceive audience members:

> The Tax Foundation determines an *average* [*mean*] tax rate . . . simply by dividing all taxes paid by the total of everyone's income. For example, if four middle-income families pay $3,000, $4,000, $5,000, and $6,000, respectively, in taxes, and one very wealthy family pays $82,000 in taxes, the *average* [*mean*] tax paid by these five families is $20,000 ($100,000 in total taxes divided by five families). But four of the five families [actually] have a tax bill equaling $6,000 or less. . . . [Many] analysts would [more accurately] define a *median* income family—a family for whom half of all families have higher income and half have lower income—to be the "typical family." . . .[16]

Present Statistics Ethically

Offering listeners inaccurate statistics is unethical. Following are steps you can take to reduce the likelihood of using false or misleading statistics:

- *Use only reliable statistics.* Include statistics from the most authoritative source you can locate, and evaluate the methods used to generate the data.
- *Present statistics in context.* Inform listeners of when the data were collected and by whom, the method used to collect the data, and the scope of the research:

  These figures represent data collected by the U.S. Department of Education during 2015 from question-naires distributed to all public and private schools in the United States with students in at least one of grades 9–12 in the fifty states and the District of Columbia.

QUICK TIP

Avoid Cherry-Picking

Politicians are often accused of **cherry-picking**—selecting only those statistics that buttress their own arguments while ignoring competing data.[17] To present the mean when in fact one of the other averages is the better indicator of what your data represent, is an instance of cherry-picking. To be fair to audience members avoid misrepresenting the truth by offering only one-sided data. Present statistics accurately and in context, or not at all.

- *Avoid confusing statistics with "absolute truth."* Even the most recent data available will change the next time data are collected. Nor are statistics necessarily any more accurate than the human who collected them. Offer data as they appropriately represent your point, but refrain from declaring that these data are definitive.

◉ Refer Orally to Your Sources

Clearly identify the source of your information and provide enough context (including approximate date of publication) to accurately interpret it. For guidelines on orally citing your sources, see Chapter 10, "Citing Sources in Your Speech."

> ✓ **CHECKLIST**
> ## Evaluating Your Research Needs
>
> Do you need . . .
>
> ❑ Examples to illustrate, describe, or represent your ideas?
>
> ❑ A story or an anecdote to drive your point home?
>
> ❑ Firsthand findings, in the form of testimony, to illustrate your points or strengthen your argument?
>
> ❑ Relevant facts, or documented occurrences, to substantiate your statements?
>
> ❑ Statistics to demonstrate relationships?

CHAPTER 9 ●●●●

Finding Credible Sources in Print and Online

The search for supporting material—for the examples, facts and statistics, opinions, stories, and testimony described in Chapter 8—can be one of the most enjoyable parts of putting together a speech. It is at this stage that you can delve into your subject, sift through sources, and select relevant and audience-centered material to support your thesis and speech points. Every speech will suggest a different mix of sources, so before beginning your search, reflect on what might work best for your particular rhetorical situation.

◉ Use a Library Portal to Access Credible Sources

Easy access to the Internet may lead you to rely heavily or even exclusively on sources you find through popular search engines such as Google and Bing. In doing so, however, you risk overlooking key sources not found through those sites and finding biased and/or false information. To circumvent this, begin your search at your school's or town's **library portal**, or electronic entry point into its holdings (e.g., the library's home page).

A key benefit of beginning your research at a library portal is the ability to access scholarly research articles and peer-reviewed journals, which contain some of the most cutting-edge and reliable research on almost any topic. Not only that, but libraries purchase access to proprietary databases and other resources that form part of the **deep Web**—the large portion of the Web that general search engines cannot access because the information is licensed and/or fee-based.

As with its shelved material, a library's e-resources are built through careful and deliberate selection. Librarians track, sort, and organize the millions of articles and book titles, both print and electronic, competing for your attention. They select only what is of value, according to well-defined standards and in consultation with faculty.[1] No such standards exist for popular Web search engines. The following table lists resources typically found on library portals.

TYPICAL RESOURCES FOUND ON LIBRARY PORTALS

- Full text databases (newspapers, periodicals, journals)
- General reference works (dictionaries, encyclopedias, atlases, almanacs, fact books, biographical reference works, quotation resources, poetry collections)
- Books, e-books, and monographs
- Archives and special collections (collected papers, objects and images, and scholarly works unique to the institution)
- Digital collections (oral histories, letters, old newspapers, image collections, audio and video recordings)
- Video and music collections

◉ Be a Critical Consumer of Online Information

Discerning the accuracy of open content is not always easy when you're surfing the Internet outside of a library portal. Anyone can post material on the Web and, with a little bit of design savvy, make a website look professional. Further, search engines such as Google cannot differentiate quality of information; only a human editor can do this. Each time you examine a document, especially one that has not been evaluated by credible editors, ask yourself, "Who put this information here, and why did they do so? What are the source's qualifications? Where is similar information found? When was the information posted, and is it timely?" (See "From Source to Speech: Evaluating Web Sources," pp. 68–69.)

Recognize Propaganda, Misinformation, and Disinformation

One way to judge a source's trustworthiness is to ask yourself: Is it reliable information, or is it propaganda, misinformation, or disinformation?[2] (See the table on p. 63.)

- **Information** is *data* that is presented in an understandable context. Data are raw and unprocessed facts; information makes sense of data. For example, a patient's vital signs (temperature, blood pressure, pulse, etc.) are data. Interpreting the vital signs in the context of health status is information. Information is neutral unto itself but is subject to manipulation, for purposes both good and bad. It then has the potential to become propaganda, misinformation, or disinformation.

- **Propaganda** is information represented in such a way as to provoke a desired response. The purpose of propaganda is to instill a particular attitude or emotion in order to gain support for a cause or issue. Usually presented as advertising or publicity, propaganda encourages you to think or act according to the ideological, political, or commercial perspective of the message source. Military posters that encourage enlistment are an example of propaganda.

- **Misinformation** always refers to something that is not true. While propaganda may include factual information, misinformation does not. For example, in the summer of 2014, rumors circulated that the Ebola virus had mutated and become airborne when in fact it had not. One common form of misinformation on the Internet is the *urban*

Information, Propaganda, Misinformation, and Disinformation	
Information	Data set in a context for relevance.
	Example: A fact
Propaganda	Information represented in such a way as to provoke a desired response.
	Example: An advertisement to conserve energy
Misinformation	Something that is not true.
	Example: An urban legend
Disinformation	Deliberate falsification of information.
	Example: A falsified profit-and-loss statement

legend—a fabricated story passed along by unsuspecting people.

- **Disinformation**, which thrives on the Internet and elsewhere, is the deliberate falsification of information. Doctored photographs and falsified profit-and-loss statements are examples of disinformation in action.

Ethical speeches are based on sound information—on facts put into context—rather than on misinformation, propaganda, or disinformation.

Use Watchdog Sites to Check the Facts

Our most trustworthy elected officials occasionally make false assertions, and even the most reliable news sources publish errors of fact or omission. So whom should you believe—Congresswoman X's dire predictions regarding Social Security or Senator Y's rosier assessment? To check the factual accuracy of information offered by key political players and major journalistic outlets, consult these websites (bearing in mind that they too are not infallible).

- **www.factcheck.org**, sponsored by the Annenberg Public Policy Center
- **www.politifact.com**, sponsored by the *Tampa Bay Times*
- Fact Checker, a blog sponsored by the *Washington Post*

◎ Investigate a Mix of Primary and Secondary Sources

Nearly all types of speeches can benefit from a mix of the two broad categories of supporting material: primary and secondary sources. **Primary sources** provide firsthand accounts or direct evidence of events, objects, or people (see below). **Secondary sources** provide analysis or commentary about things not directly observed or created. These include the vast world of news, commentary, analysis, and scholarship found in books, articles, and a myriad of sources other than the original (see below).

A speech that contains both primary and secondary sources can be more compelling and believable than one that relies on one source type alone. The firsthand nature of a credible primary source can build trust and engage audience members emotionally. Secondary sources can help listeners put the topic in perspective. A speech on an oil spill, for example, can command more attention if it includes testimony by oil riggers and other eyewitnesses (primary sources) along with analyses of the spill from magazines and newspapers (secondary sources).

◉ Explore Primary Sources

A primary source for a speech may be your own personal experience; a firsthand account found in letters, diaries, old newspapers, photographs, or other sources, often housed in a library's digital collection; or interviews or surveys that you conduct yourself.

Access Digital Collections

Chief among sources of primary speech materials are the many online digital collections of the world's libraries. Nearly all libraries now offer digital collections, which are generally organized by topic, material type, time period, and geographic area. Housed within these online repositories are oral histories, letters, old newspapers; photographs, prints, and paintings; and audio and video recordings.

QUICK TIP

Dazzle Them with Digital Collection Materials

Supporting material drawn from a library's digital collection can add great color and depth to speeches on many topics. A presentation on early African American actors, for example, might include a passage from a diary of a nineteenth-century actor and a photograph of him or her on stage. One way to discover a digital collection related to your topic is to enter your topic terms into a general search engine (e.g., African American actors AND digital collections).

Consider Personal Knowledge and Experience

Used effectively, your own knowledge and experience about your topic can serve important functions in a speech, drawing in listeners and creating a sense of connection with them. Sharing experiences and observations about work you've done, people you've known, or places you've visited can add a dimension of authenticity and credibility that a secondhand source might not.

Conduct Interviews

Oftentimes you can glean considerably more insight into a topic, and get more compelling material to bring to your audience, by speaking personally to someone who has expertise on the subject. However, getting the information you need from a subject does require research and advance

> ### ✓ CHECKLIST
> ### Finding Speeches Online
>
> Online, you can find numerous videos and audio files of speeches. These can be useful as models of speeches and primary source material.
>
> ❑ American Rhetoric (**www.americanrhetoric.com**) contains 5,000+ speeches.
> ❑ Gifts of Speech (**gos.sbc.edu**) features speeches by women from around the world since 1848.
> ❑ The Wake Forest University's Political Speeches gateway (**www.wfu.edu/~louden/Political%20Communication/Class%20Information/SPEECHES.html**) offers links to collections of political speeches.
> ❑ The United States Senate (**www.senate.gov**) includes speeches by U.S. senators.
> ❑ *Vital Speeches of the Day* (**www.vsotd.com**) features current speeches delivered in the United States and is published monthly.

planning, from deciding how you will record the interview to the questions you will ask.

- Begin by *learning about the person you will be interviewing* so that you can prepare appropriate and informed questions for him or her.
- *Prepare questions for the interview* in advance of the interview date.
- *Word questions carefully:*
  - Avoid *vague questions,* those that don't give the person being interviewed enough to go on. Vague questions waste the interviewee's time and reflect the interviewer's lack of preparation.
  - Avoid *leading questions,* those that encourage, if not force, a certain response and reflect the interviewer's bias (e.g., "Like most of us, are you going to support candidate X?"). Likewise, avoid *loaded questions,* those that are phrased to reinforce the interviewer's agenda or that have a hostile intent (e.g., "Isn't it true that you've never supported school programs?").
  - Focus on asking *neutral questions,* those that don't lead the interviewee to a desired response. Usually, this will consist of a mix of open, closed, primary, and secondary questions. See pages 42–43 for more details on open- and closed-ended questions.

- *Establish a spirit of collaboration at the start:*
  - Acknowledge the interviewee and express respect for his or her expertise.
  - Briefly summarize your topic and informational needs.
  - State a (reasonable) goal—what you would like to accomplish in the interview—and reach agreement on it.
  - Establish a time limit for the interview and stick to it.
- *Use active listening strategies (see Chapter 5):*
  - Don't break in when the subject is speaking or inter-ject with leading comments.
  - Paraphrase the interviewee's answers when you are unclear about meaning and repeat back to him or her.
  - Ask for clarification and elaboration when necessary.
- *End the interview by rechecking and confirming:*
  - Confirm that you have covered all the topics (e.g.,"Does this cover everything?").
  - Briefly offer a positive summary of important things you learned in the interview.
  - Offer to send the interviewee the results of the interview.

✅ CHECKLIST

Preparing for the Interview

- ❑ Have I researched my interviewee's background and accomplishments?
- ❑ Do I have a written set of questions?
- ❑ Can the questions be answered within a reasonable time frame?
- ❑ Are my questions relevant to the purpose of my speech?
- ❑ Are my questions posed in a well-thought-out sequence?
- ❑ Are my questions free of bias or hostile intent?
- ❑ Are controversial questions reserved until the end of the interview?
- ❑ Have I obtained advance permission to record the interview?
- ❑ Do I have a working writing implement and ample notepaper, or functioning laptop or tablet?
- ❑ Have I made certain that any recording equipment I plan to use is in working order?

Distribute Surveys

A survey can be useful as both a tool to investigate audience attitudes and a source of primary material for your speech. Surveys are an especially effective source for speech topics focused on the attitudes and behavior of people in your immediate environment, such as fellow students' opinions on issues on or off campus or community members' attitudes toward local initiatives (for guidelines on creating surveys, see Chapter 6.)

◉ Explore Secondary Sources

Along with possible primary sources, your speeches will most likely require the support of secondary sources as found in books, newspapers, periodicals, government publications, print or online reference works (such as encyclopedias, almanacs, biographical reference works, books of quotations, poetry collections, and atlases), and reputable blogs and social news sites.

🅜 LaunchPadSolo For detailed information about locating credible secondary sources, visit macmillanhighered.com /pocketspeak5e

Wikipedia—Dos and Don'ts

When it comes to online research, it is impossible to ignore the presence of Wikipedia, the world's largest experimental free encyclopedia, written collaboratively and often anonymously by anyone who wishes to contribute to it. Though Wikipedia's instant accessibility and vast range make it tantalizingly easy to consult, bear in mind that information may or may not be accurate at any given moment, as people edit material at will. As with any encyclopedia, Wikipedia may provide an initial overview of a topic, but to ensure accuracy, it should serve only as a starting-off point for further research.[3] The references cited in a Wikipedia article can serve as potential research leads—*if* you follow the links provided and carefully evaluate the information for trustworthiness Be sure to compare the information in the article to credible sources *not* supplied in the entry itself, and do not offer Wikipedia—or any encyclopedia entry—as a source to audience members.

Blogs and Social News Sites

Blogs and social news sites can be important sources of information of unfolding events and new trends and ideas, if the source is reputable. A *blog* is a site containing journal-type entries maintained by individuals or groups in which newest entries appear first. A **social news site** allows users to submit

FROM SOURCE TO SPEECH

Evaluating Web Sources

Check the Most Authoritative Websites First

Seek out the most authoritative websites on your topic. If your speech explores the NBA draft, start with the NBA's official website. For information on legislation, government statistics, health, the environment, and other relevant topics, check government-sponsored sites at the official U.S. government portal, **www.usa.gov**. Government-sponsored sites are free of commercial influence and contain highly credible primary materials.

Evaluate Authorship and Sponsorship

1 *Examine the domain in the Web address*—the suffix at the end of the address that tells you the nature of the site: educational (.edu), government (.gov), military (.mil), nonprofit organization (.org), business/commercial (.com), and network (.net). A tilde (~) in the address usually indicates that it is a personal page rather than part of an institutional website. Make sure to assess the credibility of each site, whether it is operated by an individual, a company, a government agency, or a nonprofit group.

2 *Look for an "About" link that describes the organization or a link to a page that gives more information.* These sections can tell a great deal about the nature of the site's content. Be wary of sites that do not include such a link.

3 *Identify the creator of the information.* If an individual operates the site—and such sites are now prolific in the form of blogs and professional profile pages—does the document provide relevant biographical information, such as links to a résumé or a listing of the author's credentials? Look for contact information. A source that doesn't want to be found, at least by e-mail, is not a good source to cite.

Check for Currency

4 *Check for a date that indicates when the page was placed on the Web and when it was last updated.* Is the date current? Websites that do not have this information may contain outdated or inaccurate material.

Check That the Site Credits Trustworthy Sources

5 *Check that the website documents its sources.* Reputable websites document the sources they use. Follow any links to these sources, and apply the same criteria to them that you did to the original source document. Verify the information you find with at least two other independent, reputable sources.

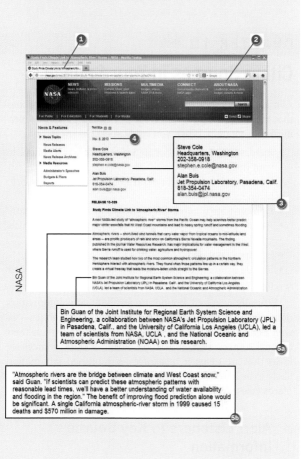

Steve Cole
Headquarters, Washington
202-358-0918
stephen.e.cole@nasa.gov

Alan Buis
Jet Propulsion Laboratory, Pasadena, Calif.
818-354-0474
alan.buis@jpl.nasa.gov

Bin Guan of the Joint Institute for Regional Earth System Science and Engineering, a collaboration between NASA's Jet Propulsion Laboratory (JPL) in Pasadena, Calif., and the University of California Los Angeles (UCLA), led a team of scientists from NASA, UCLA , and the National Oceanic and Atmospheric Administration (NOAA) on this research.

"Atmospheric rivers are the bridge between climate and West Coast snow," said Guan. "If scientists can predict these atmospheric patterns with reasonable lead times, we'll have a better understanding of water availability and flooding in the region." The benefit of improving flood prediction alone would be significant. A single California atmospheric-river storm in 1999 caused 15 deaths and $570 million in damage.

NASA

news stories, articles, and videos to share with other users of the site. The most popular items win more visibility.

Reference only those sites that are affiliated with reputable (local, regional, or national) news agencies and media outlets, or by well-known bloggers with serious reputations. A blog-specific search engine can help you find what you need. Technorati's core product was previously an Internet search engine for searching blogs. The website stopped indexing blogs and assigning authority scores in May of 2014 with the launch of its new website, which is focused on online publishing and advertising.

CHAPTER 10 ●●●●

Citing Sources in Your Speech

Alerting the audience to the sources you use and offering ones that they will find authoritative is a critical aspect of delivering a presentation. When you credit speech sources, you:

- Increase the odds that audience members will believe in your message.
- Demonstrate the quality and range of your research to listeners.
- Demonstrate that reliable sources support your position.
- Avoid plagiarism and gain credibility as an ethical speaker who acknowledges the work of others.
- Enhance your own authority.
- Enable listeners to locate your sources and pursue their own research on the topic.

Ethically you are bound to attribute any information drawn from other people's ideas, opinions, and theories—as well as any facts and statistics gathered by others—to their original sources. Remember, you need not credit sources for ideas that are *common knowledge*—established information likely to be known by many people and described in multiple places (see p. 24).

◎ Alert Listeners to Key Source Information

An **oral citation** credits the source of speech material that is derived from other people's ideas. For each source, plan on briefly alerting the audience to the following:

1. The *author* or *origin of the source* ("documentary filmmaker *Ken Burns* . . ." or "on the *National Science Foundation website* . . .")

2. The *type of source* (journal article, book, personal interview, website, blog, online video, etc.)

3. The *title* or a *description of the source* ("In the book *Endangered Minds . . .*"; or "In *an article on sharks . . .*")

4. The *date of the source* ("The article, published in the *October 10th, 2015*, issue . . ." or "According to a report on revising the SAT, posted online September 28, 2015, on the *Daily Beast . . .*")

Spoken citations need not include a complete bibliographic reference (exact title, full names of all authors, volume, and page numbers); doing so will interrupt the flow of your presentation and distract listeners' attention. However, do keep a running list of source details for a bibliography to appear at the end of your speech draft or outline. (See Appendix A.)

Establish the Source's Trustworthiness

Too often, inexperienced speakers credit their sources in bare-bones fashion, offering a rote recitation of citation elements. For example, they might cite a source's name, but leave out key details about the source's background that could convince the audience to trust the source as credible (believable) and his or her conclusions as true (accurate).

Source credibility refers to our level of trust in a source's credentials and track record for providing accurate information. If you support a scientific claim by crediting it to an obscure personal blog, for example, listeners won't find it nearly as reliable as if you credited it to a scientist affiliated with a reputable institution.

Be aware that while a source that is credible is usually accurate, this is not always so.[1] Sometimes we have information that contradicts what we are told by a credible source. For instance, a soldier might read an article in the *Washington Post* about a conflict in which he or she participated. The soldier knows the story contains inaccuracies because the soldier was there. In general, however, the soldier finds the *Washington Post* a credible source. Therefore, *since even the most credible source can sometimes be wrong, it is always better to offer a variety of sources, rather than a single source, to support a major point.* This is especially the case when your claims are controversial.

Qualify the Source

A simple and straightforward way to demonstrate a source's credibility is to include a brief description of the source's qualifications to address the topic (a "**source qualifier**"), along with your oral citation (e.g., "researcher at Duke Cancer Institute," "columnist for the *Wall Street Journal*"). This will allow the audience to put the source in perspective. To see how you can orally cite sources in ways that listeners will accept and believe in them, see "From Source to Speech: Demonstrating Your Source's Credibility and Accuracy."

QUICK TIP

Consider Audience Perception of Sources

Not every trustworthy source is necessarily appropriate for every audience. For example, a politically conservative audience may reject information from a liberal publication. Thus, audience analysis should factor in your choice of sources. In addition to checking that your sources are reliable, consider whether they will be seen as credible by your particular audience.[2]

◉ Avoid a Mechanical Delivery

Acknowledging sources need not interrupt the flow of your speech. On the contrary, audience members will welcome information that adds backing to your assertions. The key is to avoid a formulaic, or mechanical, delivery. Varying the wording and order in which you introduce a citation can help.

Vary the Wording

Avoid a rote delivery of sources by varying your wording. If you introduce one source with the phrase "According to . . . ," switch to another construction ("As reported by . . .") for the next one. Alternating introductory phrases contributes to a natural delivery and provides the necessary variety listeners need.

Vary the Order

Vary the order in which you introduce a citation. Occasionally discuss the findings first, before citing the source. For example, you might state that "Caffeine can cause actual intoxication" and provide evidence to back it up before revealing the source(s) of it—"A chief source for this argument is a report in the July 5, 2015, issue of the *New England Journal of Medicine*. . . ."

◉ Types of Sources and Sample Oral Citations

Following are common types of sources cited in a speech, the specific citation elements to mention, and examples of how you might refer to these elements in a presentation. Note that each example includes an underlined source qualifier describing the source's qualifications to address the topic—for instance, "director of undergraduate studies for four years" or "research scientist at Smith-Kline." Including a source qualifier can make the difference between winning or losing acceptance for your supporting material.

Book

If a book has *two* or *fewer* authors, state first and last names, source qualifier, title, and date of publication. If *three* or *more authors*, state first and last name of first author and "coauthors."

> *Example:* In the book *1948: The First Arab-Israeli War*, published in *2008*, noted Israeli historian Benny Morris claims that . . .

> *Example:* In *The Civic Potential of Video Games*, published in 2009, Joseph Kahne, noted professor of education and director of the Civic Education Research Group at Mills College, and his two coauthors, both educators, wrote that . . .

Reference Work

For a reference work (e.g., atlas, directory, encyclopedia, almanac), note title, date of publication, author or sponsoring organization, and source qualifier.

> *Example:* According to *Literary Market Place 2015*, the foremost guide to the U.S. book publishing industry, Karen Hallard and her coeditors report that . . .

Print Article

When citing from a print article, use the same guidelines as you do for a book.

> *Example:* In an article entitled "How Junk Food Can End Obesity," published in the July 2013 issue of the *Atlantic* magazine, David H. Freedman, a journalist and author of the book *Wrong: Why the Experts Keep Failing Us*, argues that fast food chains such as McDonald's can offer lower-cost healthy foods than higher-priced health food stores. . . .

Online-Only Publications

For online-only publications, use the book guidelines, and identify the publication as "online magazine," "online newspaper," or "online journal."

> *Example:* In an article on massive online open courses (MOOCs) posted on July 23, 2013, on the online magazine *Slate*, Gabriel Kahn, a professor at the University of Southern California and director of the Future of Journalism at Annenberg Innovation Lab . . .

FROM SOURCE TO SPEECH

Demonstrating Your Sources' Credibility and Accuracy

How Can I Lead the Audience to Accept My Sources as Credible and Accurate?

- If the source is affiliated with a respected institution, identify that affiliation.
- If citing a study linked to a reputable institution, identify the institution.
- If a source has relevant credentials, note the credentials.
- If the source has relevant real-life experience, mention that experience.

In the following excerpt from a speech about becoming a socially conscious consumer, the speaker omits information about his key sources that would help convince the audience that his evidence and sources are trustworthy:

> The force behind this new kind of partnership is called "cause marketing." According to the *Financial Times*, cause marketing is when a company and a consumer group—or a charity—tackle a social or environmental problem and create business value for the company at the same time. A survey on consumer responses to cause marketing was conducted by Nielsen. The poll found that two-thirds of consumers around the world would say they prefer to buy products and services from companies that have programs that give back to society. And over 46 percent of consumers were willing to pay more for goods and services from companies that are giving back.

Below we see a much more convincing use of the same sources.

> The force behind this new kind of partnership is called "cause marketing." According to the *Financial Times* Lexicon, an online dictionary found at the publication's website, in *cause marketing* a company and a consumer group—or a charity—tackle a social or environmental problem and create business value for the company at the same time. In March of 2012, the global marketing firm Nielson, which studies consumer behavior in more than one hundred countries, conducted a world-wide study on cause marketing. It found that two-thirds of consumers around the world say they prefer to buy products and services from companies that have programs that give back to society. And over 46 percent said that they were, and I'm quoting here from the survey question, "willing to pay more for goods and services from companies that are giving back."

1 The speaker states the date of the study in cause marketing and shows that it is relatively recent research.

2 Rather than merely mentioning the source's name (Nielsen), the speaker identifies the source as a reputable global marketing firm. Listeners are more likely to trust the source if it is connected to a trusted entity.

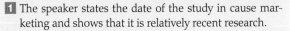

03.27.2012

nielsen   NEWSWIRE REPORTS SOLUTIONS TOPTEN ABOUT

NEWSWIRE

THE GLOBAL, SOCIALLY CONSCIOUS CONSUMER

GLOBAL | 03.27.2012

Around the world, companies have invested time, talent, and treasure in social and environmental efforts for a range of complementary reasons. For many companies, cause marketing—the use of social and environmental efforts to build a brand and increase profits—has been a secondary if not primary motivation.

Cause marketing won't work with all customer segments—some simply don't care—but research suggests that there is a segment of socially conscious consumers that cause marketers should pay attention to. But who are these socially conscious consumers? What causes are most important to them? What's the best way to reach them?

New findings from a Nielsen survey of more than 28,000 online respondents from 56 countries around the world provide fresh insights to help businesses better understand the right audience for cause marketers, which programs resonate most strongly with this audience, and what marketing methods may be most effective in reaching these consumers.

In the study, respondents were asked if they prefer to buy products and services from companies that implement programs that give back to society. Anticipating a positive response bias, respondents were also asked whether they would be willing to pay extra for those services. For the purposes of this study, Nielsen defines the "socially conscious consumer" as those who say they would be willing to pay the extra.

Two thirds (66%) of consumers around the world say they prefer to buy products and services from companies that have implemented programs to give back to society. That preference extends to other matters, too: they prefer to work for these companies (62%), and invest in these companies (59%). A smaller share, but still nearly half (46%) say they are willing to pay extra for products and services from these companies. These are the "socially conscious consumers," as defined by and focused upon in this report.

RELATED NEWS

Can Doing Good Be Good For Business?

Successful Brands Care The Case for Cause Marketing

Hunger Action Month Reminds us that Hunger is Closer than we Think

The Green Gap Between Environmental Concerns and the Cash Register

Global Concerns for Climate Change Dips Amid Other Environmental and Economic Concerns

RELATED REPORTS

Sustainable Efforts & Environmental Concerns

3 Interested in learning more?

Contact Us

Two thirds (66%) of consumers around the world say they prefer to buy products and services from companies that have implemented programs to give back to society. That preference extends to other matters, too: they prefer to work for these companies (62%), and invest in these companies (59%). A smaller share, but still nearly half (46%) say they are willing to pay extra for products and services from these companies. These are the "socially conscious consumers," as defined by and focused upon in this report.

3 The speaker directly quotes from the source instead of paraphrasing, which provides stronger evidence and further credits the argument.

4 The speaker includes stronger language, like "a worldwide study," to emphasize the breadth of the agency's research.

Organization Website

Name the website, source qualifier, section of website cited (if applicable), and last update.

> *Example:* On its website, last updated September 18, 2015, the Society of Interventional Radiology, a national organization of physicians and scientists, explains that radio waves are harmless to healthy cells. . . .

If website content is undated or not regularly updated, review the site for credibility before use, using the criteria listed on pp. 68–69, "From Source to Speech: Evaluating Web Sources."

Blog

Name the blogger, source qualifier, affiliated website (if applicable), and date of posting.

> *Example:* In a July 8, 2015, posting on *Talking Points Memo,* a news blog that specializes in original reporting on government and politics, editor Josh Marshall notes that . . .

Television or Radio Program

Name the program, segment, reporter, source qualifier, and date aired.

> *Example:* Judy Woodruff, PBS Newshour co-anchor, described in a segment on the auto industry aired on June 2, 2015 . . .

Online Video

Name the online video source, program, segment, source qualifier, and date aired (if applicable).

> *Example:* In a session on "Mindfulness in the World" delivered at the Wisdom 2.0 Conference on February 26th, 2015, and broadcast on YouTube, Jon Kabat-Zinn, scientist, renowned author, and founding director of the Stress Reduction Clinic . . .

QUICK TIP

Credit Sources in Presentation Aids

Just as you acknowledge the ideas of others in the verbal portion of your speech, be sure to credit such material used in any accompanying presentation aids. When reproducing copyrighted material, such as a table or photograph, label it with a copyright symbol (©) and the source information. Even if it is not copyrighted, supporting material listed on a visual aid may require citation. You may cite this material orally, print the citation unobtrusively on the aid, or both.

Testimony (Lay or Expert)

Name the person, source qualifier, and date and context in which information was offered.

> *Example:* On July 17, 2014, in Congressional testimony before the U.S. Senate Foreign Relations Committee, Thomas A. Shannon Jr., an attorney with the U.S. Department of State, described the exodus of unaccompanied minors from Central America. . . .

Interview and Other Personal Communication

Name the person, source qualifier, and date of the interview/communication.

> *Example:* In an interview I conducted last week, Tim Zeutenhorst, Chairman of the Orange City Area Health System Board, at Orange City Hospital in Iowa, said . . .

> *Example:* In a June 23rd e-mail/letter/memorandum from Ron Jones, a researcher at the Cleveland Clinic . . .

✓ CHECKLIST

Offering Key Source Information

- ❑ Have I identified the author or origin of the source?
- ❑ Have I indicated the type of source?
- ❑ Have I offered the title or description of the source?
- ❑ Have I noted the date of the source?
- ❑ Have I qualified the source to establish its reliability and credibility?

part

Organization

11. **Organizing the Body of the Speech** 80

12. **Selecting an Organizational Pattern** 89

13. **Outlining the Speech** 95

CHAPTER 11

Organizing the Body of the Speech

A speech structure is simple, composed of just three basic parts: an introduction, a body, and a conclusion. The **introduction** establishes the purpose of the speech and shows its relevance to the audience. The **body** of the speech presents main points that are intended to fulfill the speech purpose. The **conclusion** brings closure to the speech by restating the purpose, summarizing main points, and reiterating the speech thesis and its relevance to the audience. In essence, the introduction of a speech tells listeners where they are going, the body takes them there, and the conclusion lets them know the journey has ended.

Chapter 14 describes how to create effective introductions and conclusions. Here we focus on the elements of the speech body: *main points, supporting points,* and *transitions.*

◎ Use Main Points to Make Your Claims

Main points express the key ideas of the speech. Their function is to represent each of the major ideas or claims being made in support of the speech thesis. To create main points, identify the most important ideas you want to convey. What major findings emerge from your research? Each of these ideas should be expressed as a main point.

Restrict the Number of Main Points

Research indicates that audiences are most comfortable taking in between two and seven main points.[1] For most speeches, and especially those delivered in the classroom, between two and five main points should be sufficient. As a rule, the fewer main points in a speech, the greater the odds that you will maintain your listeners' attention. If you have too many main points, further narrow your topic (see Chapter 7) or check the points for proper subordination (see pp. 82–83).

Restrict Each Main Point to a Single Idea

A main point should not introduce more than one idea. If it does, split it into two (or more) main points:

Incorrect:	**I.** West Texas has its own Grand Canyon, and south Texas has its own desert.
Correct:	**I.** West Texas boasts its own Grand Canyon.
	II. South Texas boasts its own desert.

QUICK TIP

Save the Best for Last—or First

Listeners have the best recall of speech points made at the end of a speech (a phenomenon termed the "recency effect") and at the beginning of a speech (the "primacy effect") than of those made in between (unless the ideas made in between are much more striking than the others).[2] If it is especially important that listeners remember certain ideas, introduce those ideas near the beginning of the speech and reiterate them at the conclusion.

Main points should be mutually exclusive of one another. If they are not, consider whether a main point more properly serves as a subpoint.

Express each main point as a *declarative sentence*—one that asserts or claims something. For example, if one of your main points is that children need more vitamin D, clearly state, "According to the American Academy of Pediatrics, children from infants to teens should consume more vitamin D." In addition, state your main points (and supporting points; see below) in *parallel form*—that is, in similar grammatical form and style (see p. 123). Phrasing points in parallel form helps listeners follow your ideas more easily while lending a rhythmic elegance to your words.

Use the Purpose and Thesis Statements as Guides

Main points should flow directly from your specific purpose and thesis statements (see pp. 50–51), as in the following example:

Specific Purpose:
What you want the audience to learn or do as a result of your speech

"To show my audience, through a series of easy steps, how to meditate."

Thesis:
The central idea of the speech

"When performed correctly using just three steps, meditation is an effective and easy way to reduce stress."

Main Points:

I. The first step of meditation is the "positioning."

II. The second step of meditation is "breathing."

III. The third step of meditation is "relaxation."

◎ Use Supporting Points to Demonstrate Your Claims

Supporting points organize the evidence you have gathered to explain (in an informative speech) or justify (in a persuasive speech) the main points. Generate these points with the supporting material you've collected in your research—examples, narratives, testimony, facts, and statistics (see Chapter 8).

In an outline, supporting points appear in a subordinate position to main points. This is indicated by *indentation*. Arrange supporting points in order of their importance or relevance to the main point.

✓ CHECKLIST

Reviewing Main and Supporting Points

- ❑ Do the main points flow directly from the speech goal and thesis?
- ❑ Do the main points express the key points of the speech?
- ❑ Is each main point truly a main point or a subpoint of another main point?
- ❑ Is each main point substantiated by at least two supporting points—or none?
- ❑ Do you spend roughly the same amount of time on each main point?
- ❑ Are the supporting points truly subordinate to the main points?
- ❑ Does each main point and supporting point focus on a single idea?
- ❑ Are the main and supporting points stated in parallel form?

◎ Pay Close Attention to Coordination and Subordination

Outlines reflect the principles of **coordination and subordination**—the logical placement of ideas relative to their importance to one another. Ideas that are *coordinate* are given equal weight; **coordinate points** are indicated by their parallel alignment. An idea that is *subordinate* to another is given relatively less weight; **subordinate points** are indicated by their indentation below the more important points.

The most common format for outlining points is the **roman numeral outline**. Main points are enumerated with uppercase roman numerals (I, II, III . . .), while supporting points are enumerated with capital letters (A, B, C . . .), Arabic numerals (1, 2, 3 . . .), and lowercase letters (a, b, c . . .), as seen in the following example (in phrase outline form; see p. 96) from a speech about using effective subject lines in business-related e-mails:

I. Subject line most important, yet neglected part of e-mail

  A. Determines if recipient reads message

    1. Needs to specify point of message

    2. Needs to distinguish from spam

  B. Determines if recipient ignores message

    1. May ignore e-mail with missing subject line

    2. May ignore e-mail with unclear subject line

II. Use proven techniques for effective subject lines

  A. Make them informative

    1. Give specific details

    2. Match central idea of e-mail

    3. Be current

  B. Check for sense

    1. Convey correct meaning

    2. Reflect content of message

  C. Avoid continuing subject line in text

    1. May annoy the reader

    2. May be unclear

      a. Could be confused with spam

      b. Could be misinterpreted

PRINCIPLES OF COORDINATION AND SUBORDINATION

- Assign equal weight to ideas that are coordinate.
- Assign relatively less weight to ideas that are subordinate.
- Indicate coordinate points by their parallel alignment.
- Indicate subordinate points by their indentation below the more important points.
- Every point must be supported by at least two points or none at all (consider how to address one "dangling" point by including it in the point above it).

QUICK TIP

Spend Time Organizing Speech Points

Don't skimp on organizing speech points. Listeners' understanding of information is directly linked to how well it is organized,[3] and they will quickly lose interest when the speech is disorganized.[4] Listeners also find speakers whose speeches are well organized more believable than those who present poorly organized ones.[5]

◉ Strive for a Unified, Coherent, and Balanced Organization

A well-organized speech is characterized by unity, coherence, and balance. Try to adhere to these principles as you arrange your speech points.

A speech exhibits *unity* when it contains only those points implied by the specific purpose and thesis statements (see pp. 50–51). The thesis is supported by main points, main points are strengthened by supporting points, and supporting points consist of carefully chosen evidence and examples.

A speech exhibits *coherence* when it is organized clearly and logically, using the principles of coordination and subordination to align speech points in order of importance (see "Principles of Coordination and Subordination," below). In addition, the speech body should expand upon the introduction, and the conclusion should summarize the body. Within the body of the speech itself, main points should support the thesis statement, and supporting points should enlarge upon the main points. Transitions serve as mental bridges that help establish coherence.

Inexperienced speakers may give overly lengthy coverage to one point and insufficient attention to others; or they might provide scanty evidence in the speech body after presenting an impressive introduction. The principle of *balance* suggests that appropriate emphasis or weight be given to each part of the speech relative to the other parts and to the theme. The body of a speech should always be the longest part, and the introduction and conclusion should be of roughly the same length. Stating the main points in parallel form is one aspect of balance. Assigning each main point at least two supporting points is another. If you have only one subpoint, consider how you might incorporate it into the superior point. Think of a main point as a body and supporting points as legs; without at least two legs, the body cannot stand.

◎ Use Transitions to Give Direction to the Speech

Transitions are words, phrases, or sentences that tie the speech ideas together and enable the listener to follow the speaker as he or she moves from one point to the next. Transitions (also called *connectives*) are a truly critical component of speeches because listeners cannot go back and re-read what they might have missed. As you develop your speech, focus on creating transitions to shift listeners from one point to the next and signal to the audience that a new point will be made. Transitions can take the form of full sentences, phrases, or single words.

Use Transitions between Speech Points

Use transitions to move between speech points: from one main point to the next, and from one subpoint to another.

When moving from one *main point* to another, **full-sentence transitions** are especially effective. For example, to move from main point I in a speech about sales contests (*"Top management should sponsor sales contests to halt the decline in sales over the past two years"*) to main point II (*"Sales contests will lead to better sales presentations"*), the speaker might use the following transition:

> Next, let's look at exactly what sales contests can do for us.

Transitions between *supporting points* can be handled using single words, phrases, or full sentences as in the following:

> Next, . . .
> First, . . . (second, third, and so forth)
> Similarly, . . .
> We now turn . . .
> If you think that's shocking, consider this . . .

Transitions can also serve the dual function of signaling shifts between speech points and indicating relationships between ideas, as seen in the table on page 88.

Use Internal Previews and Summaries as Transitions

Previews briefly introduce audience members to the ideas that the speaker will address. In a speech introduction, the **preview statement** briefly mentions the main points and thesis of the speech (see p. 98 and p. 112). Within the body

FROM POINT TO POINT

Using Transitions to Guide Your Listeners

Transitions direct your listeners from one point to another in your speech, leading them forward along a logical path while reinforcing key ideas along the way. Plan on using transitions to move between:

- The introduction and the body of the speech
- The main points
- The subpoints, whenever appropriate
- The body of the speech and the conclusion

Introduction

  I. Today I'll explore the steps you can take to create a greener campus . . .

(Transition: So how do you go green?)

Body

  A. Get informed—understand what is physically happening to your planet

(Transition: Understanding the issues is only part of going green, however. Perhaps most important, . . .)

  B. Recognize that change starts here, on campus, with you. . . .

While transitions help guide your listeners from point to point, they can also do a lot more, including:

- Introduce main points
- Illustrate cause and effect
- Signal explanations and examples
- Emphasize, repeat, compare, or contrast ideas
- Summarize and preview information
- Suggest conclusions from evidence

Following is an excerpt from a working outline on a speech about campuses going green. Note how the student edits himself to ensure that he (1) uses transitions to help listeners follow along and retain his speech points and (2) uses transitions strategically to achieve his goal of persuading the audience.

(**Transition:** Why are environmentalists targeting college campuses?)

I. College campuses generate the waste equivalent of many large towns . . .

(**Transition:** As a result . . .)

   A. Colleges face disposal issues, especially of electronics . . .

   B. Administrators face decisions about mounting energy costs . . .

(**Transition:** Following are some ideas to create a greener campus. First . . .)

I. Promote a campus-wide recycling program

(**Transition:** For example . . .)

   A. Decrease the availability of bottled water and disposable . . .

   B. Insist on recycling bins at all residence halls . . .

   C. Encourage computer centers to recycle . . .

(**Transition:** Recycling is a critical part of going green. Decreasing the consumption of plastic and paper, installing recycling bins, and responsibly disposing of print cartridges will make a huge difference. Another aspect of going green is using sustainable energy . . .)

II. Lobby administrators to investigate solar, wind, and geothermal . . .

   A. Make an argument for "eco-dorms . . ."

   B. Explore alternative heating . . .

(**Transition:** So far, we've talked about practical actions we can take to encourage a greener lifestyle on campus, but what about beyond the campus?)

III. Get involved at the town government level

   A. Town-grown communities . . .

   B. Speak up and voice your concerns . . .

(**Transition:** As you can see, we have work to do . . .)

Conclusion

I. If we want our children and our children's children to see a healthy earth, we must take action now . . .

USE TRANSITIONAL WORDS AND PHRASES

- **To show comparisons:** Similarly; In the same way; Likewise; Just as

- **To contrast ideas:** On the other hand; And yet; At the same time; In spite of; However; In contrast

- **To illustrate cause and effect:** As a result; Hence; Because; Thus; Consequently

- **To illustrate sequence of time or events:** First, second, third . . . ; Following this; Later; Earlier; At present; In the past

- **To indicate explanation:** For example; To illustrate; In other words; To simplify; To clarify

- **To indicate additional examples:** Not only; In addition to; Let's look at

- **To emphasize significance:** Most important; Above all; Remember; Keep in mind

- **To summarize:** In conclusion; In summary; Finally; Let me conclude by saying

itself, speakers use an **internal preview** to signal a shift from one main point or idea to another:

> Victoria Woodhull was a pioneer in many respects. Not only was she the first woman to run her own brokerage firm, she was also the first to run for the presidency of the United States, though few people know this. Let's see how she accomplished these feats.

Similar to the internal preview, the **internal summary** draws together important ideas before the speaker proceeds to another speech point. Often, a speaker will transition from one major idea or main point to the next by using an internal summary and internal preview together:

> We've seen that mountain bikes differ from road bikes in the design of the tires, the seat, the gears, the suspension systems, and the handlebars. (*internal summary*) Now let's take a look at the different types of mountain bikes themselves. As you will see, mountain bikes vary according to the type of riding they're designed to handle—downhill, trails, and cross-country. Let's begin with cross-country. (*internal preview*)

See Chapter 13, "Outlining the Speech," for guidance on including transitions in the outline of your speech.

CHAPTER 12

Selecting an Organizational Pattern

Of all of the aspects of speechmaking, the idea of organizational arrangements may seem the most confusing. But selecting and organizing speech points into a pattern is easier and more natural than it might seem. An organizational pattern helps the audience follow the speaker's ideas and link points together to maximum effect. Studies confirm that the way you organize your ideas affects your audience's understanding of them, so you'll want to make use of a pattern.[1] A good time to select one is after you've researched the speech and prepared preliminary main points.

Speeches make use of at least a dozen different organizational arrangements of main and supporting points. Here we look at six commonly used patterns: chronological, spatial, causal (cause-effect), problem-solution, topical, and narrative. In Chapter 23, you will find three additional patterns of organization designed specifically for persuasive speeches: *Monroe's motivated sequence, comparative advantage*, and *refutation*.

◉ Arranging Speech Points Chronologically

Some topics lend themselves well to the arrangement of main points according to their occurrence in time relative to one another. A **chronological pattern**, also called a *temporal pattern*, follows the natural sequential order of the topic under consideration. Topics that describe a series of events in time (such as events leading to development of a new vaccine) or follow a set of instructions (such as steps in installing solar panels) call out for this pattern. A speech describing the development of the World Wide Web, for example, calls for a chronological, or time-ordered, sequence of main points:

Thesis Statement:	The Internet evolved from a small network designed for military and academic scientists into a vast array of networks used by billions of people around the globe.
Main Points:	I. The Internet was first conceived in 1962 as the ARPANET to promote the sharing of research among scientists in the United States.
	II. In the 1980s, a team created TCP/IP, a language that could link networks, and the Internet as we know it was born.

> **III.** At the end of the Cold War, the ARPANET was decommissioned, and the World Wide Web constituted the bulk of Internet traffic.[2]

◉ Arranging Speech Points Using a Spatial Pattern

When describing the physical arrangement of a place, a scene, or an object, logic suggests that the main points can be arranged in order of their physical proximity or direction relative to one another. This calls for a **spatial pattern**. For example, you can select a spatial arrangement when your speech provides the audience with a "tour" of a particular place:

Thesis Statement:	El Morro National Monument in New Mexico is captivating for its variety of natural and historical landmarks.
Main Points:	**I.** Visitors first encounter an abundant variety of plant life native to the high-country desert.
	II. Soon visitors come upon an age-old watering hole that has receded beneath the 200-foot cliffs.
	III. Beyond are the famous cliff carvings made by hundreds of travelers over several centuries of exploration in the Southwest.

In a speech describing a geothermal heating and cooling company's market growth across regions of the country, a speaker might use the spatial arrangement as follows:

Thesis Statement:	Sales of geothermal systems have grown in every region of the country.
Main Points:	**I.** Sales are strongest in the Eastern Zone.
	II. Sales are growing at a rate of 10 percent quarterly in the Central Zone.
	III. Sales are up slightly in the Mountain Zone.

◉ Arranging Speech Points Using a Causal (Cause-Effect) Pattern

Some speech topics represent cause-effect relationships. Examples include (1) events leading to higher interest rates, (2) reasons students drop out of college, and (3) effects of skipping vaccinations. The main points in a **causal (cause-effect) pattern of arrangement** usually take the following form:

    I. Cause

    II. Effect

Sometimes a topic can be discussed in terms of multiple causes for a single effect, or a single cause for multiple effects:

Multiple Causes for a Single Effect (Reasons Students Drop Out of College)	Single Cause for Multiple Effects (Reasons Students Drop Out of College)
I. Cause 1 (lack of funds)	**I.** Cause (lack of funds)
II. Cause 2 (unsatisfactory social life)	**II.** Effect 1 (lowered earnings over lifetime)
III. Cause 3 (unsatisfactory academic performance)	**III.** Effect 2 (decreased job satisfaction over lifetime)
IV. Effect (drop out of college)	**IV.** Effect 3 (increased stress level over lifetime)

Some topics are best understood by presenting listeners with the effect(s) before the cause(s). In a speech on health care costs, a student speaker arranges his main points as follows:

Thesis Statement:	In response to rising health care costs, large employers are shifting part of the expense to workers.
Main Points:	**I.** (Effect) Workers are now seeing higher co-pays and deductibles.
Main Points:	**II.** (Effect) Raising the amount employees must contribute has restricted employer costs to just 5 percent this year.

QUICK TIP

Blend Organizational Patterns

The pattern of organization for your subpoints can differ from the pattern you select for your main points. *Do keep your main points in one pattern — this will be the predominant pattern for the speech* — but feel free to use other patterns for subpoints when it makes sense to do so. For instance, for a speech about the history of tattooing in the United States, you may choose a chronological pattern to organize the main points but use a cause-effect arrangement for some of your subpoints regarding why tattooing is on the rise today.

    III. (Cause) The Affordable Care Act mandates that large employers offer more of their workers health care plans.

    IV. (Cause) Rising health care costs have lead to more expensive plans at all levels of coverage.

◉ Arranging Speech Points Using a Problem-Solution Pattern

The **problem-solution pattern** organizes main points to demonstrate the nature and significance of a problem followed by a proposed solution. Most often used in persuasive speeches, the problem-solution pattern can be arranged as simply as two main points:

    I. Problem (define what it is)

    II. Solution (offer a way to overcome the problem)

But many problem-solution speeches require more than two points to adequately explain the problem and to substantiate the recommended solution:

    I. The nature of the problem (identify its causes, incidence, etc.)

    II. Effects of the problem (explain why it's a problem, for whom, etc.)

    III. Unsatisfactory solutions (discuss those that have not worked)

    IV. Proposed solution (explain why it's expected to work)

Following is a partial outline of a persuasive speech about cyber-bullying arranged in a problem-solution format (for more on using the problem-solution pattern in persuasive speeches, see Chapter 24).

Thesis Statement:	To combat cyber-bullying, we need to educate the public about it, report it when it happens, and punish the offenders.
Main Point:	**I.** Nature of cyber-bullying

        A. Types of activities involved

            1. Name-calling, insults

            2. Circulation of embarrassing pictures

            3. Sharing private information

            4. Threats

B. Incidence of bullying

C. Profile of offenders

Main Point: **II.** Effects of cyber-bullying on victims

   A. Acting out in school

   B. Feeling unsafe in school

   C. Skipping school

   D. Experiencing depression

Main Point: **III.** Unsuccessful attempts at solving cyber-bullying

   A. Let offenders and victims work it out on their own

   B. Ignore problem, assuming it will go away

Main Point: **IV.** Ways to solve cyber-bullying

   A. Educate in schools

   B. Report incidents to authorities

   C. Suspend or expel offenders

◉ Arranging Speech Points Topically

When each of the main points is a subtopic or category of the speech topic, try the **topical pattern** (also called **categorical pattern**). Consider an informative speech about choosing Chicago as a place to establish a career. You plan to emphasize three reasons for choosing Chicago: the strong economic climate of the city, its cultural variety, and its accessible public transportation. Since these three points are of relatively equal importance, they can be arranged in any order without affecting one another or the speech purpose negatively. For example:

Thesis
Statement: Chicago is an excellent place to establish a career.

Main Points: **I.** Accessible transportation

   II. Cultural variety

   III. Multiple industries

This is not to say that, when using a topical arrangement, you should arrange the main points without careful consideration. Any number of considerations can factor in your ordering of points, not least of which should be the audience's most immediate needs and interests. Perhaps you have determined that listeners' main concern is the city's multiple industries, followed by an interest in its cultural variety and accessible transportation.

QUICK TIP

Find Freedom with the Topical Pattern

Topical arrangements give you the greatest freedom to structure main points according to the way you wish to present your topic. You can approach a topic by dividing it into two or more categories, for example. You can lead with your strongest evidence or leave your most compelling points until you near the conclusion. If your topic does not call out for one of the other patterns described in this chapter, be sure to experiment with the topical pattern.

◉ Arranging Speech Points Using the Narrative Pattern

Storytelling is often a natural and effective way to get your message across. In the **narrative pattern**, the speech consists of a story or series of short stories complete with character, setting, brief plot, and vivid imagery.

In practice, a speech built largely upon a story (or series of stories) is likely to incorporate elements of other designs. You might organize the main points of the story in an effect-cause design, in which you first reveal the outcome of what

✓ CHECKLIST

Determining an Organizational Pattern

Does your speech . . .

❑ Describe a series of developments in time or a set of actions that occur sequentially? Use the *chronological pattern*.

❑ Describe or explain the physical arrangement of a place, a scene, or an object? Use the *spatial pattern*.

❑ Explain or demonstrate a topic in terms of its underlying causes or effects? Use the *causal pattern*.

❑ Demonstrate the nature and significance of a problem and justify a proposed solution? Use the *problem-solution pattern*.

❑ Stress natural divisions or categories of a topic, in which points can be moved to emphasize audience needs and interests? Use a *topical pattern*.

❑ Convey ideas through a story, using character, plot, and settings? Use a *narrative pattern*, perhaps in combination with another pattern.

happened (such as a drunken driving accident) and then describe the events that led up to the accident (the causes).

Whatever the structure, simply telling a story is no guarantee of giving a good speech. Any speech should include a clear thesis, well-organized main points, and effective transitions, so be certain to include these elements as you organize the speech.

CHAPTER 13 ● ● ●●

Outlining the Speech

Outlines are enormously helpful in putting together a speech, providing a framework for your speech materials and a blueprint for your presentation. In an **outline** you separate main and supporting points—the major speech claims and the evidence to support them—into larger and smaller divisions and subdivisions. Plotting ideas into hierarchical fashion based on their relative importance to one another and using indentation to visually represent this hierarchy will allow you to examine the underlying logic and relationship of ideas to one another. (For a review of the principles and of the mechanics of outlining, see Chapter 11.)

◉ Plan on Creating Two Outlines

As you develop a speech, plan on creating two outlines: a working outline (also called a *preparation or rough outline*) and a speaking, or delivery, outline. Use the **working outline** to organize and firm up main points and, with the research you've gathered, develop supporting points to substantiate them. Completed, the working outline should contain your entire speech, organized and supported to your satisfaction.

Use a **speaking outline** to practice and actually present the speech. Speaking outlines contain the working outline in condensed form and are much briefer. Figure 13.1 provides an overview of the steps involved in outlining a speech.

Use Sentences, Phrases, or Key Words

Speeches can be outlined in sentences, phrases, or key words. Working outlines typically contain sentences, reflecting much of the text of the speech; speaking outlines use key words or short phrases.

In the **sentence outline format**, each main and supporting point is stated in sentence form as a declarative statement (e.g., one that makes an assertion about something). Following is an excerpt in sentence format from a speech by Mark B. McClellan on keeping prescription drugs safe:[1]

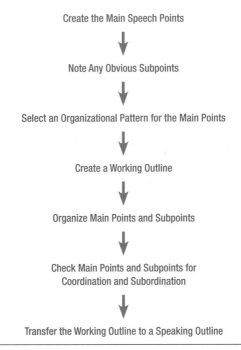

Create the Main Speech Points

⬇

Note Any Obvious Subpoints

⬇

Select an Organizational Pattern for the Main Points

⬇

Create a Working Outline

⬇

Organize Main Points and Subpoints

⬇

Check Main Points and Subpoints for
Coordination and Subordination

⬇

Transfer the Working Outline to a Speaking Outline

FIGURE 13.1 **Steps in Organizing and Outlining the Speech**

I. The prescription drug supply is under attack from a variety of increasingly sophisticated threats.

   A. Technologies for counterfeiting—ranging from pill molding to dyes—have improved across the board.

   B. Inadequately regulated Internet sites have become major portals for unsafe and illegal drugs.

A **phrase outline** uses partial construction of the sentence form of each point. McClellan's sentence outline would appear as follows in phrase outline form:

I. Drug supply under attack

   A. Counterfeiting technologies more sophisticated

   B. Unregulated Internet sites

The **key-word outline** uses the smallest possible units of understanding to outline the main and supporting points. Keyword outlines encourage you to become familiar enough with your speech points that a glance at a few words is enough to remind you of exactly what to say:

I. Threats

   A. Counterfeiting

   B. Internet

Use a Key-Word Outline for Optimal Eye Contact

The type of outline you select will affect how you deliver a speech. The less you rely on reading any outline, the more eye contact you can have with audience members—an essential aspect of a successful speech. For this reason, experts recommend outlines containing key words or phrases over sentences, with the succinct key-word outline often being the preferred format. Key-word outlines permit not only the greatest degree of eye contact but also greater freedom of movement and better control of your thoughts and actions than either sentence or phrase outlines. With sufficient practice, the key words will jog your memory so that the delivery of your ideas becomes more natural.

◎ Create a Working Outline First

Begin with a working outline before transferring your ideas to a speaking outline containing key words or shortened phrases, editing and rearranging as necessary as you work through the mass of information you've collected.

Prepare the body of the speech *before* the introduction, keeping the introduction (and the conclusion) *separate from* the main points (see sample outlines in this chapter). Since introductions serve to preview main points, you will first need to finalize them in the body. Introductions must also gain the audience's attention, introduce the topic and thesis, and establish the speaker's credibility (see Chapter 14). To ensure that you address these elements, use such labels as *Attention Getter*, *Topic and Thesis*, *Credibility Statement*, and *Preview Statement*.

SAMPLE WORKING OUTLINE

The following working outline is from a speech delivered by public speaking student Zachary Dominque. It includes all elements of the speech, including transitions, and reminders to show presentation aids (SHOW SLIDE) in magenta.

The History and Sport of Mountain Biking

Zachary Dominque
St. Edwards University

Topic:	Mountain Biking
General Speech Purpose:	To inform my listeners about the sport of mountain biking
Specific Purpose:	To help my audience gain an overview of and appreciation for mountain biking

Thesis Statement: Mountain biking is a relatively new, exciting, and diverse sport.

Introduction
(Attention Getter)

   I. Imagine that you're on a bike, plunging down a steep, rock-strewn mountain, yet fully in control.

   II. Adrenaline courses through your body as you hurtle through the air, touch down on glistening pebbled streams and tangled grasses, and rocket upward again.

   III. You should be scared, but you're not; in fact, you're having the time of your life.

   IV. Like we say, Nirvana.

   V. How many of you like to bike—ride to campus, bike for fitness, or cycle just for fun?

   VI. You might own a bike with a lightweight frame and thin wheels, and use it to log some serious mileage—or possibly a comfort bike, with a nice soft seat and solid tires.

   VII. Good morning, folks. My name is Zachary Dominque, and I'm a mountain biker.

   VIII. I've been racing since I was eight years old and won state champion three years ago, so this topic is close to my heart.

(Preview Statement)

   IX. Today, I'm going to take you on a tour of the exciting sport of mountain biking: I'll be your engine—your driver—in mountain bike–speak.

   X. Our ride begins with a brief overview of mountain biking; then we'll do a hopturn—a turn in reverse—to learn about the sport's colorful history.

   XI. Pedalling ahead in this beautiful autumn air, we'll chat about the various differences in design and function between mountain bikes and road bikes.

   XII. We'll conclude our tour at a local bike shop, where you can compare downhill, trail, and cross-country mountain bikes.

   XIII. These are the three main types of mountain bikes, designed for the three major types of mountain biking.

   XIV. I hope by then that you'll catch a little bit of mountain biking fever and see why I find it such an exciting, intense, and physically challenging sport.

Transition: Mountain biking is a sport that can be extreme, recreational, or somewhere in between. But no matter what kind of rider you are, it's always a great way to get out in the natural world and get the adrenaline going. To start, let me briefly define mountain biking.

Body

I. The website ABC of Mountain Biking offers a good basic definition: "Mountain biking is a form of cycling on off-road or unpaved surfaces such as mountain trails and dirt roads; the biker uses a bicycle with a sturdy frame and fat tires."

  A. The idea behind mountain biking is to go where other bikes won't take you.

    1. Mountain bikers ride on backcountry roads and on single-track trails winding through fields or forests.

    2. They climb up steep, rock-strewn hills and race down over them.

    3. The focus is on self-reliance, because these bikers often venture miles from help.

  B. According to the National Bicycle Dealers Association website, in 2013 mountain bikes accounted for 25 percent of all bikes sold in the United States.

    1. If you factor in sales of the comfort bike, which is actually a mountain bike modified for purely recreational riders, sales jump to nearly 38 percent of all bikes sold.

    2. Some 50 million Americans love riding their mountain bikes, according to data collected by the New England Mountain Bike Association.

Transition: So you see that mountain biking is popular with a lot of people. But the sport itself is fairly new.

II. The history of mountain biking is less than 50 years old, and its founders are still around.

  A. The man in this picture is Gary Fisher, one of the founders of mountain biking. (SHOW PHOTO)

  B. According to *The Original Mountain Bike Book*, written in 1998 by pioneering mountain bikers Rob van der Plas and Charles Kelly, they, along with Fisher, Joe Breeze, and other members of the founding posse from the Marin County, California, area, were instrumental in founding the modern sport of mountain biking in the early 1970s.

C. Mountain bikes—called MTBs or ATBs (for all-terrain bikes)—didn't exist then as we now know them, so as you can see in this picture of Gary Fisher, he's riding a modified one-speed Schwinn cruiser. (SHOW GARY)

    1. Cruisers, or "ballooners," aren't made to go off road at all.

    2. Nothing equips them to navigate trails, and their brakes aren't remotely equipped to handle stops on steep descents.

    3. But this is the type of bike Fisher and others started out with.

D. By the mid-1970s, growing numbers of bikers in California got into using modified cruisers to race downhill on rocky trails.

    1. They'd meet at the bottom of Mount Tamalpais, in Corte Madera, California.

    2. They'd walk their bikes a mile or two up its steep slopes, and hurl on down.

E. As even more people got involved, Charles Kelly and others organized the famed Repack Downhill Race on Mt. Tam.

    1. Held from 1976 to 1979, the Repack race became a magnet for enthusiasts and put the sport on the map, according to *The Original Mountain Bike Book.*

Transition: The reason why the race was called "Repack" is a story in itself.

    2. The trail in the Repack race plummeted 1,300 feet in less than 2 miles, according to the Marin Museum of Biking website.

        a. Such a steep drop meant constant braking, which in turn required riders to replace, or "repack," their bikes' grease after nearly each run.

        b. As Breeze recounts in his own words: "The bikes' antiquated hub coaster brake would get so hot that the grease would vaporize, and after a run or two, the hub had to be repacked with new grease."

Transition: As you might imagine, these early enthusiasts eventually tired of the routine.

F. The bikers had tinkered with their bikes from the start, adding gearing, drum brakes, and suspension systems.

G. In 1979, Joe Breeze designed a new frame—called the "Breezer"—which became the first actual mountain bike.

H. By 1982, as van der Plas and Kelly write in *The Original Mountain Bike Book*, standardized production of mountain bikes finally took off.

Transition: Now that you've learned a bit of the history of mountain biking, let's look at what today's mountain bike can do. To make things clearer, I'll compare them to road bikes. Road bikes are the class of bikes that cyclists who compete in the Tour de France use.

III. Mountain bikes and road bikes are built for different purposes.

A. Mountain bikes are built to tackle rough ground, while road bikes are designed to ride fast on paved, smooth surfaces.

 1. To accomplish their task, mountain bikes feature wide tires with tough tread.

 2. In contrast, road bike tires are ultrathin and their frames extremely lightweight.

 a. If you take a road bike off-road, chances are you'll destroy it.

 b. Without the knobby tread and thickness found on mountain bike tires, road bike tires can't grip onto the rocks and other obstacles that cover off-road courses.

B. The handlebars on the bikes also differ, as you can see here. (SHOW HANDLEBARS)

 1. Mountain bikes feature flat handlebars; these keep us in an upright stance, so that we don't flip over when we hit something.

 2. The drop handlebars on road bikes require the cyclist to lean far forward; this position suits road cycling, which prizes speed.

C. The gears and suspension systems also differentiate mountain bikes from road bikes.

 1. Mountain bikes use lower gears than road bikes and are more widely spaced, giving them more control to ride difficult terrain.

 2. As for suspension, road bikes generally don't have any kind of suspension system that can absorb power.

 a. That is, they don't have shock absorbers because they're not supposed to hit anything.

 b. Imagine riding over rocks and roots without shocks; it wouldn't be pretty.

3. Many mountain bikes have at least a great front shock absorbing suspension system.

    a. Some have rear-suspension systems.

    b. Some bikes have dual systems.

Transition: I hope by now you have a sense of the mountain bike design. But there are finer distinctions to draw.

IV. There are actually three different types of mountain bikes, designed to accommodate the three major kinds of mountain biking—downhill, trails, and cross-country.

Transition: Let's start with downhill. (SHOW BIKE)

A. Downhill bikes have the fewest gears of the three types of mountain bikes and weigh the most.

    1. That's because downhill biking is a daredevil sport—these bikers are crazy!

    2. They slide down hills at insane speeds, and they go off jumps.

B. As described on the website **Trails.com**, downhill racers catch a shuttle going up the mountain, then speed downhill while chewing up obstacles.

C. Think of downhill racing as skiing with a bike.

Transition: Now let's swing by trails biking.

D. Trails bikes look quite different than either downhill or cross-country bikes. (SHOW TRAIL BIKE)

    1. They have very small wheels, measuring either 20, 24, or 26 inches, and smaller frames.

    2. These differences in design help trail bikers do what they do best: jump over obstacles—cars, rocks, and large logs.

E. The trail biker's goal is to not put a foot down on the ground.

F. Trail bike racing is one of the few types of biking that's done by time, not all at a mass start.

Transition: The third major type of mountain biking, cross-country, or XC cycling, is my sport. (SHOW XC)

G. Cross-country biking is also the most common type of mountain biking—and the one sponsored by the Olympics.

      1. That's right. According to **Olympic.org**, in 1996, mountain biking became an Olympic sport.

      2. This was just two decades after its inception.

  H. With cross-country, you get the best of all worlds, at least in my humble opinion.

      1. The courses are creative, incorporating hills and valleys and rough to not-so-rough terrain.

      2. If done competitively, cross-country biking is like competing in a marathon.

      3. Done recreationally, it offers you the chance to see the great outdoors while getting, or staying, in great shape.

  I. Cross-country bikes come in two forms.

      1. XC bikes are very lightweight, with either full or partial suspension.

      2. The Trails/Marathon XC hybrid bikes are a bit heavier, with full suspension; XC bikes are designed for seriously long rides.

Transition: Well, it has been quite a tour, folks. *(Signals close of speech)*

Conclusion

  I. Our course began with an overview of mountain biking and a hopturn into a brief history of the sport.

 II. We also learned about the differences between mountain bikes and road bikes, and the three major categories of mountain bikes. *(Summarizes main points)*

III. To me, mountain biking, and especially cross-country, is the perfect sport—fulfilling physical, spiritual, and social needs.

 IV. It's a great sport to take up recreationally. *(Leaves audience with something to think about)*

  V. And if you decide to mountain bike competitively, just remember: ride fast, drive hard, and leave your blood on every trail. *(Memorable close)*

Works Cited

"Cycling, Mountain Biking," **Olympics.org** website, accessed February 15, 2015, **www.olympic.org/Assets/OSC%20Section/pdf/QR_sports_summer/Sports_Olympiques_VTT_eng.pdf**.

"The Economics and Benefits of Mountain Biking," New England Mountain Bike Association, accessed February 15, 2015, **www.nemba.org**.

"History of Mountain Biking," Marin Museum of Biking web-site, accessed February 15, 2015 **http://mmbhof.org/mtn-bike-hall-of-fame/history**.

"Industry Overview, 2013," National Bicycle Dealers Association, accessed February 15, 2015, **http://nbda.com/articles /industry-overview-2012-pg34.htm**.

"Types of Mountain Bikes," **Trails.com**, accessed February 15, 2015, **www.trails.com/types-of-mountain-bikes.html**.

Van der Plas, Rob, and Charles Kelly. *The Original Mountain Bike Book*. Minneapolis: Motorbooks, 1998.

"What Is Mountain Biking," ABC of Mountain Biking website, accessed February 15, 2015, **www.abc-of-mountainbiking .com/mountain-biking-basics/whatis-mountain-biking.asp**.

◉ Prepare a Speaking Outline for Delivery

Using the same numbering system as the working outline, condense long phrases or sentences into key words or short phrases, including just enough words to jog your memory. Include any *delivery cues* that will be part of the speech (see below). Place the speaking outline on large (at least 4 × 6-inch) notecards, 8.5 × 11-inch sheets of paper, or in a speaker's notes software program or app (see Chapter 21). Print large enough, or use large-enough fonts, so that you can see the words at a glance.

Indicate Delivery Cues

Include any **delivery cues** that will be part of the speech. To ensure visibility, capitalize the cues, place them in parentheses, and/or highlight them.

Delivery Cue	Example
Transitions	(TRANSITION)
Timing	(PAUSE) (SLOW DOWN)
Speaking Rate/Volume	(SLOWLY) (LOUDER)
Presentation Aids	(SHOW MODEL) (SLIDE 3)
Source	(ATLANTA CONSTITUTION, August 2, 2015)
Statistic	(2015, boys to girls = 94,232; U.S. Health Human Services)
Quotation	Eubie Blake, 100: "If I'd known I was gonna live this long, I'd have taken better care of myself."

Practice the Speech

The key to the successful delivery of a speech using a key-word outline is practice. For more information on practicing the speech, see Chapter 18.

SAMPLE SPEAKING OUTLINE

The History and Sport of Mountain Biking

Zachary Dominque
St. Edwards University

Introduction

(Attention Getter)

    I. Imagine on bike, plunging rock-strewn, yet control.

    II. Adrenaline, hurtle, touch downstream, rocket.

  III. Be scared, but not—time of life.

   IV. Nirvana.

    V. How many bike, fitness, fun?

   VI. Might own lightweight, thin wheels, serious mileage—or comfort, soft seat, solid tires.

  VII. Morning, Zachary, MTBer.

 VIII. Eight; champion, heart.

(Preview Statement)

   IX. Today, tour, exciting sport of . . . engine, driver, MTB-speak.

    X. Ride begins brief overview; do hopturn—colorful history.

   XI. Pedaling ahead autumn, chat differences between mountain, road.

  XII. Conclude shop, compare MTBs.

 XIII. Three types bikes, designed for three . . .

 XIV. Hope catch fever, exciting, intense, and physically.

    Transition: MTB sport extreme . . . in-between. But no matter, always great way natural world, adrenaline. Start, define.

Body

    I. ABC/MB def: "MTB is a form of cycling on off-road or unpaved surfaces such as mountain trails and dirt roads; the biker uses a bicycle with a sturdy frame and fat tires."

    A. The idea—go where others.

      1. MTBs ride backcountry, single-track winding fields, forests.

    2. Climb steep, rock-strewn, race down.

    3. Self-reliance, miles from help.

  B. National Bicycle Dealers Assoc., 2013 MTBs 25 percent sold.

    1. Factor comfort, actually MTB modified recreational, sales 38 percent.

    2. 50 million love riding, data gathered NE MTB Assn.

Transition: So MTB popular people. But fairly new.

II. History MTB less 50, founders.

  A. Gary Fisher, founders MTB. (SHOW PICTURE)

  B. *Original Mountain Bike Book*, written 1998 by van der Plas, Kelly; they, along with Fisher, Breeze, other members posse Marin, instrumental founding modern sport early 1970s.

  C. MTBs or ATBs (terrain)—didn't exist, so picture Fisher, modified Schwinn cruiser. (SHOW PICTURE)

    1. Cruisers, "ballooners," off-road.

    2. Nothing equips navigate, brakes equipped stops descents.

    3. But bike Fisher, others started.

  D. Mid-1970s, growing numbers using modified race downhill.

    1. Meet bottom Tamalpais, CA.

    2. Walk bikes mile up steep, hurl.

  E. Even involved, Kelly, others organized Repack.

    1. 1976–1979, magnet enthusiasts, on map, *Original MTB*.

Transition: Reason called "Repack" story itself.

    2. Trail plummeted 1,300 feet 2 miles, according Breeze article posted MTB Fame website.

      a. Such drop constant braking, required riders replace, "repack," grease each run.

      b. Breeze recounts: "The bikes' antiquated hub coaster brake would get so hot that the grease would vaporize, and after a run or two, the hub had to be repacked with new grease."

Transition: Might imagine, early enthusiasts tired.

  F. Bikers tinkered, gearing, drum, suspension.

  G. 1979, Breeze new frame—"Breezer"—first actual MTB.

  H. 1982, as van der Plas, Kelly write in *Original MTB*, standardized took off.

Transition: Now learned history, let's look today's can do. Clearer, compare road. Class cyclists Tour de France use.

III. MTB, road built different purposes.

    A. MTB tackle rough, road designed fast, paved, smooth.

        1. Accomplish task, wide tire, tough tread.

        2. In contrast, road ultrathin, frames lightweight.

          a. Take off-road, destroy.

          b. Without knobby tread, thickness MTB tires, road can't grip rocks, obstacles.

    B. Handlebars differ.

        1. MTB flat; upright stance, don't flip.

        2. Drop handlebars require lean forward; suits road cycling, prizes speed.

    C. Gears, suspension also differentiate.

        1. MTB lower gears, widely spaced — more control difficult terrain.

        2. As for suspension, road don't, absorb power.

          a. That is, don't have shock, not supposed to.

          b. Imagine without shocks; wouldn't be pretty.

        3. Many MTBs at least a great front.

          a. Some rear.

          b. Some dual.

Transition: Hope sense MTB design. But finer distinctions to draw.

IV. Actually three types MTB, accommodate three kinds.

Transition: Let's start with downhill.

    A. Downhill fewest gears, weigh most.

        1. Because downhill daredevil — crazy!

        2. Slide insane, off jumps.

    B. **Trails.com**, downhill racers catch shuttle going up, speed downhill chewing up.

    C. Think racing skiing bike.

Transition: Now let's swing by trails biking.

    D. Trails bikes look different than either.

        1. Small wheels, 20, 24, or 26, smaller frames.

        2. Differences design help trail do best — jump obstacles — cars, rocks, large logs.

    E. Trail goal not foot on ground.

    F. Trail racing few types done by time, not mass.

Transition: Third major type MTB, cross-country, or XC.

    G. Cross-country most common — Olympics.

        1. That's right. In 1996 . . .

        2. Just two decades inception.

    H. With XC, best all worlds, humble.

        1. Courses creative, incorporating hills, valleys, rough, not-so.

        2. Competitively, XC like marathon.

        3. Recreationally, chance see outdoors, shape.

    I. XC two forms.

        1. Lightweight, full or partial.

        2. Trails/Marathon XC hybrids heavier, full suspension; designed seriously long.

Transition: Quite tour. *(Signals close of speech)*

Conclusion

    I. Course began overview, hopturn history sport.

   II. Also learned differences: mountain, road, three major categories of MTB, three types MTB accommodate fans. *(Summarizes main points)*

  III. To me, MTB, especially XC, perfect — fulfilling physical, spiritual, social needs.

  IV. Great take up recreationally. *(Leaves audience with something to think about)*

   V. Decide bike competitively, remember: ride fast, drive hard, leave blood. *(Memorable close)*

✓ CHECKLIST

Steps in Creating a Speaking Outline

- ❏ Create the outline on sheets of paper, large notecards, or software app.
- ❏ Write large and legibly using at least a 14-point font or easy-to-read ink and large letters.
- ❏ For each main and subpoint, choose a key word or phrase that will jog your memory accurately.
- ❏ Include delivery cues.
- ❏ Write out full quotations or other critical information.
- ❏ Using the speaking outline, practice the speech at least five times, or as needed.

part

Starting, Finishing, and Styling

14. Developing the Introduction and Conclusion 110

15. Using Language 117

CHAPTER 14

Developing the Introduction and Conclusion

A compelling introduction and conclusion, although not a substitute for a well-developed speech body, are nevertheless essential to its success. A good opening previews what's to come in a way that engages listeners in the topic and speaker. An effective conclusion ensures that the audience remembers the message and reacts in a way that the speaker intends.

Any kind of supporting material—examples, stories, testimony, facts, or statistics; see Chapter 8—can be used to open and conclude a speech as long as it accomplishes these objectives.

◉ Preparing the Introduction

The choices you make about the introduction can affect the outcome of the entire speech. In the first several minutes (one speaker pegs it at twenty seconds),[1] audience members will decide whether they are interested in the topic of your speech and whether they will believe what you say.

A speech introduction serves to:

- Arouse the audience's attention and willingness to listen.
- Introduce the topic and purpose.
- Establish your credibility to speak on the topic.
- Preview the main points.
- Motivate the audience to accept your speech goals.

✓ CHECKLIST

Guidelines for Preparing the Introduction

❏ Prepare the introduction after you've completed the speech body so you will know exactly what you need to preview.

❏ Keep the introduction brief—as a rule, no more than 10 to 15 percent of the entire speech.

❏ Practice delivering your introduction until you feel confident you've got it right.

Gain Audience Attention

An introduction must first of all win the audience's attention. They must believe the speech will interest them and offer them something of benefit. Some time-honored techniques of doing this include sharing a compelling story, establishing common ground, providing unusual information, posing a question, using humor, and offering a quotation.

TELL A STORY   Noted speechwriter and language expert William Safire once remarked that stories are "surefire attention getters."[2] Stories, or *narratives*, that are directly relevant to your message encourage audience identification and involvement. Speeches that begin with brief stories of interesting, humorous, or real-life incidents also boost speaker credibility and promote greater understanding and retention of the speaker's message.[3] You can relate an entire story (if brief) in the introduction, or, alternatively, offer part of one, indicating you will return to it further on in the speech.

QUICK TIP

Show Them the Transformation

Stories often feature transformation—how people overcome obstacles or otherwise experience change.[4] One powerful means of gaining audience involvement is to tell a story in which others were changed by adopting beliefs and behaviors similar to those you are proposing in your speech. If you can think of a story that does this, your message is likely to be doubly persuasive.

ESTABLISH COMMON GROUND   Refer to the occasion that has brought you together, and use your knowledge of the audience to touch briefly on areas of shared experience. Audiences are won over when speakers express interest in them and show that they share in the audience's concerns and goals. This creates goodwill and a feeling of common ground (or *identification;* see also Chapter 6).

OFFER UNUSUAL INFORMATION   "Sean Connery wore a wig in every single one of his Bond performances." Surprising audience members with unusual facts is one of the surest ways to get their attention. Some the most effective statements are based in statistics, a powerful means of illustrating consequences and relationships that can quickly bring points into focus, as in this opener by Chef James Oliver: "Sadly, in the next eighteen minutes when I do our chat, four Americans that are alive will be dead from the food they eat."[5]

POSE A PROVOCATIVE QUESTION   "How long do you think our water supply will last?" Posing a question of vital interest to the audience can be an effective way to draw the audience's attention to what you are about to say. These sorts of questions are usually rhetorical, in that they do not invite actual responses, but instead make the audience think.

Sometimes a speaker will use a series of **rhetorical questions** to introduce different aspects of his or her topic.

USE HUMOR   Handled well, humor can build rapport and set a positive tone for the speech. But humor can also easily backfire. Telling a series of unrelated jokes without making a relevant point will detract from your purpose, and few things turn an audience off more quickly than tasteless humor. Strictly avoid humor or sarcasm that belittles others—whether on the basis of race, sex, ability, or otherwise. A good rule of thumb is that speech humor should always match the rhetorical situation.

USE A QUOTATION   A Czech proverb says, "Do not protect yourself by a fence but rather by your friends." A quotation that elegantly and succinctly expresses a theme of the speech will draw the audience's attention. Quotations can be culled from literature, poetry, and film, or directly from people you know.

State the Topic and Purpose

Once you've gained the audience's attention, use the introduction to alert listeners to the speech topic and purpose. Declare what your speech is about and what you hope to accomplish.

Topic and purpose are clearly revealed in this introduction by Marvin Runyon, former postmaster general of the United States:

> This afternoon, I want to examine the truth of that statement—"Nothing moves people like the mail, and no one moves the mail like the U.S. Postal Service." I want to look at where we are today as a communications industry, and where we intend to be in the days and years ahead.[6]

Establish Credibility as a Speaker

During the introduction, audience members make a decision about whether they are interested not just in your topic but also in you. They want to feel that they can trust what you have to say—that they can believe in your *ethos*, or good character. To build credibility, offer a simple statement of your qualifications for speaking on the topic. Briefly emphasize some experience, knowledge, or perspective you have that is different from or more extensive than that of your audience.

Preview the Main Points

Once you've revealed the topic and purpose and established your credibility, briefly preview the main points of the speech. This helps audience members mentally organize the speech as they follow along. An introductory **preview statement** is straightforward. You simply tell the audience what the main points will be and in what order you will address them. Save your in-depth discussion of each one for the body of your speech.

Robert L. Darbelnet effectively introduces his topic, purpose, and main points with this preview statement:

> My remarks today are intended to give you a sense of AAA's ongoing efforts to improve America's roads. Our hope is that you will join your voices to ours as we call on the federal government to do three things:
>
> Number one: Perhaps the most important, provide adequate funding for highway maintenance and improvements.
>
> Number two: Play a strong, responsible, yet flexible role in transportation programs.
>
> And number three: Invest in highway safety.
>
> Let's see what our strengths are, what the issues are, and what we can do about them.[7]

Motivate the Audience to Accept Your Goals

A final and critical function of the introduction is to motivate the audience to care about your topic and make it relevant to them. You may choose to convey what the audience stands to gain by the information you will share or convince audience members that your speech purpose is consistent with their motives and values. A student speech about the value of interview training shows how this can be accomplished:

> Why do you need interview training? It boils down to competition. As in sports, when you're not training, someone else is out there training to beat you. All things being equal, the person who has the best interviewing skills has got the edge.

✓ CHECKLIST

Craft an Effective Introduction

- ❑ Use stories, unusual facts, quotes, or humor to capture the audience's attention and stimulate their interest.
- ❑ Establish a positive common bond with listeners, perhaps by referring to the purpose of the occasion.
- ❑ Alert listeners to the speech purpose and topic.
- ❑ Establish your credibility to address the topic.
- ❑ Preview the main points of the speech.
- ❑ Motivate listeners to accept your speech goals by conveying the benefits of your topic.

◉ Preparing the Conclusion

Just as a well-crafted introduction gets your speech effectively out of the starting gate, a well-constructed conclusion gives you the opportunity to drive home your purpose and leave the audience inspired to think about and even to act upon your ideas. The conclusion consists of several elements that end the speech effectively. Conclusions serve to:

- Signal that the speech is coming to an end and provide closure.
- Summarize the key points.
- Reiterate the thesis or central idea of the speech.
- Remind the audience of how your ideas will benefit them.
- Challenge the audience to remember and possibly act upon your ideas.
- End the speech memorably.

Signal the End of the Speech and Provide Closure

People who listen to speeches are taking a journey of sorts, and they want and need the speaker to acknowledge the journey's end. They look for logical and emotional closure.

One signal that a speech is about to end is a transitional word or phrase: *finally, looking back, in conclusion, let me close by saying* (see Chapter 11). You can also signal closure by adjusting your manner of delivery; for example, you can vary

---

✓ CHECKLIST

Guidelines for Preparing the Conclusion

❑ As with the introduction, prepare the conclusion after you've completed the speech body.

❑ Do not leave the conclusion to chance. Include it with your speaking outline.

❑ Keep the conclusion brief—as a rule, no more than 10 to 15 percent, or about one-sixth, of the overall speech. Conclude soon after you say you are about to end.

❑ Carefully consider your use of language. More than in other parts of the speech, the conclusion can contain words that inspire and motivate (see Chapter 15).

❑ Practice delivering your conclusion until you feel confident you've got it right.

❑ Once you've signaled the end of your speech, conclude in short order (though not abruptly).

your tone, pitch, rhythm, and rate of speech to indicate that the speech is winding down (see Chapters 17 and 18).

Summarize the Key Points

One bit of age-old advice for giving a speech is "Tell them what you are going to tell them (in the introduction), tell them (in the body), and tell them what you told them (in the conclusion)." The idea is that emphasizing the main points three times will help the audience to remember them. A restatement of points in the conclusion brings the speech full circle and gives the audience a sense of completion. Consider how Holger Kluge, in a speech titled "Reflections on Diversity," summarizes his main points:

> I have covered a lot of ground here today. But as I draw to a close, I'd like to stress three things.
>
> First, diversity is more than equity. . . .
>
> Second, weaving diversity into the very fabric of your organization takes time. . . .
>
> Third, diversity will deliver bottom line results to your businesses and those results will be substantial. . . .[8]

Reiterate the Topic and Speech Purpose

The conclusion should reiterate the topic and speech purpose—to imprint it on the audience's memory. In the conclusion to a speech about the U.S. immigration debate, Elpidio Villarreal reminds his listeners of his central idea:

> Two paths are open to us. One path would keep us true to our fundamental values as a nation and a people. The other would lead us down a dark trail; one marked by 700-mile-long fences, emergency detention centers and vigilante border patrols. Because I really am an American, heart and soul, and because that means never being without hope, I still believe we will ultimately choose the right path. We have to.[9]

Challenge the Audience to Respond

A strong conclusion challenges audience members to put to use what the speaker has shared with them. In an *informative speech*, the speaker challenges audience members to use what they've learned in a way that benefits them. In a *persuasive speech*, the challenge usually comes in the form of a **call to action**. Here the speaker challenges listeners to act in response to the speech, see the problem in a new way, or change both their actions and their beliefs about the problem.

Hillary Rodham Clinton makes a strong call to action in her conclusion to an address presented to the United Nations World Conference on Women:

We have seen peace prevail in most places for a half century. We have avoided another world war. But we have not solved older, deeply rooted problems that continue to diminish the potential of half the world's population. *Now it is time to act on behalf of women everywhere.* If we take bold steps to better the lives of women, we will be taking bold steps to better the lives of children and families too. . . . Let this conference be our—and the world's—call to action.[10]

QUICK TIP

Bring Your Speech Full Circle

Picking up on a story or an idea you mentioned in the introduction can be a memorable way to close a speech and bring the entire presentation full circle. You can provide the resolution of the story ("what happened next?") or reiterate the link between the moral (lesson) of the story and the speech theme.

Make the Conclusion Memorable

A speech that makes a lasting impression is one that listeners are most likely to remember and act on. To accomplish this, make use of the same devices for capturing attention described for use in introductions—quotations, stories, questions, startling statements, humor, and references to the audience and the occasion.

✓ CHECKLIST

Craft an Effective Conclusion

- ❏ Signal the start of the conclusion with a transition.
- ❏ End your speech soon after you signal you're about to close.
- ❏ Plan for a conclusion that is no more than about one-sixth of the time spent on the body of the speech.
- ❏ Reiterate your main points.
- ❏ Remind listeners of the speech topic and purpose.
- ❏ Reiterate the benefits of your topic.
- ❏ Include a challenge or call to action to motivate the audience to respond to your ideas or appeals, particularly if your goal is to persuade.
- ❏ Consider referring back upon story, unusual fact, or quotations you used in your introduction to provide a sense of closure and make a lasting impression.

CHAPTER 15

Using Language

Words are the public speaker's tools of the trade, and the ones you choose to style your speech will play a crucial role in creating a dynamic connection with your audience. The right words help listeners understand, believe in, and retain your message.

◉ Use an Oral Style

Speeches require an **oral style**—the use of language that is simpler, more repetitious, more rhythmic, and more interactive than written language.[1] Speeches therefore must be prepared for the ear—to be *heard* rather than read. This is particularly important because unlike readers, listeners have only one chance to get the message.

Strive for Simplicity

To ensure understanding, express yourself simply, without pretentious language or unnecessary **jargon** (the specialized, "insider" language of a given profession). Speak in commonly understood terms and choose the simpler of two synonyms: "guess" rather than "extrapolate;" "use" rather than "utilize." Use fewer rather than more words, and shorter sentences rather than longer ones. As speechwriter Peggy Noonan notes in her book *Simply Speaking:*

> Good hard simple words with good hard clear meanings are good things to use when you speak. They are like pickets in a fence, slim and unimpressive on their own but sturdy and effective when strung together.[2]

Make Frequent Use of Repetition

Repetition is key to oral style, serving to compensate for natural lapses in listening and to reinforce information. Even very brief speeches repeat key words and phrases. Repetition

---

QUICK TIP

Experiment with Phrases and Sentence Fragments

In line with an oral style, experiment with using phrases and sentence fragments in place of full sentences. This speaker, a physician, demonstrates how short phrases can add punch to a speech: "I'm just a simple bone-and-joint guy. I can set your broken bones. Take away your bunions. Even give you a new hip. But I don't mess around with the stuff between the ears. . . . That's another specialty."[3]

adds emphasis to important ideas, helps listeners follow your logic, and imbues language with rhythm and drama.

Use Personal Pronouns

Audience members want to know what the speaker thinks and feels, and to be assured that he or she recognizes them and relates them to the message. The direct form of address, using the personal pronouns such as *we, us, I,* and *you,* helps to create this feeling of recognition and inclusion. Note how Sheryl Sandberg, Chief Operating Officer of Facebook, uses personal pronouns to begin a speech on why there are too few women leaders:

> So for any of *us* in this room today, let's start out by admitting *we're* lucky. *We* don't live in the world *our* mothers lived in, *our* grandmothers lived in, where career choices for women were so limited. . . . But all that aside, *we* still have a problem. . . . Women are not making it to the top of any profession anywhere in the world.[4]

◉ Choose Concrete Language and Vivid Imagery

Concrete words and vivid imagery engage audience members' senses, enlivening a speech. **Concrete language** is specific, tangible, and definite. Words such as "mountain," "spoon," "dark," and "heavy" describe things we can physically sense (see, hear, taste, smell, and touch). In contrast, **abstract language** is general or nonspecific, leaving meaning open to interpretation. Abstract words, such as "peace," "freedom," and "love," are purely conceptual; they have no physical reference. Politicians use abstract language to appeal to mass audiences, or to be noncommittal: "We strive for peace." In most speaking situations, however, listeners will appreciate concrete nouns and verbs.

Note how concrete words add precision and color:

Abstract: The old road was bad.

Concrete: The road was pitted with muddy craters and nearly swallowed up by huge outcroppings of dark gray granite.

Offer Vivid Imagery

Imagery is concrete language that brings into play the senses of smell, taste, sight, hearing, and touch to paint mental pictures. Vivid imagery is more easily recalled than colorless language,[5] and speeches containing ample imagery elicit more positive responses than those that do not.[6]

Choose Strong Verbs

Mundane	Verb Colorful Alternative
look	behold, gaze, glimpse, peek, stare
walk	stride, amble, stroll, skulk
throw	hurl, fling, pitch
sit	sink, plop, settle
eat	devour, inhale, gorge

Adding imagery into your speech need not be difficult if you focus on using concrete and colorful adjectives and strong verbs. Substitute passive forms of the verb "to be" (e.g., *is, are, was, were, will be* . . .) with more active verb forms. Rather than "the houses were empty," use "the houses stood empty." You can use descriptive adjectives to modify nouns as well as verbs, as in "*dilapidated* house." President Franklin D. Roosevelt famously did this when he portrayed the Japanese bombing of Pearl Harbor as "the dark hour,"[7] conveying with one simple adjective the gravity of the attack.

Use Figures of Speech

Figures of speech, including similes, metaphors, and analogies, make striking comparisons that help listeners visualize, identify with, and understand the speaker's ideas. A **simile** explicitly compares one thing to another, using *like* or *as:* "He works like a dog," and "The old woman's hands were as soft as a baby's." A **metaphor** also compares two things, but does so by describing one thing as actually *being* the other: "Time is a thief."

An **analogy** is simply an extended metaphor or simile that compares an unfamiliar concept or process to a more familiar one. For example, African American minister Phil

QUICK TIP

Avoid Clichés and Mixed Metaphors

Try to avoid predictable and stale metaphors and similes, known as **clichés**, such as "sold like hotcakes" (a clichéd simile) and "pearly white teeth" (a clichéd metaphor). Beware, too, of **mixed metaphors**, or those that compare unlike images or expressions: for example, "Burning the midnight oil at both ends" incorrectly joins the expressions "burning the midnight oil" and "burning the candle at both ends." Other figures of speech that contribute to vivid imagery include personification, understatement, irony, allusion, hyperbole, and onomatopoeia.

Wilson used metaphoric language when he preached about the dangers of AIDS:

> Our house is on fire! The fire truck arrives, but we won't come out, because we're afraid the folks from next door will see that we're in that burning house. AIDS is a fire raging in our community and it's out of control![8]

As useful as analogies are, they can mislead audience members if used carelessly. A **faulty analogy** is an inaccurate or misleading comparison suggesting that because two things are similar in some ways, they are necessarily similar in others. (See Chapter 23 for examples of this and Chapter 24 for other logical fallacies to avoid.)

◎ Choose Words That Build Credibility

Audiences expect speakers to be competent and credible. To project these qualities, use language that is appropriate, accurate, assertive, and respectful.

Use Words Appropriately

The language you use in a speech should be appropriate to the audience, the occasion, and the subject matter. Listeners view speakers who use General American (GA) English as more competent — though not necessarily more trustworthy or likable — than those who speak in a distinctive dialect (regional variation of speech).[9] At times, however, it may be appropriate to mix casual language, dialects, or even slang into your speech. Done carefully, the selective use of dialect, sometimes called **code-switching**, can imbue your speech with friendliness, humor, earthiness, honesty, and nostalgia.[10] The key is to ensure that your meaning is clear and your use is appropriate for your audience. Consider the following excerpt:

> On the gulf where I was raised, *el valle del Rio Grande* in South Texas — that triangular piece of land wedged between the river *y el golfo* which serves as the Texas–U.S./Mexican border — is a Mexican *pueblito* called Hargill.[11]

Use Words Accurately

Audiences lose confidence in speakers who misuse words. Check that your words mean what you intend, and beware of **malapropisms** — the inadvertent, incorrect uses of a word or phrase in place of one that sounds like it[12] ("It's a strange receptacle" for "It's a strange spectacle").

Use the Active Voice

Voice is the feature of verbs that indicates the subject's relationship to the action. Speaking in the active rather than passive voice will make your statements—and the audience's perception of you as the speaker—clear and assertive instead of indirect and weak. A verb is in the *active voice* when the subject performs the action, and in the *passive voice* when the subject is acted upon or is the receiver of the action:

Passive:	A test was announced by Ms. Carlos for Tuesday.
	A president is elected every four years.
Active:	Ms. Carlos announced a test for Tuesday.
	The voters elect a president every four years.

Use Culturally Sensitive and Gender-Neutral Language

Be alert to using language that reflects respect for audience members' cultural beliefs, norms, and traditions. Review and eliminate any language that reflects unfounded assumptions, negative descriptions, or stereotypes of a given group's age, class, gender, ability, and geographic, ethnic, racial, or religious characteristics. Consider, too, whether certain seemingly well-known names and terms may be foreign to some listeners, and include brief explanations for them. Sayings specific to a certain region or group of people—termed **colloquial expressions** or *idioms*—such as "back the wrong horse" and "ballpark figure" can add color and richness to a speech, but only if listeners understand them.

Word your speech with gender-neutral language: Avoid the third-person generic masculine pronouns *(his, he)* in favor of inclusive pronouns such as *his* or *her, he* or *she, we, our, you, your,* or other gender-neutral terms.

QUICK TIP

Denotative versus Connotative Meaning

When drafting your speech, choose words that are both denotatively and connotatively appropriate to the audience. The **denotative meaning** of a word is its literal, or dictionary, definition. The **connotative meaning** of a word is the special (often emotional) association that different people bring to bear on it. For example, you may agree that you are "angry," but not "irate," and "thrifty" but not "cheap." Consider how the connotative meanings of your word choices might affect the audience's response to your message, including those of non-native speakers of English.

◉ Choose Words That Create a Lasting Impression

Language artfully arranged and infused with rhythm draws listeners in and leaves a lasting impression on audience members. You can create a cadenced arrangement of language through **rhetorical devices** such as repetition, alliteration, and parallelism.

Use Repetition to Create Rhythm

Repeating key words, phrases, or even sentences at various intervals throughout a speech creates a distinctive rhythm and thereby implants important ideas in listeners' minds. Repetition works particularly well when delivered with the appropriate voice inflections and pauses.

In a form of repetition called *anaphora*, the speaker repeats a word or phrase at the beginning of successive phrases, clauses, or sentences. In his speech delivered in 1963 in Washington, DC, Dr. Martin Luther King Jr. repeated the phrase "I have a dream" eleven times in eight successive sentences, each with an upward inflection followed by a pause. Speakers have made use of anaphora since earliest times. For example, Jesus preached:

> Blessed are the poor in spirit. . . .
> Blessed are the meek. . . .
> Blessed are the peacemakers. . . .[13]

Repetition can help to create a thematic focus for a speech. Speakers often do this by using both anaphora and *epiphora* in the same speech. In **epiphora** (also called *epistrophe*) the repetition of a word or phrase appears at the end of successive statements. In a speech to his New Hampshire supporters, President Barack Obama used both anaphora and epiphora to establish a theme of empowerment (italics added):

> *It was* a creed written into the founding documents that declared the destiny of a nation: *Yes we can.*
>
> *It was* whispered by slaves and abolitionists as they blazed a trail toward freedom through the darkest of nights: *Yes we can.*
>
> *It was* sung by immigrants as they struck out from distant shores and pioneers who pushed westward against an unforgiving wilderness: *Yes we can.*[14]

Use Alliteration for a Poetic Quality

Alliteration is the repetition of the same sounds, usually initial consonants, in two or more neighboring words or syllables. Alliteration lends speech a poetic, musical rhythm.

Classic examples of alliteration in speeches include phrases such as Jesse Jackson's "Down with dope, up with hope" and former U.S. Vice-President Spiro Agnew's disdainful reference to the U.S. press as "nattering nabobs of negativism."

Experiment with Parallelism

The arrangement of words, phrases, or sentences in a similar form is known as **parallelism**. Parallel structure can help the speaker emphasize important ideas, and can be as simple as orally numbering points ("first, second, and third"). Like repetition, it also creates a sense of steady or building rhythm. Speakers often make use of three parallel elements, called a *triad:*

> . . . of the people, by the people, and for the people . . .
>
> —*Abraham Lincoln*

Parallelism in speeches often makes use of **antithesis**—setting off two ideas in balanced (parallel) opposition to each other to create a powerful effect:

> One small step for a man, one giant leap for mankind.
>
> —*Neil Armstrong on the moon, 1969*

> For many are called, but few are chosen.
>
> —*Matthew 22:14*

✓ CHECKLIST
Using Effective Oral Style

- ❑ Use familiar words, easy-to-follow sentences, and straightforward syntax.
- ❑ Root out culturally insensitive and gender-biased language.
- ❑ Avoid unnecessary jargon.
- ❑ Use fewer rather than more words to express your thoughts.
- ❑ Make striking comparisons with *similes, metaphors,* and *analogies.*
- ❑ Use the active voice.
- ❑ Repeat key words, phrases, or sentences at the beginning of successive sentences (*anaphora*) and at their close (*epiphora*).
- ❑ Experiment with *alliteration*—words that repeat the same sounds, usually initial consonants, in two or more neighboring words or syllables.
- ❑ Experiment with *parallelism*—arranging words, phrases, or sentences in similar form.

part

Delivery

16. **Methods of Delivery**   126

17. **Your Voice in Delivery**   129

18. **Your Body in Delivery**   134

CHAPTER 16

Methods of Delivery

For most of us, anticipating the actual delivery of a speech feels unnerving. In fact, effective delivery rests on the same natural foundation as everyday conversation, except that it is more rehearsed and purposeful. By focusing on four key qualities of effective delivery, you can reduce your fears and make your presentations more authentic.

◉ Keys To Effective Delivery

Effective delivery is the controlled use of voice and body to express the qualities of naturalness, enthusiasm, confidence, and directness.[1] Audiences respond most favorably to speakers who project these characteristics during delivery. As you practice delivering your speech, focus on these key qualities:

- *Strive for naturalness.* Rather than behaving theatrically, act naturally. Think of your speech as a particularly important conversation.
- *Show enthusiasm.* Inspire your listeners by showing enthusiasm for your topic and for the occasion. An enthusiastic delivery helps you feel good about your speech, and it focuses your audience's attention on the message.
- *Project a sense of confidence.* Focus on the ideas you want to convey rather than on yourself. Inspire the audience's confidence in you by appearing confident to them.
- *Be direct.* Engage directly with audience members. Demonstrate your interest and concern for listeners by establishing eye contact, using a friendly tone of voice, and animating your facial expressions, especially positive ones such as smiling and nodding whenever appropriate. (See Chapters 17 and 18 on techniques for using voice and body in a speech.)

◉ Select a Method of Delivery

For virtually any type of speech or presentation, you can choose from four basic methods of delivery: speaking from manuscript, speaking from memory, speaking impromptu, and speaking extemporaneously.

Speaking from Manuscript

When **speaking from manuscript**, you read a speech *verbatim*—that is, from prepared written text that contains the entire speech, word for word. As a rule, speaking from manuscript restricts eye contact and body movement, and may also limit expressiveness in vocal variety and quality. Watching a speaker read a speech can be monotonous and boring for the audience.

If you must read from prepared text—for example, when you need to convey a precise message, when you will be quoted and must avoid misinterpretation, or when addressing an emergency and conveying exact descriptions and direction—do what you can to deliver the speech naturally:

- Vary the rhythm of your words (see Chapter 17).
- Become familiar enough with the speech so that you can establish some eye contact.
- Use a large font and double- or triple-space the manuscript so that you can read without straining.
- Consider using some compelling presentation aids (see Chapter 20).

Speaking from Memory

The formal name for **speaking from memory** is **oratory**. In oratorical style, you put the entire speech, word for word, into writing and then commit it to memory. Memorization is not a natural way to present a message. True eye contact with the audience is unlikely, and the potential for disaster exists because there is always the possibility of forgetting. Some kinds of brief speeches, however, such as toasts and introductions, can be well served by memorization. Sometimes it's helpful to memorize a part of the speech, especially when you use direct quotations as a form of support. If you do use memorization, practice that portion of your speech so completely that you can convey enthusiasm and directness.

Speaking Impromptu

Impromptu speaking, a type of delivery that is unpracticed, spontaneous, or improvised, involves speaking on relatively short notice with little time to prepare. Many occasions require that you make remarks on the spur of the moment. An instructor may ask you to summarize key points from an assignment, for example, or a boss may invite you to take the place of an absent co-worker who was scheduled to speak on a new project.

Try to anticipate situations that may require you to speak impromptu, and prepare some remarks beforehand. Otherwise, maximize the time you do have to prepare on the spot:

- *Think first about your listeners.* Consider their interests and needs, and try to shape your remarks accordingly. For example, who are the people present, and what are their views on the topic?

- *Listen to what others around you are saying.* Take notes in a key-word or phrase format (see p. 96) and arrange them into main points from which you can speak.
- *Acknowledge the previous speaker.* If your speech follows someone else's, acknowledge that person's statements. Then make your points.
- *Stay on the topic.* Don't wander off track.
- *Use Transitions.* Use signal words such as "first," "second," and "third" to organize points and help listeners follow them.

As much as possible, try to organize your points into a discernible pattern. If addressing a problem, for example, such as a project failure or glitch, consider the *problem-solution pattern*—state problem(s), then offer solution(s); or the *cause-effect pattern* of organizational arrangement—state cause(s) first, then address effect(s); see Chapter 12 for various ways of using these patterns. If called upon to defend one proposal as superior to another, consider using the *comparative advantage pattern* to illustrate various advantages of your favored proposal over the other options (see p. 186).

Speaking Extemporaneously

When speaking extemporaneously, you prepare and practice in advance, giving full attention to all facets of the speech—content, arrangement, and delivery alike. However, in an **extemporaneous speech**, instead of memorizing or writing the speech word for word, you speak from an outline of key words and phrases that isolates the main ideas that you want to communicate (see Chapter 13).

Because extemporaneous delivery is most conducive to achieving a natural, conversational quality, most speakers prefer it among the four types of delivery. Knowing your ideas well enough to present them without memorization or manuscript gives you greater flexibility in adapting to the specific speaking situation. You can modify wording, rearrange your points, change examples, or omit information in keeping with the audience and the setting. You can have more eye contact, more direct body orientation, greater freedom of movement, and generally better control of your thoughts and actions than any of the other delivery methods allow.

Speaking extemporaneously does present a possible drawback. Occasionally, even a glance at your speaking notes may fail to jog your memory on a point you wanted to cover, and you find yourself searching for what to say next. The remedy for this potential pitfall is frequent practice—rehearsing the speech about six times—using a key-word or phrase outline (see p. 96).

Choosing a Method of Delivery

When . . .	Method of Delivery
You want to avoid being misquoted or misconstrued, or you need to communicate exact descriptions and directions . . .	Consider *speaking from manuscript* (read the part of your speech requiring precise wording from fully prepared text).
You must deliver a short special occasion speech, such as a toast or an introduction, or you plan on using direct quotations . . .	Consider *speaking from memory* (memorize part or all of your speech).
You are called upon to speak without prior planning or preparation . . .	Consider *speaking impromptu* (organize your thoughts with little or no lead time).
You have time to prepare and practice developing a speech or presentation that achieves a natural conversational style . . .	Consider *speaking extemporaneously* (develop your speech in working outline and then practice and deliver it with a phrase or key-word outline).

✓ CHECKLIST
Successful Delivery

- ❑ Strive for naturalness.
- ❑ Show enthusiasm.
- ❑ Project a sense of confidence and composure.
- ❑ Engage your audience by being direct.
- ❑ If you must read from a prepared text, do so naturally.
- ❑ In general, don't try to memorize entire speeches.
- ❑ When speaking impromptu, maximize any preparation time.

CHAPTER 17 ●●●●

Your Voice in Delivery

When delivering a speech, voice matters. Used properly, your voice is a powerful instrument of expression that can signal confidence and control, and enable you to communicate meaning exactly as you intend. As you practice, you can learn to modulate each of the elements of vocal delivery: volume, pitch, speaking rate, pauses, vocal variety, and pronunciation and articulation.

◉ Adjust Your Speaking Volume

Volume, the relative loudness of a speaker's voice while delivering a speech, is usually the most obvious vocal element we notice about a speaker, and with good reason. We need to hear the speaker at a comfortable level. *The proper volume for delivering a speech is somewhat louder than that of normal conversation.* Just how much louder depends on three factors: (1) the size of the room and of the audience, (2) whether or not you use a microphone, and (3) the level of background noise. Speaking at the appropriate volume is critical to how credible your listeners will perceive you to be, so check that audience members can hear you. Be alert to signals that your volume is slipping or is too loud and make the necessary adjustments.

QUICK TIP

Breathe from Your Diaphragm

To project your voice so that it is loud enough to be heard by everyone in the audience, breathe deeply from your diaphragm rather than more shallowly from your vocal cords. The reason? The strength of our voices depends on the amount of air the diaphragm—a large, dome-shaped muscle encasing the inner rib cage—pushes from the lungs to the vocal cords.

◉ Vary Your Intonation

Pitch is the range of sounds from high to low (or vice versa). Anatomy determines a person's natural pitch—a bigger or smaller voice box produces a lower- or higher-pitched voice. But within these natural constraints, you can and should control pitch through **intonation**—the rising and falling of sound across phrases and sentences. Intonation is important in speechmaking because it powerfully affects the meaning associated with spoken words. For example, say "stop." Now, say "Stop!" Varying intonation conveys two very distinct meanings.

As you speak, intonation conveys your mood, level of enthusiasm, concern for the audience, and overall commitment to the occasion. Without intonation, speaking becomes monotonous. A monotone voice is a death knell to any speech.

The best way to avoid speaking in monotone is to practice and listen to your speeches with a recording device. If you have a recording device on your smart phone, you can use it to test your voice. You will readily identify instances that require better intonation.

◎ Adjust Your Speaking Rate

Speaking rate is the pace at which you convey speech. The normal rate of speech for native English-speaking adults is roughly between 120 and 150 words per minute, but there is no standard, ideal, or most effective rate. If the rate is too slow, it may lull the audience to sleep. If your speech is too fast, listeners may see you as unsure about your control of the speech.[1]

Being alert to the audience's reactions is the best way to know whether your rate of speech is too fast or too slow. Some serious topics benefit from a slower speech rate; a lively pace generally corresponds with a lighter tone. An audience will get fidgety, bored, listless, perhaps even sleepy if you speak too slowly. If you speak too rapidly, listeners will appear irritated and confused, as though they can't catch what you're saying.

QUICK TIP

Control Your Rate of Speaking

To control your speaking rate, choose 150 words from your speech and time yourself for one minute as you read them aloud. If you fall very short of finishing, increase your pace. If you finish well before the minute is up, slow down. Practice until you achieve a comfortable speaking rate.

◎ Use Strategic Pauses

Many novice speakers are uncomfortable with pauses. Like intonation, however, pauses can be important strategic elements of a speech. **Pauses** enhance meaning by providing a type of punctuation, emphasizing a point, drawing attention to a thought, or just allowing listeners a moment to contemplate what is being said.

As you practice delivering your speech, focus on avoiding unnecessary and undesirable **vocal fillers** such as "uh," "hmm," "you know," "I mean," and "it's like." These so-called disfluencies will make you appear unprepared and cause audience members to be distracted from the message. Rather than vocal fillers, use silent pauses for strategic effect.

◉ Strive for Vocal Variety

Rather than operating separately, all the vocal elements described so far—volume, pitch, speaking rate, and pauses—work together to create vocal variety. Indeed, the real key to effective vocal delivery is to vary all these elements with a tone of enthusiasm. For example, as the great civil rights leader Martin Luther King Jr. spoke the now famous words "I have a dream," the pauses were immediately preceded by a combination of reduced speech rate and increased volume and pitch. Vocal variety comes quite naturally when you are excited about what you are saying to an audience, when you feel it is important and want to share it with them.

✓ CHECKLIST

Practice Check for Vocal Effectiveness

- ❑ As you practice, is your vocal delivery effective?
- ❑ Is your voice too loud? Too soft?
- ❑ Do you avoid speaking in a monotone? Do you vary the stress or emphasis you place on words to clearly express your meaning?
- ❑ Is your rate of speech comfortable for listeners?
- ❑ Do you avoid unnecessary vocal fillers, such as "uh," "hmm," "you know," and "I mean"?
- ❑ Do you use silent pauses for strategic effect?
- ❑ Does your voice reflect a variety of emotional expressions? Do you convey enthusiasm?

◉ Carefully Pronounce and Articulate Words

Few things distract an audience more than improper pronunciation or unclear articulation of words. **Pronunciation** is the correct formation of word sounds—examples of *mispronunciation* include, "aks" for "asked" (*askt*), and "jen yu wine" for "genuine" (jen yu *in*). **Articulation** is the clarity or forcefulness with which the sounds are made, regardless of whether they are pronounced correctly. Incorrect pronunciation and poor articulation are largely a matter of habit.

A common pattern of poor articulation is **mumbling**—slurring words together at a low level of volume and pitch so that they are barely audible. Sometimes the problem is **lazy speech**. Common examples are saying "fer" instead of "for" and "wanna" instead of "want to."

Like any habit, poor articulation can be overcome by unlearning the problem behavior:

- If you mumble, practice speaking more loudly and with emphatic pronunciation.
- If you tend toward lazy speech, put more effort into your articulation.
- Consciously try to say each word clearly and correctly.
- Practice clear and precise enunciation of proper word sounds. Say "articulation" several times until it rolls off your tongue naturally.
- Do the same for these words: "want to," "going to," "Atlanta," "chocolate," "sophomore," "California."

✅ CHECKLIST

Tips on Using a Microphone

- ❑ Perform a sound check with the microphone several hours before delivering your speech.
- ❑ When you first speak into the microphone, ask listeners if they can hear you clearly.
- ❑ Speak directly into the microphone; if you turn your head or body, you won't be heard.
- ❑ To avoid broadcasting private statements, beware of "open" mikes.
- ❑ When wearing a **lavaliere microphone** attached to clothing, speak as if you were addressing a small group. The amplifier will do the rest.
- ❑ When using a *handheld* or *fixed microphone*, beware of *popping*. Popping occurs when you use sharp consonants such as *"p," "t,"* and *"d"* and the air hits the mike. To prevent popping, move the microphone slightly below your mouth and about six inches away.[2]

◉ Use Dialect (Language Variation) with Care

Every culture has subcultural variations, or **dialects**, on the preferred pronunciation and articulation of its languages. In the United States, there is so-called "standard" or "General American English" (GAE), Ebonics (African American English), and Tex-Mex (a combination of Spanish and English spoken with a distinct Texas drawl). Although dialects are neither superior nor inferior to standard language patterns, the audience must be able to understand and relate to the speaker's language. As you practice your delivery, ensure that your pronunciation and word usage can be understood by all audience members.

CHAPTER 18 ●●●●

Your Body in Delivery

As we listen to a speaker, we simultaneously use our eyes and ears to evaluate messages sent by his or her **nonverbal communication**—body movements, physical appearance, and qualities of voice. As much if not more than listening to a speaker's words, we respond to his or her visual and aural cues. Thus it is vital to plan not only the words you will say but the physical manner in which you will deliver them.

◉ Pay Attention to Body Language

Research confirms the importance of **body language**—facial expressions, eye behavior, gestures, and general body movements during the delivery of a speech. For example, audiences are more readily persuaded by speakers who emphasize eye contact, nodding at listeners, and standing with an open body position than by those who minimize these nonverbal cues.[1] Additionally, when speakers talk about their feelings and attitudes, one study suggests that the audience derives a mere 7 *percent* of the speakers' meaning from the words they utter. The balance comes from the speakers' use of voice (38 percent) and body language and appearance (55 percent).[2]

Animate Your Facial Expressions

From our facial expressions, audiences can gauge whether we are excited about, disenchanted by, or indifferent to our speech—and the audience to whom we are presenting it.

Few behaviors are more effective for building rapport with an audience than *smiling*.[3] A smile is a sign of mutual welcome at the start of a speech, of mutual comfort and interest during the speech, and of mutual goodwill at the close of a speech. In addition, smiling when you feel nervous or otherwise uncomfortable can help you relax and gain heightened composure. Of course, facial expressions need to correspond

> ### ✔ CHECKLIST
> ## Tips for Using Effective Facial Expressions
>
> ❑ Use animated expressions that feel natural and express your meaning.
> ❑ Avoid a deadpan expression.
> ❑ Never use expressions that are out of character for you or inappropriate to the speech occasion.
> ❑ In practice sessions, loosen your facial features with exercises such as widening the eyes and moving the mouth.
> ❑ Establish rapport with the audience by smiling naturally when appropriate.

to the tenor of the speech. Doing what is natural and normal for the occasion should be the rule.

Maintain Eye Contact

If smiling is an effective way to build rapport, maintaining eye contact is mandatory in establishing a positive relationship with your listeners. Having eye contact with the audience is one of the most, if not *the* most, important physical actions in public speaking, at least in Western cultures. Eye contact does the following:

- Maintains the quality of directness in speech delivery.
- Lets people know they are recognized.
- Indicates acknowledgment and respect.
- Signals to audience members that you see them as unique human beings.

While it may be impossible to look at every listener, you can make the audience feel recognized by using a technique called **scanning**—moving your gaze from one listener to another and from one section to another, pausing to gaze at one person long enough to complete one thought. Be certain to give each section of the room equal attention.

Use Gestures That Feel Natural

Words alone seldom suffice to convey what we want to express. Physical gestures fill in the gaps, as in illustrating the size or shape of an object (e.g., by showing the size of it by extending two hands, palms facing each other), or expressing the depth of an emotion (e.g., by pounding a fist on a podium). Gestures should arise from genuine emotions and should conform to your personality.[4]

✅ CHECKLIST
Using Gestures Effectively

❑ Use natural, spontaneous gestures.

❑ Avoid exaggerated gestures, but use gestures that are broad enough to be seen by each audience member.

❑ Eliminate distracting gestures, such as fidgeting with pens, jingling coins in pockets, drumming your fingers on a podium or table, or brushing back hair from your eyes.

❑ Analyze your gestures for effectiveness in practice sessions.

❑ Practice movements that feel natural to you.

Create a Feeling of Immediacy

In most Western cultures, listeners learn more from and respond most positively to speakers who create a perception of physical and psychological closeness, called **nonverbal immediacy**, between themselves and audience members.[5] The following behaviors encourage immediacy:

- Use an enthusiastic vocal delivery.
- Make frequent eye contact.
- Animate your facial expressions.
- Use natural body movements.

QUICK TIP

Use Movement to Connect

Audience members soon tire of listening to a **talking head** that remains steadily positioned in one place behind a microphone or a podium, so even in formal situations, use natural body movements. Use your physical position vis-à-vis audience members to adjust your relationship with them, establishing a level of familiarity and closeness that is appropriate to the rhetorical situation. Movement towards listeners stimulates a sense of informality and closeness; remaining behind the podium fosters a more formal relationship of speaker to audience.

Stand Straight

A speaker's posture sends a definite message to the audience. Listeners perceive speakers who slouch as being sloppy, unfocused, or even weak. Strive to stand erect, but not ramrod straight. The goal should be to appear authoritative but not rigid.

◉ Practice the Delivery

Practice is essential to effective delivery. The more you practice, the greater your comfort level will be when you actually deliver the speech. More than anything, it is uncertainty that breeds anxiety. By practicing your speech using a fully developed speaking outline (see Chapter 13), you will know what to expect when you actually stand in front of an audience.

Focus on the Message

The primary purpose of any speech is to get a message across, not to display extraordinary delivery skills. Keep this goal foremost in your mind. Psychologically, too, focusing on your message is likely to make your delivery more natural and confident.

Plan Ahead and Practice Often

If possible, begin practicing your speech at least several days before you are scheduled to deliver it.

- Practice with your speaking notes, revising those parts of the speech that aren't satisfactory, and altering the notes as you go.
- Record the speech (see nearby Quick Tip).
- Time each part of your speech — introduction, body, and conclusion (see Chapter 14 for guidelines).
- Include any presentation aids you plan to use.
- Practice the speech about five times in its final form.
- Visualize the setting in which you will speak, and practice the speech under realistic conditions, paying particular attention to projecting your voice to fill the room.
- Practice in front of at least one volunteer, and seek constructive criticism.
- Schedule your practice sessions early in the process so that you have time to prepare.
- Dress appropriately for the rhetorical situation.

QUICK TIP

Record Two Practice Sessions

Videorecording two practice sessions can provide valuable feedback. As you watch your initial recording, make notes of the things you'd like to change. Before rerecording, practice several more times until you are comfortable with the changes you've incorporated. No one is ever entirely thrilled with his or her image on video, so try to avoid unnecessary self-criticism. Videorecord your speech a second time, paying close attention to the areas of speech delivery that you want to improve.

part

6

Presentation Aids

19. Speaking with Presentation Aids 140

20. Designing Presentation Aids 144

21. Using Presentation Software 148

CHAPTER 19

Speaking with Presentation Aids

Used judiciously, the visual reinforcement provided by presentation aids can help listeners to understand and retain information that is otherwise difficult or time-consuming to convey in words. Indeed, research confirms that most people process information best when it is presented both verbally and visually—a principle dubbed the "multimedia effect."[1] However, no matter how powerful a photograph, chart, or other aid may be, if it is unrelated to a speech point, is poorly designed, or simply duplicates what the speaker says, the audience will become distracted and actually retain less information than without it.[2]

◉ Select an Appropriate Aid

A **presentation aid** can be an object, model, picture, graph, chart, table, audio, video, or multimedia. Choose the aid, or combination of aids, that will help your audience grasp information most effectively.

Props and Models

A **prop** can be any object, inanimate or even live, that helps demonstrate the speaker's points. A **model** is a three-dimensional, scale-size representation of an object. Presentations in engineering, architecture, and many other disciplines often make use these aids. When using a prop or model:

- In most cases, keep the prop or model hidden until you are ready to use it.
- Make sure it is big enough for everyone to see (and read, if applicable).
- Practice your speech using the prop or model.

Pictures

Pictures (two-dimensional representations) include photographs, line drawings, diagrams, maps, and posters. A *diagram* or *schematic drawing* explains how something works or is constructed or operated. *Maps* help listeners visualize geographic areas and understand relationships among them; they also illustrate the proportion of one thing to something else in different areas.

Graphs, Charts, and Tables

A **graph** represents relationships among two or more things. A *line graph* uses points connected by lines to demonstrate how something changes or fluctuates in value. A *bar and column graph* uses bars of varying lengths to compare quantities or magnitudes. *Pie graphs* depict the division of a whole into slices. Each slice constitutes a percentage of the whole.

Pictograms use picture symbols (icons) to illustrate relationships and trends; for example, a generic-looking human figure repeated in a row can demonstrate increasing enrollment in college over time.

A **chart** visually organizes complex information into compact form. A **flowchart** diagrams the progression of a process or relationship helping viewers visualize a sequence or directional flow. A **table** (tabular chart) systematically groups data in column form, allowing viewers to examine and make comparisons about information quickly.

✓ CHECKLIST
Create Effective Line, Bar, and Pie Graphs

- ❑ Label the axes of line graphs, bar graphs, and pictograms.
- ❑ Start the numerical axis of the line or bar graph at zero.
- ❑ Compare only like variables.
- ❑ Assign a clear title to the graph.
- ❑ Clearly label all relevant points of information in the graph.
- ❑ When creating multidimensional bar graphs, do not compare more than three kinds of information.
- ❑ In pie graphs, restrict the number of pie slices to a maximum of seven.
- ❑ Identify and accurately represent the values or percentages of each pie slice.
- ❑ In pictograms, clearly indicate what each icon symbolizes.
- ❑ Make all pictograms the same size.

Audio, Video, and Multimedia

Audio and video clips—including short recordings of sound, music, or speech; and clips from movies, television, and other recordings—can motivate attention and help to move among and clarify points.[3] *Multimedia*, which combines stills, sound, video, text, and data into a single production, requires familiarity with presentation software programs such as Windows Movie Maker and Apple iMovie. (See Chapter 21 for guidelines on linking audio and video clips to slides.) This rich variety of information cues can potentially boost audience attention, comprehension, and retention.[4] One application of

Best Uses of Different Types of Graphs and Charts

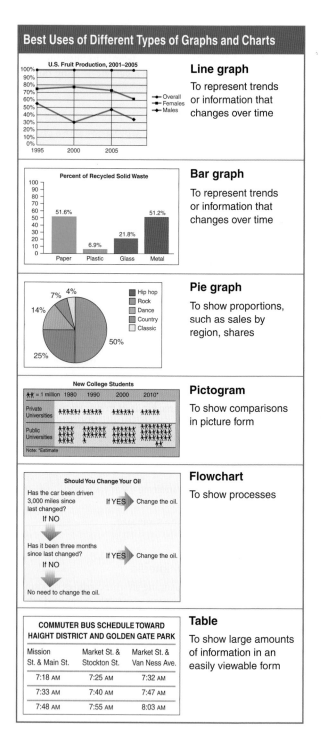

Line graph

To represent trends or information that changes over time

Bar graph

To represent trends or information that changes over time

Pie graph

To show proportions, such as sales by region, shares

Pictogram

To show comparisons in picture form

Flowchart

To show processes

Table

To show large amounts of information in an easily viewable form multimedia is **digital storytelling**—using multimedia to tell a story about yourself or others with resonance for the audience.

When incorporating audio and video into your presentation:

- Cue the audio or video clip to the appropriate segment before the presentation.
- Alert audience members to what they will be hearing or viewing before you play it back.
- Reiterate the relevance of the audio or video clip to your key points once it is over.
- Use the audio or video clip in a manner consistent with copyright.

◉ Options for Displaying Presentation Aids

Many presenters create computer-generated aids shown with digital projectors or LCD displays. On the more traditional side, display options include chalkboards and whiteboards, flip charts, posters, and handouts.

Computer-Generated Aids and Displays

With software programs such as Microsoft PowerPoint and Apple Keynote, speakers can create slides to project using LCD (liquid crystal display) panels and projectors or DLP (digital light processing) projectors. See Chapter 21 for a discussion of how to use presentation software.

Chalkboards and Whiteboards

On the lowest-tech end of the spectrum lies the writing board on which you can write with chalk (on a chalkboard) or with nonpermanent markers (on a *whiteboard*). Reserve the writing board for impromptu explanations, such as presenting simple processes that are done in steps, or for engaging the audience in short brainstorming sessions. If you have the time to prepare a speech properly, however, don't rely on a writing board. They force the speaker to turn his or her back to the audience, make listeners wait while you write, and require legible handwriting that will be clear to all viewers.

Flip Charts

A **flip chart** is simply a large (27–34 inch) pad of paper on which a speaker can write or draw. This aid is often prepared in advance; then, as you progress through the speech, you flip through the pad to the next exhibit. You can also write and draw on the pad as you speak. Sometimes a simple drawing or word written for emphasis can be as or more powerful than a highly polished slide.

QUICK TIP

Hold the Handouts

A **handout** conveys information that either is impractical to give to the audience in another manner or is intended to be kept by audience members after the presentation. To avoid distracting listeners, unless you specifically want them to read the information as you speak, wait until you are finished before you distribute the handout. If you do want the audience to view a handout during the speech, pass it out only when you are ready to talk about it.

Posters

Speakers use *posters*—large paperboards incorporating text, figures, and images, alone or in combination—to illustrate some aspect of their topic; often the poster rests on an easel. See Chapter 30 for guidelines on using posters in presentations called *poster sessions*.

✔ CHECKLIST

Incorporating Presentation Aids into Your Speech

- ❑ Practice with the aids until you are confident that you can handle them without causing undue distractions.
- ❑ Talk to your audience rather than to the screen or object—avoid turning your back to the audience.
- ❑ Maintain eye contact with the audience.
- ❑ Place the aid to one side rather than behind you, so that the entire audience can see it.
- ❑ Display the aid only when you are ready to discuss it.
- ❑ If you use a pointer, once you've indicated your point, put it down.
- ❑ In case problems arise, be prepared to give your presentation without the aids.

CHAPTER 20 ●●●●

Designing Presentation Aids

The visual appeal of a speaker's presentation aids is a critical factor in the audience's perception of his or her credibility, or ethos. Well-designed aids signal that the speaker is prepared and professional; poorly designed aids create a negative impression that is difficult to overcome.

As you generate aids, focus on keeping elements easy to read and consistently designed. Audience members can follow only one information source at a time, and visuals that are crowded or difficult to decipher will divert attention from your message.[1]

Keep the Design Simple

On average, audience members have only 30 seconds or less[2] to view an aid, so restrict text to a minimum and present only one major idea per aid:

- *Follow the six-by-six rule.* Use no more than six words in a line and six lines on one slide. This way the audience will spend less time reading the aid and more time listening to you (see "Buying a Used Car Below").
- *Word text in active verb form.* Use the active voice and parallel grammatical structure, e.g., "Gather Necessary Documents; Apply Early" (see Chapter 15 on language).
- *Avoid clutter.* Allow plenty of white space, or "visual breathing room" for viewers.[3]
- *Create concise titles.* Use titles that summarize content and reinforce your message.

Cluttered Aid	Easy-to-Read Aid
Buying a Used Car	Buying a Used Car
1. Prepare in advance—know the market value of several cars you are interested in before going to shop.	1. Know the car's market value.
2. Do not get into a hurry about buying the first car you see—be patient, there will be others.	2. Don't hurry to buy.
3. It is recommended that you shop around for credit before buying the car.	3. Shop for credit before buying.
4. Inspect the car carefully, looking for funny sounds, stains, worn equipment, dents, etc.	4. Inspect the car carefully.
5. Ask for proof about the history of the car, including previous owners.	5. Get proof of the car's history.

QUICK TIP

Beware of "Chartjunk"

Certain kinds of information—especially statistical data
and sequences of action—are best understood when visually presented. However, avoid what design expert Edward
Tufte coined as "chartjunk"[4]—slides jammed with too
many graphs, charts, and meaningless design elements that
obscure rather than illuminate information. Use fewer rather
than more slides and only those design elements that truly
enhance meaning.

◉ Use Design Elements Consistently

Apply the same design decisions you make for one presentation aid to all of the aids you display in a speech; this will
ensure that viewers aren't distracted by a jumble of unrelated
visual elements. Carry your choice of design elements—color,
fonts, upper- and lowercase letters, styling (boldface, underlining, italics), general page layout, and repeating elements
such as titles and logos—through each aid.

◉ Select Appropriate Typeface Styles and Fonts

A *typeface* is a specific style of lettering, such as Arial or Times
Roman. Typefaces come in a variety of *fonts*, or sets of sizes
(called the *point size*), and upper- and lower cases. Designers
divide the thousands of available typefaces into two major
categories: serif and sans serif. *Serif typefaces* include small
flourishes, or strokes, at the tops and bottoms of each letter.
Sans serif typefaces are more blocklike and linear; they are
designed without these tiny strokes.

Consider these guidelines when selecting and designing
type:

- Check the lettering for legibility, taking into consideration the audience's distance from the presentation. On
  slides, experiment with 36-point type for major headings, 24-point type for subheadings, and *at least* 18-point
  type for text.
- Lettering should stand apart from the background. Use
  either dark text on light background or light text on dark
  background.
- Use a typeface that is simple and easy to read, not
  distracting.
- Use standard upper- and lowercase type rather than all
  capitals.

Using Serif and Sans Serif Type

For reading a block of text, serif typefaces are easier on the eye. Small amounts of text, however, such as headings, are best viewed in sans serif type. Thus, consider a sans serif typeface for the heading and a serif typeface for the body of the text. If you include only a few lines of text, use sans serif type throughout.

- As a rule, use no more than two different typefaces in a single visual aid.
- Use **boldface**, <u>underlining</u>, or *italics* sparingly.

◎ Use Color Carefully

Skillful use of color can draw attention to key points, influence the mood of a presentation, and make things easier to see. Conversely, poor color combinations will set the wrong mood, render an image unattractive, or make it unreadable. Note the effect of these color combinations:

Effects of Color Combinations	
Color	Effect in Combination
Yellow	Warm on white, harsh on black, fiery on red, soothing on light blue
Blue	Warm on white, hard to see on black
Red	Bright on white, warm or difficult to see on black

Color affects both the legibility of text and the mood conveyed. Following are some tips for using color effectively in your presentation aids:

- Keep the *background color* constant across all slides or other aids.
- Use *bold, bright colors* to emphasize important points.
- For typeface and graphics, use colors that contrast rather than clash with or blend into the background color; check for visibility when projecting. Audiences will remember information just as easily if white text appears on dark background or dark text on light background, so long as the design is appealing.[5]
- Limit colors to no more than three, with maximum of four in complex and detailed aids.

◉ Consider Subjective Interpretations of Color

Colors can evoke distinct associations for people, so take care not to summon an unintended meaning or mood. For example, control engineers see red and think danger, whereas a financial manager will think unprofitability.

Consider, too, that the meanings associated with certain colors may differ across cultures. Western societies don black for funerals, while the Chinese use white. If you are presenting in a cross-cultural context, check the meanings of colors for the relevant nationalities.

✓ CHECKLIST

Apply the Principles of Simplicity and Continuity

❑ Concentrate on presenting one major idea per visual aid.

❑ Apply design decisions consistently to each aid.

❑ Use type that is large enough for audience members to read comfortably.

❑ Use color to highlight key ideas and enhance readability.

❑ Check that colors contrast rather than clash.

CHAPTER 21 ●●●●

Using Presentation Software

Public speakers can use a variety of powerful software tools to create and display high-quality visual aids. These programs include the familiar Microsoft PowerPoint and its Apple counterpart, Keynote, as well as the Web-based program Prezi.

◉ Develop a Plan

Often the best place to begin planning your slides is your speaking outline (see p. 104). In general, a speaking outline will contain between two and seven main points, each of which is linked to at least two subpoints. Think through which points in your speech might be better explained to your audience with some kind of visual: decide what the content of your slides should be, how many slides you'll need, and how to arrange your slides. Review and edit slides as necessary using *Slide Sorter view* (in PowerPoint), *Lightable* or *Outline view* (in Keynote), or *path tool* (in Prezi).

🅐 LaunchPadSolo For detailed guidance on creating presentations in PowerPoint, Keynote, and Prezi, go to macmillanhighered.com/pocketspeak5e

◉ Avoid Technical Glitches

Technical errors are always a hazard with presentation software and any hardware required to run it. Common risks include incompatibility of a PowerPoint or Keynote file with an operating system, an Internet connection failing while using Prezi, a display screen malfunction, or a computer drive freezing when attempting to play a media file. To avoid forcing the audience to wait as you try to fix technical problems, follow these steps:

1. Save all the files associated with your presentation (i.e., images, sound, videos) into the same folder you will use in your presentation.

2. Check that the operating system of the computer you will use during your speech (e.g., Windows XP, Mac OS X) is compatible with the operating system used to create the aids.

3. Confirm that the version of the presentation software used to create the aids corresponds to the software on the computer you will use in the presentation; this will prevent distortions in your graphics, sound, and video.

4. Verify that you've saved the files to a source—a flash drive, CD, DVD, website, or e-mail—that will be recognized by the presentation computer.

5. Familiarize yourself with the layout and functioning of the presentation computer before the speech to facilitate smooth operation during the presentation.

6. Prepare a digital backup of your presentation in case of technical challenges.

◉ Give a Speech, Not a Slide Show

Frequently we hear someone say, "I'm giving a PowerPoint (or a Prezi or Keynote) today," instead of "I'm giving a speech today." Some speakers hide behind presentation media, focusing attention on their aids rather than on the audience. They might erroneously believe that the display itself is the presentation, or that it will somehow save an otherwise poorly planned speech.[1] Other speakers become so involved in generating glitzy aids that they forget their primary mission: to communicate through the spoken word[2] and their physical presence.

Presentation aids certainly can and do help listeners process information and so enhance a speech, but only as long as you truly work to engage the audience and achieve your speech goal. Speaker and message, rather than any presentation media, must take center stage.

◎ Finding Media for Presentations

You can import still images, clip art, video, or sound directly into your aids by downloading your own files or those from the Internet. For downloadable *digital images,* try the following websites:

- Corbis Images (www.corbisimages.com): Contains more than two million photographs, prints, and paintings, 35,000 of which you can download for your personal use (for a fee).
- Google (www.google.com), Yahoo! (www.yahoo.com), and Bing (www.bing.com) offer extensive image searches.

The following sites contain free photographs and other still images:

- Flickr (www.flickr.com/creativecommons): Access to thousands of photographs shared by amateur and hobbyist photographers.
- Exalead (www.exalead.com/search/image): An innovative image search engine with over two billion images.
- American Memory (memory.loc.gov/ammem/index/html): Free access to still and moving images depicting the history of the American experience.

The following sites offer downloadable *music files* and *audio clips:*

- MP3.com (www.mp3.com)
- SoundClick (www.soundclick.com)
- Internet Archive (www.archive.org/details/audio)
- The Daily.WAV (www.dailywav.com)
- FreeAudioClips.com (www.freeaudioclips.com)
- SoundCloud (www.soundcloud.com)

The following sites contain useful *video clips:*

- CNN Video (www.cnn.com/video) and ABC News Video (abcnews.go.com/video): Especially useful for speech topics on current events or timely social issues.
- YouTube (www.youtube.com)
- New York Times (www.nytimes.com/video)
- Google Videos (video.google.com)
- Bing Videos (www.bing.com/videos/browse)
- Metacafe (www.metacafe.com)

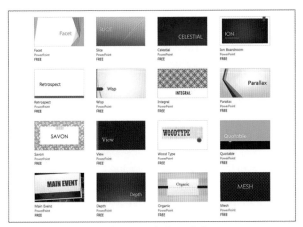

FIGURE 21.1 Design Templates in PowerPoint

FIGURE 21.2 Design Templates in Keynote

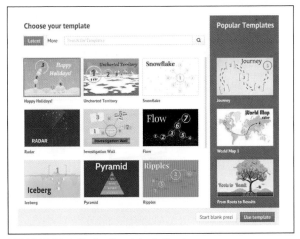

FIGURE 21.3 Design Templates in Prezi

FROM SLIDE SHOW TO PRESENTATION

Getting Ready to Deliver a PowerPoint, Keynote, or Prezi Presentation

To avoid technical glitches, practice delivering your speech with your presentation software and ensure compatibility with the venue's equipment.

Check the Venue

Before your speech, take stock of the equipment and room layout. See the annotated photo for tips on achieving a smooth delivery with digital aids.

1 **Locate power sources.** Ensure that cords can reach the presentation equipment, and consider taping them to the floor to keep them out of the way.

2 **Computer needs and compatibility.** Check that all files, from the slide show to audio and video clips, load successfully to the presentation computer. If possible, practice at least once on this computer.

(clockwise from bottom) Jeff Presnail/Getty Images; Cinoby/Getty Images; Casper Benson/Getty Images; Purestock/Getty Images

3 **Internet access.** Have wireless log-in information available and/or a cable that reaches the Internet jack.

4 **Backup plan.** Create a contingency plan in case of computer failure; for example, print overhead transparencies from slide show, prepare to put information on board, or create handouts.

5 **Audio.** Determine how you will broadcast any audio aids, and check speaker volume before the speech.

Position Yourself Carefully

Choose a place to stand that gives the audience clear sight-lines to you and your slide show. Stand such that you can face forward even when changing slides or gesturing toward your aids. This helps you connect with your audience, project your voice clearly, and prevents you from reading off your slides.

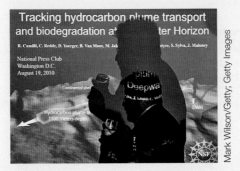

Needs improvement: This speaker's sideways stance discourages eye contact and indicates that he may be reading off his slides.

Good placement: This speaker can access the computer or gesture toward the slides without blocking the audience's sightlines.

◉ Avoid Copyright Infringement

Be certain to abide by copyright restrictions when using
visual and audio materials from the Internet or other sources.
Recognize when material is available under fair-use provi-
sions (see p. 27). Even if fair use applies, cite the source of the
material in your presentation. Consult your school's information technology (IT) office for statements of policy pertaining
to copyrighted and fair-use materials, especially from undocumented sources such as peer-to-peer (P2P) sharing:

- Cite the source of all copyrighted material in your presentation. For example, include a bibliographic footnote
  on the slide containing the material.
- Be wary of sites purporting to offer "royalty free" media
  objects; there might actually be other costs associated
  with the materials.
- When time, resources, and ability allow, create and use
  your own pictures, video, or audio for your presentation
  slides.

✔ CHECKLIST

**Tips for Successfully Using Presentation
Software in Your Speech**

- ❏ Don't let the technology get in the way of relating to
  your audience.
- ❏ Talk to your audience rather than to the screen.
- ❏ Maintain eye contact as much as possible.
- ❏ Have a backup plan in case of technical errors.
- ❏ If you use a pointer (laser or otherwise), turn it off and
  put it down as soon as you have made your point.
- ❏ Never shine a laser pointer into anyone's eyes. It will
  burn them!
- ❏ Incorporate the aids into your practice sessions until
  you are confident that they strengthen, rather than
  detract from, your core message.

part

Types of Speeches

22. **Informative Speaking** 156

23. **Principles of Persuasive Speaking** 167

24. **Constructing the Persuasive Speech** 174

25. **Speaking on Special Occasions** 192

CHAPTER 22 ● ●●

Informative Speaking

To *inform* is to communicate knowledge. The goal of **informative speaking** is to increase the audience's knowledge and deepen their understanding of some phenomenon.[1] Informative speeches bring new issues to light, offer fresh insights on familiar subjects, or provide novel ways of thinking about a topic. Your speech might be an analysis of an issue, a report of an event, or a physical demonstration of how something works. As long as the audience learns something, the options are nearly limitless.

QUICK TIP

Enlighten Rather Than Advocate

Whereas a persuasive speech would seek to modify attitudes or ask an audience to adopt a specific position, an informative speech stops short of this. Yet there are always elements of persuasion in an informative speech, and vice versa. Nevertheless, if you keep in mind the general speech purpose of sharing knowledge and deepening understanding, you will be able to deliver a speech whose primary function is to enlighten rather than to advocate.

◉ Gain and Sustain Involvement

Audience members are not simply empty vessels into which you can pour facts and figures for automatic processing. Before your listeners retain information, they must be motivated to hear it and able to recognize, understand, and relate to it.[2]

Use Audience Analysis

Use audience analysis to gauge the audience's existing knowledge of your topic and their likely interests and needs with respect to it. Then adapt your speech accordingly. (See the Chapter 6 section on "Gauge Listeners' Feelings toward the Topic.")

Present New and Interesting Information

Audiences want to learn something new from the speaker. To satisfy this drive, offer information that is fresh and compelling. Seek out unusual (but credible) sources, novel (but sound) interpretations, moving stories, compelling examples, and striking facts. If a speech does not offer audience members anything new, they will feel that their time has been wasted and will rightly be offended.[3]

QUICK TIP

Don't Overwhelm the Audience

As important as offering new information is not over-whelming audience members with too much of it. Most people will recall less than half of the information you tell them, so focus on what you most want to convey and trim material that is not vital to your central idea.[4]

◎ Look for Ways to Increase Understanding

Audience members cannot put the speaker on "pause" in order to digest information, so help them to stay on track with these basic speechmaking techniques described in previous chapters:

- *Prepare a well-organized introduction that clearly previews the thesis and main points* and a conclusion that summarizes them; this will help listeners anticipate and remember information (see Chapter 14).
- *Make liberal use of transition words and phrases* ("first," "next," "I'll now turn . . .") to signal points and verbally map the flow of ideas. Use *internal previews* to forecast key points and *internal summaries* to reinforce them (see p. 85).
- *Use rhetorical devices* such as repetition and parallelism to reinforce information and drive home key ideas (see Chapter 15).
- *Choose an organizational pattern* to help listeners mentally organize ideas and see relationships among them (see Chapters 12 and 24).
- *Use presentation aids* selectively to help listeners hear *and* see related (but not duplicated) information, as, for instance, in charts and diagrams (see Chapters 19–21).

QUICK TIP

Make the Introduction Motivating

Early on in your informative speech, give audience members a reason to care about your message. Use the introduction to point out the topic's relevance to them and to describe any concrete benefits they will gain by listening to you. Expand upon these points in the speech body, and reiterate them once more in the conclusion.

◎ Subject Matter of Informative Speeches

Informative speeches may be about *people, events, concepts, issues, processes,* or *objects* or *phenomena.* These are not hard-and-fast divisions—a speech can be about both the *process* of dance and the *people* who perform it, for example—nor are they the only way to categorize informative speeches. These subject categories, however, do indicate the range of potential subject matter suited to an informative purpose, as seen in the following table.

Subject Categories of Informative Speeches	
Subject Category	Sample Topics
Speeches about People	
Address impact of individuals or groups of people who have made a difference	• Athletes • Authors • Inventors • You, the speaker
Speeches about Current or Historical Events	
Address noteworthy occurrences, past and present	• The disappearance of Malaysia Flight 370 • The rise of the Islamic State • The Battle of Britain
Speeches about Concepts	
Address abstract or complex ideas, theories, or beliefs	• Free speech • Chaos theory • Nanotechnology
Speeches about Issues	
Address social problems or matters in dispute, about which you want to raise awareness rather than advocate a position	• Impact of long-term unemployment • Legalizing and taxing nonmedical marijuana • U.S. Immigration Policy
Speeches about Processes	
Demonstrate and/or explain how something is done, how it is made, or how it works	• Production of algae-based biofuels • Visualization in sports • Power-Yoga routine
Speeches about Objects or Phenomena	
Address aspects of non-human subjects (their history and function, for example)	• MRI-based lie detectors • e-book readers • El Niño wind patterns in the western United States

◉ Decide How to Communicate Your Information

Typically, we communicate information by defining, describing, demonstrating, and/or explaining it. Some speeches rely on a single approach (e.g., they focus on *demonstrating* how something works or *explaining* what something means). Oftentimes, we use multiple strategies. As you prepare your speech, ask yourself, "How much emphasis should I give to defining my topic, describing it, demonstrating it, or explaining its meaning?"

DEFINITION When your topic is new to the audience and/or addresses a complex concept *(What is a fractal?)*, pay particular attention to providing adequate definitions. After all, you don't want audience members spending the entire speech wondering what your topic actually means. To *define* something is to identify its essential qualities and meaning.

You can approach definition in a number of ways, including the following:

- Defining something by what it does (*operational definition*): *A computer is something that processes information.*
- Defining something by describing what it is not (**definition by negation**): *Courage is not the absence of fear.*
- Defining something by providing several concrete examples (**definition by example**): *Health professionals include doctors, nurses, EMTs, and ambulance drivers.*
- Defining something by comparing it to something synonymous (**definition by synonym**): *A friend is a comrade or a buddy.*
- Defining something by illustrating its root meaning (**definition by word origin**): *Our word* rival *derives from the Latin word* rivalis, *"one living near or using the same stream."*[5]

DESCRIPTION Whether offering your audience a "virtual tour" of the top of Mount Everest, or describing the physical ravages caused by drug abuse, the point of description is to provide a mental picture for the audience. Use concrete words and vivid imagery to help listeners visualize your depictions (see Chapter 15).

DEMONSTRATION Sometimes the purpose of an informative speech is to explain how something works or to provide an actual demonstration, similar to the many "how-to" videos and podcasts that exist on the Web. A speech may not include an actual physical demonstration (e.g., *how to use social bookmarks*), but the speaker will nevertheless rely on a verbal demonstration of the steps involved.

EXPLANATION   Many informative speech topics are built on *explanation*—providing reasons or causes, demonstrating relationships, and offering interpretation and analysis. The classroom lecture is a classic example of explanation in an informative context (see Chapter 30). But numerous kinds of speeches rely on explanation, from those that address difficult or confusing theories and processes (*What is the relationship between the glycemic index and glycemic load?*) to those that present ideas that challenge conventional thinking (*Why do researchers say that sometimes emotion makes us more rather than less logical?*). See the checklist on p. 161 for strategies for explaining complex ideas.

◉ Take Steps to Reduce Confusion

New information can be hard to grasp, especially when it addresses a difficult concept (such as *equilibrium* in engineering), a difficult-to-envision process (such as *cash-flow management* in business), or a counterintuitive idea—one that challenges commonsense thinking (such as *drinking a glass of red wine a day can be healthy*).[6]

Useful for almost any speech, the following strategies for communicating information are especially helpful when attempting to clarify complex information, as in scientific and technical concepts.

Use Analogies to Build on Prior Knowledge

Audience members will understand a new concept more easily if the speaker uses an **analogy** to relate it to something that they already know. For example, to explain the unpredictable paths that satellites often take when they fall to earth, you can liken the effect to dropping a penny into water: "Sometimes it goes straight down, and sometimes it turns end over end and changes direction. The same thing happens when an object hits the atmosphere."[7]

In the following excerpt from a speech about nanotechnology, Wolfgang Porod explains the size of a nanometer by comparing it to the diameter of the moon. Note how he attempts to reduce confusion by first *defining* the root *nano* and then comparing it to the size of the moon:

> What is a nano and what is special about a nano? *Nano* is a prefix derived from the Greek word for dwarf and it means one billionth of something. So a nanosecond is a billionth of a second. A nanometer is a billionth of a meter. Now, just saying that doesn't really tell you that much. So what does it mean to have the length scale of a billionth of a meter? Well, imagine the diameter of the moon. It just happens to be, roughly . . . a billion meters. So take that and shrink it

down to the length scale of a meter, which is what it means to go a billion size scales. So a nanometer is a billionth of a meter.[8]

QUICK TIP

Use Analogies Accurately

Linking the unfamiliar with the familiar through analogy aids understanding. But no analogy can exactly represent another concept; at a certain point, the similarities will end.[9] To ensure accuracy, state the limits of the comparison. The statement "The heart is like a pump, except that the heart actually changes size as it pushes blood out" demonstrates that, though similar, a heart and a pump are not the same.[10]

Counter Faulty Assumptions

Listeners may fail to understand a process because they believe that something "obviously" works a certain way when in fact it does not. To counter faulty assumptions, first acknowledge common misperceptions and then offer an accurate explanation of underlying causes.[11]

✓ CHECKLIST

Strategies for Explaining Complex Information

To explain a *concept or term*:
- ❑ Use analogies that link concepts to something familiar.
- ❑ Define terms in several ways.
- ❑ Simplify terminology wherever possible.

To explain a *process or structure*, do all of the above *and*:
- ❑ Make ample use of presentation aids, including models and drawings.

To explain a *counterintuitive idea*, do all of the above *and*:
- ❑ Address the commonly held assumption first.
- ❑ Acknowledge its plausibility.
- ❑ Demonstrate its limitations using familiar examples.

Appeal to Different Learning Styles

People have different **learning styles**, or preferred ways of processing information. One learning theory model suggests four preferences: visual, aural, read/write, and kinesthetic[12] (see the following table on different types of learners). Some of us are *multimodal learners*, in that we combine two or more preferences.

Audience analysis may give you a sense of individuals' learning styles. For example, mechanics of all types have strong spatial visualization abilities and thus would be classified as visual learners; they may also be kinesthetic learners who want to "test" things for themselves. Often, however, you may not have enough information to determine your listeners' learning style, *so plan on conveying and reinforcing information in a variety of modes.*

Communicating Information to Different Types of Learners	
Type	Advice for Communicating Information
Visual	Will most easily grasp ideas communicated through pictures, diagrams, charts, graphs, flowcharts, maps.
Aural	Will most easily grasp ideas communicated through the spoken word, whether in live lectures, tapes, group discussions, or podcasts.
Read/Write	Will most easily grasp ideas communicated through text-based delivery, handouts, PowerPoint with text-based slides.
Kinesthetic	Will most easily grasp ideas communicated through real-life demonstrations, simulations, and movies, and through hands-on applications.

◉ Arrange Points in a Pattern

Our understanding of a speech is directly linked to how well it is organized.[13] Informative speeches can be organized using any of the patterns described in Chapter 12, including the topical, chronological, spatial, cause-effect, and narrative patterns. (Note that although the *problem-solution* pattern may be used in informative speeches, it often is a more logical candidate for persuasive speeches.) A speech about the Impressionist movement in painting, for example, could be organized *chronologically*, in which main points are arranged in sequence from the movement's early period to its later falling out of favor. It could be organized *causally* (cause-effect), by demonstrating that Impressionism came about as a reaction to the art movement that preceded it. It could also be organized *topically* (by categories), by focusing on the major figures associated with the movement, famous paintings linked to it, or notable contemporary artists who paint in the style.

SAMPLE INFORMATIVE SPEECH

This informative speech by DJ McCabe describes a movement or cause that might be unfamiliar to his audience. To ensure understanding, he is careful to define any potentially confusing or unknown terms, including, of course, the topic term *freeganism*. DJ provides a short but effective preview of his thesis and main points, which serves both to create interest in the topic and to signal how the speech will be organized—in this case topically (see p. 93). With strong supporting material in the form of examples and statistics and a compelling conclusion based on a story of a real-life freegan, DJ is able to convey a great deal of information in an engaging way.

Freeganism: More Than a Free Lunch

DJ McCabe

LaunchPadSolo See DJ deliver his speech at LaunchPad Solo:
macmillanhighered.com/pocketspeak5e

How many people in this audience consider themselves—or know someone who is—vegetarian? How about vegan? If you're not familiar with veganism, it's the form of strict vegetarianism in which individuals do not eat food containing any animal products, including dairy, eggs, or honey. Although some vegans choose this dietary lifestyle for health reasons, most do so for ideological reasons, ranging from a commitment to animal rights to concerns about pollution resulting from animal farming.

> Beginning the speech with a rhetorical question is an effective attention-getter, especially since most people do know someone who is vegetarian.

> DJ takes care to define terms that may not be familiar to the audience, or about which they may have an incomplete understanding.

To many of you, this may seem like an extreme lifestyle choice. However, there are people who take things a step beyond veganism. How many of you are familiar with the term *freegan?* According to the website

Freegan.info, *freegan* is a combination of *free* and *vegan*. Freegans look for free products—from food to furniture—to minimize the impact of human consumerism on both the planet and other people. In fact, not all freegans are vegan; it is the "free" part that is key. Freegans oppose our consumer culture, in which we buy things we don't need and throw away things that are still usable.

During this presentation, I will introduce you to the freegan lifestyle—what the Freegan.info website defines as "living based on limited participation in" capitalism and "minimal consumption of resources." I will first describe a few of the ways that freegans try to minimize their use of resources, then discuss the reasons why some people choose to live this way, and finally explore some legitimate criticisms of the freegan lifestyle.

Here is DJ's preview statement, in which he states the thesis and main points. He also signals how he will organize the speech—in this case topically, or by focusing on different categories of his topic.

First, the heart of freeganism is a commitment to using fewer resources, and one way to do that is to throw away less trash. As reported in a 2007 article in the *New York Times* by Steven Kurutz, the Environmental Protection Agency found that we throw away nearly 250 million tons of trash per year, which translates to over 4 pounds on average, per person, every single day. Two freegan practices—waste minimization and waste reclamation—specifically deal with trash and seek to reduce the amount of garbage Americans produce every year.

DJ uses the signal word "first" to transition into the body of the speech.

Many of us already support one of the tenets of freeganism—waste minimization—through recycling; hopefully everyone in this room today will take the time to throw their empty plastic water bottles and soda cans into a recycling container. But minimizing waste isn't just about recycling. Freegans also reuse everything they can, like using that old mayonnaise jar to hold pens and pencils instead of buying a specially designed pencil holder; this option reduces the demand for resources to make the specialty item and also eliminates the need for energy consumed during recycling.

Even though this is an informative speech, it contains elements of persuasion, just as persuasive speeches also inform.

DJ provides plenty of concrete examples that both enlarge understanding and add color and interest.

Waste reclamation is just a formal term for what many of us know affectionately as "Dumpster diving."

You've engaged in this free acquisition of items that other people have thrown away if you furnished your dorm or apartment with a chair or a bookcase that someone left on the curb or in a Dumpster. But would you consider making your meals out of what other people throw away? Freegans do. In his article on food waste, Robert Fireovid notes a U.S. Department of Agriculture finding: In 2008, the amount of food wasted by restaurants and stores averaged 275 pounds per American, not including what we throw away at home. For freegans, this is unnecessary waste, and so they will reclaim any still-edible food along with other household items.

> DJ encourages engagement in his topic by showing the topic's relevance to the audience members' own lives.

> DJ continues to directly engage listeners, this time by acknowledging that most people in the audience probably wouldn't engage in the more radical practices of freeganism.

> When citing this finding, DJ should have mentioned the name of the publication, which is the journal *Agricultural Research*.

If you think it sounds gross to eat food that has been thrown away by someone else, there are certainly legitimate worries about illness from spoiled food. At the same time, recent research shows that a lot of the food thrown away by grocery stores, for example, is perfectly safe to eat. A 2013 report published by the Natural Resources Defense Council and the Harvard Law School Food Law and Policy Clinic noted that $900 million in food was thrown away by retailers in 2001 because the date listed on the product had expired. Those date labels often refer to the date until which the product will retain its highest quality, not necessarily the date after which the food is no longer safe to eat. That same report confirms that "the FDA's Center for Food Safety and Applied Nutrition has noted that most foods, when kept in optimal storage conditions, are safe to eat and of acceptable quality for periods of time past the label date."

> DJ offers trustworthy sources throughout the speech.

Yet even if freegans reclaim wasted food safely and are mindful of their health, why would people who could afford to buy food choose to dig it out of the trash?

> This rhetorical question serves as an effective transition to the next point.

As defined at the beginning of my presentation, freegans try to avoid participating in capitalism, which they believe to be inherently exploitative. As the Freegan.info website puts it, "Instead of avoiding the purchase of products from one bad company only to support another, we avoid buying anything to the greatest degree we are able." Although many health- and environmentally conscious people choose to shop at certain stores so that they can buy organic or fair-trade goods, freegans see even those efforts as problematic choices. Organic and fair-trade products still need to be shipped to stores, consuming fossil fuels and producing exhaust emissions in the process. And given the amount of food wasted unnecessarily in the United States, freegans feel an ethical obligation not to contribute to increased consumer demand when so much of the existing supply is already unused.

Despite their noble commitment to environmentalism and advocacy of a more humane economic system, freegans are not without critics. In some cities, Dumpster diving is illegal under municipal codes against trespassing and vandalism, although those laws are not often enforced against people "reclaiming" waste from Dumpsters unless the divers create a mess or property owners actively seek to have anti-trespassing laws applied. Harsher objections come from critics who argue that the freegan lifestyle does little to help the truly impoverished and may literally take food out of their mouths. In the words of Jerry Adler in a 2007 *Newsweek* article, "The freegans, most of whom are educated and capable of contributing to the economy, aren't sharing the surplus wealth of the West with those who are destitute by circumstance rather than choice. They are competing with them for it." Given both the small number of Americans who choose to live as freegans and the enormous amount of food wasted in this country, freegans are not very likely to consume all of the still-edible food thrown away by stores and restaurants. But their small numbers also mean they are not likely to have a significant impact on the environmental and economic problems their freegan lifestyle hopes to combat.

DJ signals the conclusion of the speech.

During this speech, I have introduced you to the subculture of freegans in the United States. Through their practices of waste minimization and waste reclamation, freegans hope to avoid the negative impacts of capitalist consumption on both the environment and people. Whether freegans are prophets of a better world or naive idealists living on other people's trash remains an open question, but I hope that the next time you see someone exploring a Dumpster behind a supermarket, you remember that some people do so by choice rather than because it is their only option. And so I want to close by introducing you to one woman who made that choice.

As described in the 2007 *New York Times* article by Steven Kurutz, Madeline Nelson lived a life to which many of us aspire, making over $100,000 per year as a communications director for Barnes & Noble bookstores. Frustrated that her job and daily life continued to reinforce the rat race of buying "stuff" only to throw it away before buying more, in 2005 Ms. Nelson sold her posh Manhattan apartment in favor of a small place in Brooklyn and quit her corporate job so she could live as a freegan. When asked if she misses the extravagances that once filled her life, she responds, "Most people work 40- plus hours a week at jobs they don't like to buy things they don't need." We might not wish to become freegans ourselves, but Madeline's life is quite literally food for thought.

> Concluding the speech with a real-life story of a freegan gives the topic even more relevance and leaves the audience with something to think about.

References

Adler, Jerry, "The Noble Scavenger on the Living-Room Couch." *Newsweek*, October 2007, 48.

Fireovid, Robert L. "Wasted Food: What We Are Doing to Prevent Costly Losses." *Agricultural Research*, 61, no. 3 (2013): 2.

Kurutz, Steven. "Not Buying It." *The New York Times*, June 21, 2007. Retrieved from www.lexis-nexis.com

Leib, Emily Broad, Diana Gunders, Juliana Ferro, Annika Nielsen, Grace Nosek, and Jason Qu. "The Dating Game: How Confusing Food Date Labels Lead to Food Waste in America." September 2013. Retrieved from www.nrdc.org/food/files/dating-game-report.pdf

"What Is a Freegan?" (n.d.). Retrieved from http://freegan.info

CHAPTER 23 ● ● ●●

Principles of Persuasive Speaking

To persuade is to advocate, to ask others to accept your views. A **persuasive speech** is meant to influence audience members' attitudes, beliefs, values, and/or behavior by appealing to some combination of their needs, desires, interests, and even fears.

When you speak persuasively, you aim to produce some shift in the audience's emotions and reasoning about an issue — to arouse involvement and perhaps motivate action for an issue or a cause, or to strengthen (or weaken) beliefs about a certain controversy. Whatever the topic, the goal is to reinforce, stimulate, or change the audience's attitudes and beliefs about the issue in question to more closely match that of your own.

◎ Persuasive Speeches Appeal to Human Psychology

Success in persuasive speaking requires attention to human psychology — to what motivates listeners. Audience analysis is therefore extremely important in persuasive appeals, both to identify what your target audience cares about and to build common ground (see Chapter 6). But persuasion is a complex process, and getting people to change their minds, even a little, is challenging.

Research confirms that you can increase the odds of influencing the audience in your direction if you:

- Set modest goals. Expect minor rather than major changes in your listeners' attitudes and behavior.[1]
- Establish your credibility and build common bonds to encourage the audience's trust in and identification with you (see p. 37).
- Make your message personally relevant to the audience.
- Expect to be more successful when addressing an audience whose position differs only moderately from your own.[2] The more strongly audience members feel about a given issue, the less likely they are to be persuaded of an alternative viewpoint.[3]
- Demonstrate how any change you propose will benefit the audience.

QUICK TIP

Reap the Rewards

Skilled persuasive speakers achieve positions of leadership for their motivational abilities and earn the respect of their communities for making a difference. They are able to make their voices count during public conversations about issues of importance to them. Practiced persuasive speakers also tend to be skilled evaluators of persuasive messages. By learning strategies of effective and ethical persuasion, they become more educated critical thinkers, consumers, voters, and citizens.[4]

Persuasion is both ancient art and modern science, with roots in Greek and Roman *rhetoric,* as persuasion was first named, and branches in contemporary social science. Both classical and contemporary perspectives recognize that successful persuasion requires a balance of reason and emotion, and that audience members must be well disposed toward the speaker.

◉ Classical Persuasive Appeals: Ethos, Pathos, and Logos

Aristotle explained that persuasion could be brought about by the speaker's use of three types of *persuasive appeals* or "proofs"—termed logos, pathos, and ethos. The first appeal uses *reason and logic,* the second targets listeners' *emotions,* and the third enlists *speaker credibility* (see "Applying Aristotle's Three Persuasive Appeals," on p. 171). According to Aristotle, and generations who followed him to the present day, you can build an effective persuasive speech with any one or a combination of these appeals or proofs, but the most effective persuasive speeches generally make use of all three.

Appeal to Reason

Many persuasive speeches focus on issues that require considerable thought. Aristotle used the term **logos** to refer to persuasive appeals directed at the audience's systematic reasoning on a topic. Should the United States enact stricter immigration laws? Does the U.S. government endanger our privacy with its surveillance programs? When you ask audience members to reach a conclusion regarding a complicated issue, whether political or personal, they will look to you to provide solid reasons and evidence—to offer appeals to logos. You can evoke logos in a speech with evidence and reasoning, within the framework of an argument (see Chapter 24 on constructing arguments).

Appeal to Emotion

A second powerful means of persuasion is **pathos**—appealing to listeners' emotions. Feelings such as love, compassion, anger, and fear underlie many of our actions and motivate us to think and feel as we do. Appealing to these emotions helps establish a personal connection with the audience and makes your claims more relatable.

You can also evoke emotion through *vivid imagery, compelling stories* (especially ones that touch upon shared values such as patriotism, selflessness, faith, and hope), *repetition and parallelism* (to create drama and rhythm), and other stylistic devices of language (see Chapter 15). You can see this in the following excerpt from a speech by Winston Churchill, delivered in June 1940 to the British House of Commons, in which Churchill seeks to motivate the nation for the battles ahead through his use of vivid imagery, emotionally charged words ("odious apparatus"), and the cadenced repetition of sentences beginning with the same phrases ("we shall" see *anaphora*, p. 198):

> Even though large tracts of Europe and many old and famous states have fallen or may fall into the grip of the Gestapo and all the odious apparatus of Nazi rule, we shall not flag or fail. We shall go on to the end, we shall fight in France, we shall fight on the seas and oceans, we shall fight with growing confidence and growing strength in the air, we shall defend our island, whatever the cost may be, we shall fight on the beaches, we shall fight on the landing grounds, we shall fight in the fields and in the streets, we shall fight in the hills; we shall never surrender. . . .[5]

Base Emotional Appeals on Sound Reasoning

Although emotion is a powerful means of moving an audience, relying solely on naked emotion to persuade will fail most of the time. What actually persuades is the interplay between emotion and logic.[6] Emotion gets the audience's attention and arouses their feelings—either positive or negative—about the issue in question. Reason provides the justification for these feelings, and emotion and reason together may dispose audience members to believe in or act upon your suggestions. For example, urging audience members to avoid an unhealthy behavior, you might describe the consequences of the behavior, offering ample evidence to back up this logical appeal; you follow this with an emotional appeal, "If not for yourself, do it for your loved ones" (see motivational warrants, p. 177).

Stress Your Credibility

Audiences want more than logical and emotional appeals from a speaker; they want what's relevant to them from someone who cares. Aristotle termed this effect of the speaker on the audience **ethos**, or the audience's perceptions of the speaker's competence, character, and concern for the audience. Modern-day scholars call it **speaker credibility**.

Audience members' perceptions of your ethos or speaker credibility strongly influence how receptive they will be to your proposals, and studies confirm that attitude change is related directly to the extent to which listeners perceive speakers to be competent and prepared.[7] Speakers perceived as high in credibility will also be regarded as more truthful than those perceived to have low credibility.[8]

Applying Aristotle's Three Persuasive Appeals

Appeal to Logos	Target audience members' rational thinking through logical reasoning.
Appeal to Pathos	Target audience members' emotions using dramatic storytelling, vivid imagery, repetition and parallelism, metaphor, and other stylistic devices of language.
Appeal to Ethos	Target audience members' feelings about the speaker's character through demonstrations of trustworthiness, competence, and concern for audience welfare.

Contemporary Persuasive Appeals: Needs and Motivations

Current research confirms the persuasive power of ethos, pathos, and logos in persuasive appeals.[9] Advertisers consciously create ads aimed at evoking an emotional response (pathos) in consumers that convince us that their company or product is reliable or credible (ethos) and which offer factual reasons (logos) for why we should buy something.[10] At the same time, today's social scientists have developed additional strategies for reinforcing or changing attitudes, including (1) targeting audience members' *motivations* for feeling and acting as they do, (2) appealing to audience members' *needs*, and (3) appealing to how they are likely to *mentally process* the persuasive message.

Appeal to What Motivates Audience Members

Winning over audience members to your point of view requires appealing to their *motives*, or predispositions to behave in certain ways.[11] Motives arise from needs and desires that we seek to satisfy (see below). If as a speaker you can convince listeners that by taking an action you propose they will be rewarded in some way, you are likely to encourage receptivity to change.

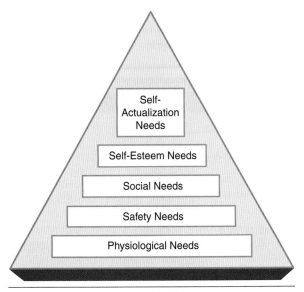

FIGURE 23.1 Maslow's Hierarchy of Needs

Appeal to Audience Members' Needs

The multibillion-dollar advertising industry focuses on one goal: appealing to consumers' needs. Likewise, one very effective way to persuade audience members is to point to some need they want fulfilled and show them a way to fulfill it. According to psychologist Abraham Maslow's classic **hierarchy of needs** (see Figure 23.1), each of us has a set of basic needs ranging from essential, life-sustaining ones to less critical, self-improvement ones. Our needs at the lower, essential levels (physiological and safety needs) must be fulfilled before the higher levels (social, self-esteem, and self-actualization needs) become important and motivating. Using Maslow's hierarchy to persuade your listeners to wear seat belts, for example, you would appeal to their need for safety.

Critics of this approach suggest that we may be driven as much by *wants* as by needs; but recent studies confirm that persuasive attempts demonstrating benefits to audience members' social needs, including an enhanced sense of belonging, self-esteem, control, and meaningful existence, are more likely to succeed than those that ignore these needs.[12] Following are Maslow's five basic needs, along with suggested actions a speaker can take to appeal to them.

Maslow's Hierarchy of Needs	
Need	Speech Action
Physiological needs (to have access to basic sustenance, including food, water, and air)	• Plan for and accommodate the audience's physiological needs—are listeners likely to be hot, cold, hungry, or thirsty?
Safety needs (to feel protected and secure)	• Appeal to safety benefits—voting for a clean air bill will remove a threat or protect audience members from harm.
Social needs (to find acceptance; to have lasting, meaningful relationships)	• Appeal to social benefits—adopting a healthier diet will lead to being more physically fit and attractive to peers.
Self-esteem needs (to feel good about ourselves; self-worth)	• Appeal to emotional benefits—volunteering as a high school mentor will make listeners feel better about themselves.
Self-actualization needs (to achieve goals; to reach our highest potential)	• Appeal to your listeners' need to fulfill their potential—daily meditation reduces stress and increases self-awareness.

Encourage Mental Engagement

Audience members will mentally process your persuasive message by one of two routes, depending on the degree of their involvement in the message.[13] According to the **elaboration likelihood model of persuasion (ELM)**, when listeners are motivated and able to think critically about a message, they engage in **central processing**. That is, listeners who seriously consider what your message means to them are the ones most likely to act on it. When audience members lack the motivation or ability to judge your argument based on its merits, they engage in **peripheral processing** of information—they pay little attention and respond to the message as being irrelevant, too complex to follow, or just plain unimportant. Listeners may buy into your message, but they do so not on the strength of the arguments but on the basis of such superficial factors as reputation, entertainment value, or the speaker's personal style. These listeners are unlikely to experience any meaningful changes in attitudes or behavior. Central processing produces more long-lasting changes in audience perspective.

Use these strategies to encourage listeners to engage in central processing and thus increase the odds that your persuasive appeal will produce lasting changes:

- Link your argument to their practical concerns and emphasize direct consequences.

  "Hybrid cars may not be the best-looking or fastest cars on the market, but when gas prices rise, they save you money."

- Present your message at an appropriate level of understanding.

  For a *general audience:* "The technology behind hybrid cars is relatively simple."

  For an *expert audience:* "To save even more gas, you can turn an EV into a PHEV with a generator and additional batteries."

- Demonstrate common bonds (i.e., foster identification) and stress your credibility to offer the claims.

  "It took me a while to convince myself to buy a hybrid, but once I did, I found I saved nearly $2,000 this year."

Consider Cultural Orientation

The audience's cultural orientation—its core values, cultural norms, cultural premises, and emotions—will significantly affect their responses to persuasion.

 LaunchPadSolo To learn more about the role of culture in persuasion, see the section on Cultural Orientation in LaunchPad Solo: macmillanhighered.com/pocketspeak5e

CHAPTER 24 ●●●●

Constructing the Persuasive Speech

In persuasive speeches, one or more arguments serve as the framework for the speaker's appeals. An **argument** is a stated position, with evidence and reasoning in support of it. The

FIGURE 24.1 Core Components of Argument

core elements of an argument consist of a claim, evidence, and warrants.[1]

1. The **claim** (*proposition*) states the speaker's conclusion about some state of affairs. The claim answers the question, "What are you trying to prove?"

2. Each claim must be supported with **evidence**, or supporting material providing grounds for belief. The evidence answers the question "What is your proof for the claim?"

3. The **warrant** provides reasons or justifications for why the evidence supports the claim; it allows audience members to evaluate whether in fact the evidence is *valid* for the claim, or *warranted*.

◉ Identify the Nature of Your Claims

In a persuasive speech, you can construct arguments based on three different kinds of claims: of *fact*, of *value*, and of *policy*. Your speech may contain only one type of claim or, often, consist of several arguments addressing different kinds of claims.

- **Claims of fact** focus on whether something is or is not true or whether something will or will not happen. They usually address issues for which two or more competing answers exist, or those for which an answer does not yet exist (called a *speculative claim*). An example of the first is, "Global warming is causing more extreme weather patterns." An example of the second is "A woman president will be elected in the next U.S. presidential election."

- **Claims of value** address issues of judgment. Speakers arguing claims of value try to show that something is right or wrong, good or bad, worthy or unworthy. Examples include "Is assisted suicide ethical?" and "Is any painting worth $100 million?" Evidence in support of a value claim tends to be more subjective than for a fact claim.

- **Claims of policy** recommend that a specific course of action be taken or approved. Legislators regularly construct arguments based on claims of policy: "Should we pass a law restricting the use of handguns/genetically modified foods/firecrackers?" Anyone can argue for a claim of policy as long as he or she advocates for or against a given plan. In claims of policy the word *should* appears; it speaks to an "ought" condition, proposing that certain better outcomes would be realized if the proposed condition were met.

✅ CHECKLIST

Identify the Nature of Your Claim

- ❏ When addressing whether something is or is not true, or whether something will or will not happen, frame your conclusion as a *claim of fact*.
- ❏ When addressing issues that rely upon individual judgment of right and wrong for their resolution, frame your conclusion as a *claim of value*.
- ❏ When proposing a specific outcome or solution to an issue, frame your conclusion as a *claim of policy*.

◉ Use Convincing Evidence

As in claims, you can choose among different types of evidence to support these claims.

Offer Secondary Sources ("External Evidence")

Chapter 8 describes several forms of evidence drawn from sources other than yourself: *examples, narratives, testimony, facts,* and *statistics.* Sometimes called "external evidence" because the knowledge comes from outside the speaker's own experience, secondary or external sources are most powerful when they impart new information that the audience has not previously used in forming an opinion.[2]

Consider Speaker Expertise as Evidence

When appropriate, consider using your own experience and knowledge as evidence. Offered in conjunction with other forms of evidence, speaker expertise can encourage audience identification and add credibility to a claim. Following is an example:

Claim:	Every college student should sign up for health insurance.
Speaker Expertise as Evidence:	Being young and healthy, I didn't believe I needed insurance until I required surgery costing thousands of dollars.

Offer Evidence That Appeals to Audience Needs and Motivations

Whether offering your own expertise or that drawn from secondary sources, try to select material that relates to the audience's needs, attitudes, and values. This is especially important when asking the audience to act on your suggestions. When urging changes in a health behavior such as diet, for example, offer evidence that listeners are likely to find personally useful and motivating.

◉ Select Warrants

As with claims and evidence, you can use different types of warrants or reasons to persuade audience members to accept your evidence as proof of a claim. Warrants can offer reasons for accepting the claim that appeal to emotion, to the source's credibility, and to factual evidence.

- **Motivational warrants** offer reasons targeted at the audience's needs and emotions. In Aristotle's terms, the motivational warrant makes use of *pathos* (see Chapter 23 for a review of *ethos*, *logos*, and *pathos*). Motivational warrants often are implied rather than stated outright:

Claim:	You can easily afford to join Organization X dedicated to ending the hunger of thousands of children.
Evidence:	The price of one soft drink can feed a child for a week.
Motivational Warrant:	You don't want any child to starve or go without proper medical care.

- **Authoritative warrants** appeal to the credibility the audience assigns to the source of the evidence; this appeal is based on *ethos*. The success or failure of authoritative warrants rests on how highly the audience regards the authority figure:

Claim:	We should contribute financially to an agency that feeds hungry children.

Evidence:	Any amount we give, however small, will go far in meeting the agency's objectives.
Authoritative Warrant:	The agency is sponsored by the U.S. senator from Arizona.

- **Substantive warrants** target the audience's faith in the speaker's factual evidence as justification for the argument; this appeal is based on *logos* and appeals to the audience's rational thinking on a matter:

Claim:	Climate change is linked to stronger hurricanes.
Evidence:	We have seen a consistent pattern of stronger hurricanes and warmer oceans.
Substantive Warrant:	Hurricanes and tropical storms get their energy from warm water.

Two common types of substantive warrants are **warrant ("reasoning") by cause** and **warrant ("reasoning") by analogy**; see section on inductive reasoning below.

Warrants reflect the assumptions, beliefs, or principles that underlie the claim. If the audience does not accept them, they won't accept your warrants justifying the link between evidence and claim. If your claim addresses a charged topic such as "Prayer should be permitted in public schools," audience members' beliefs about the separation of church and state may be such that no warrant would change their minds. For less controversial claims, the warrants may be shared by most people and thus not even necessary to state. For example, when urging people to take care of their teeth, the warrant may be as straightforward as "You want to protect your health."[3]

◉ Use Effective Lines of Reasoning

Warrants reflect the speaker's line of **reasoning**, or process of drawing conclusions from evidence. You can strengthen your claims by matching them to effective lines of reasoning.[4] The two basic forms of reasoning are deduction and induction.

Deductive Reasoning: General to Specific

Arguments using **deductive reasoning** begin with a general case ("major premise"), supported by one or more specific examples of the case ("minor premise"), which leads to the conclusion. In a classic form of deduction called the **syllogism**, if you accept the general and specific cases, you must accept the conclusion:

General Case:	Regular aerobic exercise improves heart health.
Specific Case:	Swimming is a form of aerobic exercise.
Conclusion:	Swimming regularly will improve your cardiovascular health.

Conclusions based on syllogistic reasoning can be *valid* or *invalid* and *true* or *false*. Syllogisms are valid — but not necessarily true — if and only if the conclusion necessarily follows the premises. The example above is both valid and true. Following is one that is valid but untrue:

General Case:	All lacrosse players are wealthy, prep-school kids.
Specific Case:	Roger is a lacrosse player.
Conclusion:	Roger is a wealthy, prep-school kid.

Here the conclusion is false because the general case is unfounded — in this instance, there is a **hasty generalization**, or logical fallacy that an isolated case is true for all individuals or conditions concerned (see p. 184). Ethically, a deductive argument's premises must be both valid *and* true.

Inductive Reasoning: Specific to General

Although some claims can be made with certainty, most claims in a persuasive speech address issues that lead to conclusions that can be *strong* or *weak;* that is, listeners may decide the claim is probably true, largely untrue, or somewhere in between. Arguments based on **inductive reasoning** build from specific cases (e.g., pieces of evidence) to a general case or claim supported by them. The speaker offers evidence that points to a conclusion that *appears to be*, but *is not necessarily*, true:

Specific Case:	In St. Lucia, fair-trade growers receive almost double the old rate for their produce.
Specific Case:	Fair-trade growers in Chile saw a similar rise.
Specific Case:	In Kenya, fair-trade growers make a third more than other growers.
Conclusion:	By purchasing goods from fair-trade producers, you can help ensure that they are justly compensated.

Two common forms of inductive reasoning frequently used in persuasive speeches are *reasoning by cause* and *reasoning by analogy.* In **causal reasoning**, the speaker offers a cause-and-effect relationship as proof of the claim, arguing that one event, circumstance, or idea (the cause) is the reason (effect) for another. The substantive warrant above about climate change (see p. 178) offers an instance of causal reasoning. This *warrant by cause* substantiates the relationship of cause (climate change) to effect (stronger hurricanes) on the scientific (i.e., factual) basis of the process of hurricane formation.

In **reasoning by analogy**, the speaker compares two similar cases and implies that what is true in one case is true in the other. The assumption is that the characteristics of Case A and Case B are similar, if not the same, and that what is true for B must also be true for A. As noted earlier, you can use analogical reasoning with a substantive warrant, as in this example:

Claim:	Lifting economic sanctions on Iran in exchange for a temporary halt in its pursuit of nuclear weapons risks creating another North Korea.
Evidence:	Under the Clinton Administration, North Korea used the loosening of sanctions as an opportunity to redouble its program, just as the Iranians are doing now under the Obama Administration.
Warrant *(by Analogy):*	Iran, like Korea, is an anti-American theocratic regime that cannot be trusted to do as it says.

◎ Include a Call to Action

In any speech asking audience members to do something, be sure to include a **call to action** in the conclusion of your speech (see p. 115). Make an explicit appeal to take the specific action — *buy only those products that meet fair-trade conditions, register to vote, join a charity*, and so forth. Lower barriers to action by telling the audience precisely what they need to do to accomplish the act, and remind them of the benefits to themselves of taking the action.

◎ Counterarguments: Addressing the Other Side

All attempts at persuasion are subject to counterargument. A persuasive speaker can choose to offer only one side of the argument(s) or acknowledge opposing views. A **one-sided message** does not mention opposing claims; a **two-sided message** mentions opposing points of view and sometimes refutes them. Research suggests that two-sided messages generally are more persuasive than one-sided messages, as long as the speaker adequately refutes opposing claims.[5]

If listeners are aware of opposing claims and you ignore them, you risk a loss of credibility. This is especially the case when speaking with people who disagree with your position. Yet you need not painstakingly acknowledge and refute all opposing claims. Instead, raise and refute the most important counterclaims and evidence that the audience would know about. Ethically, you can ignore counterclaims that don't significantly weaken your argument.[6] Nor do you necessarily have to address counterclaims when addressing a sympathetic audience. "Persuasive Strategies for Appealing to Different Audience Types" below describes four types of potential audiences, from hostile to critical to sympathetic to uninformed, and suggests various persuasive strategies (including those for addressing counterarguments) for appealing to them.[7]

Persuasive Strategies for Appealing to Different Audience Types*

Audience Type	Persuasive Strategies
Hostile audience or those that strongly disagree	• Stress areas of agreement. • Don't expect major change in attitudes. • Wait until the end before asking the audience to act, if at all. • Reason inductively: start with evidence, leaving conclusion until last ("tuition should be raised").
Counterargument strategies:	• Consider the *refutation* organizational pattern. • Raise counterarguments, focusing on those the audience is most likely to disagree with and try to win support.
Critical and conflicted audience	• Present strong arguments and evidence.
Counterargument strategies:	• Address major counterarguments and refute them; introduce new evidence as above.

Audience Type	Persuasive Strategies
Sympathetic audience	• Use motivational stories and emotional appeals to reinforce positive attitudes. • Stress your commonality with listeners. • Clearly tell the audience what you want them to think or do. • Consider the *narrative* (storytelling) pattern.
Counterargument strategies:	• Unnecessary to raise counterarguments if no time; otherwise, briefly address only most important ones.
Uninformed, less-educated, or apathetic audience	• Focus on capturing their attention. • Stress personal credibility and "likeability." • Stress the topic's relevance to listeners.
Counterargument strategies:	• If you have time, briefly raise only key counterarguments audience may hear in future and offer counterarguments.

*Audience types based on Herbert Simons, *Persuasion in Society*, 2nd ed. (New York: Routledge, 2011).

✓ CHECKLIST
Strategies for Addressing Counterarguments

❑ Gently challenge preconceptions associated with the counterarguments, but do not insult the audience.

❑ Acknowledge counterclaims the audience is most likely to disagree with and demonstrate why those claims are weaker than your argument.

❑ If you can introduce new evidence to demonstrate that the counterclaim is outdated or inaccurate, do so.

❑ Consider where in the speech to introduce the counterclaims: when addressing a hostile audience about a controversial topic, addressing the counterclaim early in the speech and revisiting it just before the conclusion works well; otherwise, you can address counterclaims just before the conclusion.

◎ Avoid Fallacies in Reasoning

A **logical fallacy** is either a false or erroneous statement or an invalid or deceptive line of reasoning.[8] In either case, you need to be aware of fallacies in order to avoid making them in your own speeches and to be able to identify them in the speeches of others. Many fallacies of reasoning exist; the following table lists several that occur frequently in communication.

Common Logical Fallacies	
Logical Fallacy	**Examples**
Begging the question An argument that is stated in such a way that it cannot help but be true, even though no evidence has been presented.	"Intelligent Design is the correct explanation for biological change over time because we can see godly evidence in our complex natural world."
Bandwagoning An argument that uses (unsubstantiated) general opinion as its (false) basis.	"Everybody on campus is voting for her so you should, too."
Either-or fallacy *("false dichotomy")* An argument stated in terms of only two alternatives, even though there may be many additional alternatives.	"Either you're with us or against us."
Ad hominem argument An argument that targets a person instead of the issue at hand in an attempt to incite an audience's dislike for that person.	"I'm a better candidate than X because, unlike X, I work for a living."
Red herring An argument that introduces an irrelevant or unrelated topic into the discussion to divert attention from the issue at hand.	"Immigration reform is unnecessary at this time because the president's approval ratings are low and the Keystone Pipeline will create more jobs."

Logical Fallacy	Examples
Hasty generalization An argument that uses an isolated instance to make an unwarranted general conclusion.	"My neighbor who is the manager of a Walmart is untrustworthy; therefore, Walmart is not a trustworthy company."
Non sequitur ("does not follow") An argument in which the conclusion does not connect to the reasoning.	"If we can send a person to the moon, we should be able to cure cancer in five years."
Slippery slope A faulty assumption that one case will lead to a series of events or actions.	"Helping refugees from Syria today will force us to help refugees across the Middle East and worldwide."

◉ Strengthen Your Case with Organization

Once you've developed your arguments, with claims as main points, focus on structuring your speech using one (or more) of the organizational patterns described in Chapter 12 and those introduced here designed specifically for persuasive speeches. There is no one "right" way to organize a persuasive speech—or any kind of speech—but only choices that will be more or less effective for your particular message, audience, and objective.

Some claims clearly suggest a specific pattern. A speech arguing for limiting the sale of "junk," foods in school cafeterias implies that unrestricted sales of these foods represent a problem and that limiting them represents a solution; many such *claims of policy* fit naturally into the *problem-solution pattern*. However, you could organize the same topic using the *comparative advantage pattern*, in which you offer a series of compelling advantages associated with limiting junk food over not doing so (see this chapter below).

As demonstrated in the table on appealing to different audiences on pp. 181–82, your target audience's attitudes toward the topic is yet another factor to consider. The **refutation pattern**, for example (see p. 187), is particularly effective when persuading audience members hostile to your position. Experimenting with the various patterns can help you to decide; often an effective choice will become apparent fairly quickly.

Problem-Solution Pattern

The **problem-solution pattern** is a commonly used design for persuasive speeches, especially those based on *claims of policy* (see p. 176). Here you organize speech points to demonstrate the nature and significance of a problem and then to provide justification for a proposed solution:

   I. Problem (define what it is)

 II. Solution (offer a way to overcome the problem)

Most problem-solution speeches require more than two points to adequately explain the problem and to substantiate the recommended solution. Thus a **problem-cause-solution pattern** may be in order:

    I. The nature of the problem (define what it is)

  II. Reasons for the problem (explain why it's a problem, for whom, etc.)

III. Proposed solution (explain why it's expected to work)

When arguing a claim of policy, it may be important to demonstrate the proposal's *feasibility*. To do this, use a four-point **problem-cause-solution-feasibility pattern**.

This organization can be seen in the following claim of policy about the nation's Social Security program:

Thesis Stated as Need or Problem:	Serious financial challenges to our nation's Social Security program require that we take steps to ensure it will be able meet its obligations to citizens.
Main Points:	**I.** To keep Social Security funded, we need to raise the full benefits age and early eligibility age. **(Need/problem)**
	II. People are living longer in retirement, thus collecting Social Security over a longer period. **(Reasons for the problem; can offer single or multiple reasons)**
	III. Congress should raise early eligibility age from 62 to 67 and normal retirement age from 67 to 70. **(Solution to the problem)**
	IV. Social Security programs in countries X and Y have done this successfully. **(Evidence of solution's feasibility)**

Monroe's Motivated Sequence

The **motivated sequence pattern**, developed in the mid-1930s by Alan Monroe,[9] is a five-step sequence that begins with arousing listeners' attention and ends with calling for action. This pattern is particularly effective when you want the audience to do something—buy a product, donate to a cause, and so forth.

STEP 1: ATTENTION   The *attention step* addresses listeners' core concerns, making the speech highly relevant to them.

STEP 2: NEED   The *need step* isolates the issue to be addressed. If you can show the members of an audience that they have an important need that must be satisfied or a problem that must be solved, they will have a reason to listen to your propositions.

STEP 3: SATISFACTION   The *satisfaction step* identifies the solution. This step begins the crux of the speech, offering the audience a proposal to reinforce or change their attitudes, beliefs, and values regarding the need at hand.

STEP 4: VISUALIZATION   The *visualization step* provides the audience with a vision of anticipated outcomes associated with the solution. The purpose of this step is to carry audience members beyond accepting the feasibility of your proposal to seeing how it will actually benefit them.

STEP 5: ACTION   Finally, in the *action step* the speaker asks audience members to act according to their acceptance of the message. This may involve reconsidering their present way of thinking about something, continuing to believe as they do but with greater commitment, or implementing a new set of behaviors.

For an example of using Monroe's motivated sequence in a speech, see "Becoming a Socially Conscious Consumer" on p. 188.

Comparative Advantage Pattern

Another way to organize speech points is to show how your viewpoint or proposal is superior to one or more alternative viewpoints or proposals. The **comparative advantage pattern** is most effective when your audience is already aware of the issue or problem and agrees that a need for a solution (or an alternative view) exists. To maintain credibility, identify alternatives that your audience is familiar with and ones supported by opposing interests.

Using the comparative advantage pattern, the main points in a speech addressing the best way to control the deer population might look like these:

Thesis: Rather than hunting, fencing, or contraception alone, the best way to reduce the deer population is by a dual strategy of hunting *and* contraception.

   I. A combination strategy is superior to hunting alone because many areas are too densely populated by humans to permit hunting; in such cases, contraceptive darts and vaccines can address the problem. (*Advantage over alternative #1*)

   II. A combination strategy is superior to relying solely on fencing because fencing is too expensive for widespread use. (*Advantage over alternative #2*)

   III. A dual strategy is superior to relying solely on contraception because only a limited number of deer are candidates for contraceptive darts and vaccines. (*Advantage over alternative #3*)

Refutation Pattern

Similar to debate, the refutation pattern of arrangement addresses each main point and then refutes (disproves) an opposing claim to your position. This pattern can effectively address counterarguments (see p. 180).

Refutation may influence audience members who either disagree with you or are conflicted about where they stand. Note that it is important to refute *strong* rather than *weak* objections to the claim, since weak objections won't sway the audience.[10] Consider this pattern when you are confident that the opposing argument is weak and vulnerable to attack.

Main points arranged in a refutation pattern follow a format similar to this:

Main Point I: State the opposing position.

Main Point II: Describe the implications or ramifications of the opposing claim.

Main Point III: Offer arguments and evidence for your position.

Main Point IV: Contrast your position with the opposing claim to drive home the superiority of your position.

🔀 LaunchPadSolo For more details on the Refutation pattern of arrangement, see the section Refutation Pattern on LaunchPad Solo: macmillanhighered.com/pocketspeak5e

SAMPLE PERSUASIVE SPEECH

In this carefully planned persuasive speech, Jacob Hahn offers strong evidence and reasons for his claims in support of socially responsible consumerism. Jacob organizes the speech using Monroe's five-step motivated sequence. He begins with the attention step, making the speech relevant to listeners, and ends with the action step, demonstrating clearly what audience members can do. Note Jacob's persuasive use of language throughout, especially in the strong imagery that helps listeners visualize the tragedy that occurred in a factory in Bangladesh ("bodies, bricks, and garments left in the rubble") and use of personal pronouns to involve audience members personally.

Becoming a Socially Conscious Consumer

Jacob Hahn

 LaunchPadSolo See Jacob deliver his speech at LaunchPad: macmillanhighered.com/pocketspeak5e

It started with a few cracks in the wall. But then, on April 24, 2013, it became the worst disaster in the history of the garment industry. According to BBC News, on that day the Rana Plaza garment factory in Dhaka, Bangladesh, completely collapsed, leading to the deaths of over 1,100 people.

> Jacob starts the persuasive speech with a dramatic story line ("a few cracks . . .") that serves as an effective attention getter.

Along with the bodies, bricks, and garments left in the rubble, questions remained about who was to blame for the tragedy. Sure, there were the obvious culprits—the plaza owner, the construction company. But there were other suspects too. What about the companies whose goods were manufactured there?

> Continuing with the "story" keeps the audience involved and wanting to know more.

As Emran Hossain and Dave Jamieson pointed out in their May 2, 2013, *Huffington Post* article, garment industry insiders partially blame Western retailers for the tragedy. They claim that it is retailer demand for low-priced labor that creates these poorly constructed and unsafe work factories, which then leads to disasters like the factory collapse.

The thousands of miles that separate us from tragedies like this can make them seem unrelated to our everyday lives. But what if they are not? What if, by purchasing the products these companies make, individuals such as you and me are also somewhat responsible for what happened?

> Step 1, the *attention* step of Monroe's sequence, demonstrates the topic's relevance to audience members.

As we'll see today, there is evidence to support the idea that consumers and companies share a responsibility to ensure safer conditions for factory workers. This is why I encourage all of you to become socially conscious consumers and help convince companies to adopt ethical manufacturing standards. Being a socially conscious consumer means being aware of the issues communities face worldwide and actively trying to correct them.

> Jacob states his thesis.

Why would companies do business with factories that allow dangerous working conditions? It's actually quite simple: Corporations want bigger profit margins. The cheaper the production costs, the more money they make when the product sells. And since consumers show more interest in buying lower-priced products than in thinking about how such items are produced, the pressure is on to provide inexpensive goods. The only way to do this and still make money is to make the goods at the lowest cost possible.

But there is a way to break this cycle of cheap labor and deadly working conditions. You, me, all of us as consumers, must be willing to step up and take an active role in the system.

> Step 2, the *need* step, shows listeners why they should listen to the speaker's propositions.

We can do this in two ways: First, we can pressure companies to improve working conditions for factory laborers, and second, we can pay fairer prices. Some consumer groups are now signaling their willingness to do this, and corporations are responding.

> Step 3, the *satisfaction* step, identifies how to meet the need.

The force behind this new kind of partnership is called "cause-related marketing." According to the *Financial Times, cause-related marketing* is when a company and a charity (or a consumer group) tackle a social or an environmental problem and create business value for the company at the same time.

> Jacob clearly defines a potentially confusing term, offering an explanation from a credible source.

In March 2012, the global marketing firm Nielsen conducted a worldwide study on consumer responses to cause marketing. The poll found that two-thirds of consumers around the world say they prefer to buy products and services from companies that give back to society. Nearly 50 percent of consumers said that they were, and I'm quoting here, "willing to pay more for goods and services from companies that are giving back."

> Jacob provides convincing evidence from a credible source.

The fact that large numbers of consumers are concerned enough about fairness to pay more for products is key to solving the problems that surround the ethical manufacture of clothing. Corporations can appeal to this group of socially conscious consumers, as they are called, by addressing concerns about ethical manufacturing. What do corporations gain by meeting these concerns? It allows them to charge more for their products while also raising their profit margins and improving their brand image. This means that as socially conscious consumers, we can set the standards that corporations must meet if they wish to maximize their profit from our purchasing power.

> Step 4: *visualization.* Jacob offers a vision of outcomes associated with the proposed solution.

You may find yourself asking, Can this actually work? The answer is a simple yes. In both the food and apparel industries, calls for changes in working conditions led to the now widely known nonprofit organization Fair Trade USA. According to its website, Fair Trade USA is an organization that seeks "to inspire the rise of the [socially] Conscious Consumer and eliminate exploitation" worldwide. If products are stamped with the Fair Trade logo, it means the farmers and workers who created those products were fairly treated and justly compensated through an internationally established price.

Fair Trade USA made its mark in the food industry through its relationship to coffee production in third-world nations. Its success helped major companies such as Starbucks and Whole Foods recognize the strength of cause marketing: If you appeal to the high ethical standards of socially conscious consumers, they will pay more for your product.

Appealing to high ethical standards is often directly related to tragedies like the one that occurred in Bangladesh. After the factory collapsed, the major apparel sellers faced intense criticism over their lax labor practices. In response, these companies are now much more interested in establishing their products as Fair Trade to meet socially conscious consumer standards. For example, as Jason Burke, Saad Hammadi, and Simon Neville report in the May 13, 2013, edition of the *Guardian*, major fashion chains like H&M, Zara, C&A, Tesco, and Primark have pledged to help raise the standards for working conditions. According to the article, they will be helping to "finance fire safety and building improvements in the factories they use in Bangladesh."

Note that Jacob provides evidence in support of his claim.

So, what exactly can you do to help bring about ethical labor practices within the clothing industry? The two steps I encourage you to take are these: Become informed, and ask questions about what you're buying—whether it's shoes, a t-shirt, or any other type of apparel.

Step 5 of Monroe's motivated sequence—the *action* step—is a direct request of listeners ("call to action") to act on the speaker's suggestions and concrete directions for doing so.

To be informed, go to websites such as fairtradeusa.org, thirdworldtraveler .com, and tenthousandvillages.com, which list and sell products from clothing manufacturers who have worked to meet the Fair Trade conditions. This list grows monthly, and by supporting these companies through your purchases, you can become a socially conscious consumer.

Additionally, ask questions of other retailers. Whether you shop online or at local retail stores, ask direct questions before purchasing clothes—for example, Where are your products made? Do you have proof of Fair Trade practices? Where can I find this information before I make my purchase? Such questions define the socially conscious consumer, and they ensure that you will not be directly contributing to unsafe and unfair labor practices.

Although several factors contributed to the tragedy in Bangladesh, there is one clear way to help prevent future disasters: become a socially conscious consumer. By being informed and asking questions, you, too, can make a difference in the lives of workers around the world.

Jacob concludes by reinforcing his call to action and leaves the audience with a new perspective to consider.

CHAPTER 25

Speaking on Special Occasions

Special occasions stand out from the ordinary rhythm of life, marking passages, celebrating life's highlights, and commemorating events. Such occasions often include the observance of important ceremonies and rituals as well as speeches.

◉ Functions of Special Occasion Speeches

A **special occasion speech** is one that is prepared for a specific occasion and for a purpose dictated by that occasion. Awards ceremonies call for presentation speeches that acknowledge accomplishments, for example, and acceptance speeches that display gratitude. Special occasion speeches can be either informative or persuasive or, often, a mix of both. However, neither of these functions is the main goal; the underlying function of a special occasion speech is to *entertain, celebrate, commemorate, inspire,* or *set a social agenda:*

- In speeches that *entertain,* listeners expect a lighthearted, amusing speech; they may also expect the speaker to offer a certain degree of insight into the topic at hand. Typical venues for the delivery of speeches that entertain include banquets, awards dinners, and roasts.
- In speeches that *celebrate* (a person, a place, or an event), listeners look to the speaker to praise the subject of the celebration; they also anticipate a degree of ceremony in accordance with the norms of the occasion. Weddings, anniversaries, retirement parties, and awards ceremonies call for speeches that celebrate.
- In speeches that *commemorate* an event or a person (at dedications of memorials or at gatherings held in someone's honor), listeners expect the speaker to offer remembrance and tribute.
- In speeches that *inspire* (including inaugural addresses, keynote speeches, and commencement speeches), listeners expect to be motivated by examples of achievement and heroism.
- In speeches that *set social agendas* (such as occur at gatherings of cause-oriented organizations, fund-raisers, campaign banquets, conferences, and conventions), listeners expect the articulation and reinforcement of the goals and values of the group.

⦿ Types of Special Occasion Speeches

Special occasion speeches include (but are not limited to) introductions, speeches of acceptance, award presentations, roasts and toasts, eulogies and other speeches of tribute, after-dinner speeches, and speeches of inspiration.

Speeches of Introduction

A **speech of introduction** is a short speech with two goals: to prepare or "warm up" the audience for the speaker and to motivate audience members to listen to what the main speaker has to say. A good speech of introduction balances four elements: the speaker's background, the subject of the speaker's message, the occasion, and the audience.

- *Describe the speaker's background and qualifications for speaking.* Relate something about the speaker's achievements, offices held, and other facts to demonstrate why the speaker is relevant to the occasion. The object is to heighten audience interest and build the speaker's credibility.
- *Briefly preview the speaker's topic.* Give the audience a sense of why the subject is of interest, bearing in mind that it is not the introducer's job to evaluate the speech. The rule is: Get in and out quickly with a few well-chosen remarks.
- *Ask the audience to welcome the speaker.* This can be done simply by saying something like "Please welcome Cesar Cruz."
- *Be brief.* Speak just long enough to accomplish the goals of preparation and motivation. One well-known speaker recommends a two-minute maximum.[1]

✔ CHECKLIST
Guidelines for Introducing Other Speakers

❑ Identify the speaker correctly. Assign him or her the proper title, such as "vice president for public relations" or "professor emeritus."

❑ Practice a difficult-to-pronounce name beforehand.

❑ Contact the speaker ahead of time to verify any facts about him or her that you plan to cite.

Speeches of Acceptance

A **speech of acceptance** is made in response to receiving an award. Its purpose is to express gratitude for the honor bestowed on the speaker. The speech should reflect that gratitude.

QUICK TIP

Respond to the Introduction

Whenever you are introduced by another speaker, acknowledge and thank him or her for the introduction. Common methods of responding include "I appreciate those kind words" and "Thank you for making me feel welcome. . . ." Accept praise with humility and perhaps even with humor: "Your description was so gracious that I did not realize you were speaking about me. . . ."

- *Prepare in advance.* If you know or even suspect that you are to receive an award, decide before the event what you will say.
- *Express what the award means to you.* Convey to the audience the value you place on the award. Express yourself genuinely and with humility.
- *Express gratitude.* Thank by name each of the relevant persons or organizations involved in giving you the award. Acknowledge any team players or others who helped you attain the achievement for which you are being honored.

Speeches of Presentation

The goal of the **speech of presentation** is twofold: to communicate the meaning of the award and to explain why the recipient is receiving it.

- *Convey the meaning of the award.* Describe what the award is for and what it represents. Mention the sponsors and describe the link between the sponsors' goals and values and the award.
- *Explain why the recipient is receiving the award.* Describe the recipient's achievements and special attributes that qualify him or her as deserving of the award.

Roasts and Toasts

A **roast** is a humorous tribute to a person, one in which a series of speakers jokingly poke fun at him or her. A **toast** is a brief tribute to a person or an event being celebrated. Both roasts and toasts call for short speeches whose goal is to celebrate an individual and his or her achievements.

- *Prepare.* Impromptu though they might appear, the best roasts and toasts reflect time spent drafting and, importantly, rehearsing. As you practice, time the speech.

- *Highlight remarkable traits of the person being honored.* Restrict your remarks to one or two of the person's most unusual or recognizable attributes. Convey the qualities that have made him or her worthy of celebrating.
- *Be positive and be brief.* Even if the speech is poking fun at someone, as in a roast, keep the tone positive. Remember, your overall purpose is to pay tribute to the honoree. Also, be considerate of the other speakers by refraining from taking up too much time. This is particularly important for toasts, which are expected to be very brief.

At the 2014 annual White House Correspondents' Dinner, President Barack Obama used self-deprecating humor to poke fun at himself: "I admit it—last year was rough. Sheesh. At one point things got so bad, the 47 percent called Mitt Romney to apologize."[2]

Eulogies and Other Tributes

The word **eulogy** derives from the Greek word meaning "to praise." Those delivering eulogies, usually close friends or family members of the deceased, are charged with celebrating and commemorating the life of someone while consoling those who have been left behind.

- *Balance delivery and emotions.* The audience looks to the speaker for guidance in dealing with the loss and for a sense of closure, so stay in control. If you do feel that you are about to break down, pause, take a breath, and focus on your next thought.
- *Refer to the family of the deceased.* Families suffer the greatest loss, and a funeral is primarily for their benefit. Show respect for the family, mentioning each member by name.
- *Be positive but realistic.* Emphasize the deceased's positive qualities while avoiding excessive praise.

QUICK TIP

Commemorate Life—Not Death

A eulogy should pay tribute to the deceased as an individual and remind the audience that he or she is still alive, in a sense, in our memories. Rather than focus on the circumstances of death, focus on the life of the person. Talk about the person's contributions and achievements, and demonstrate the person's character. Consider telling an anecdote that illustrates the type of person you are eulogizing. Even humorous anecdotes may be appropriate if they effectively humanize the deceased.

After-Dinner Speeches

Its name notwithstanding, the contemporary **after-dinner speech** is just as likely to occur before, during, or after a lunch seminar or other type of business, professional, or civic meeting as it is to follow a formal dinner. In general, an after-dinner speech is expected to be lighthearted and entertaining. At the same time, listeners expect to gain insight into the topic at hand and/or to hear an outline of priorities and goals for the group. Thus social agenda-setting is a simultaneous goal of many after-dinner speeches.

- *Recognize the occasion.* Connect the speech with the occasion. Delivering a speech that is unrelated to the event may leave the impression that it is a **canned speech** — one that the speaker uses again and again in different settings.
- *Balance seriousness with light-heartedness.* Even when charged with addressing a serious topic, the after-dinner speaker should make an effort to keep his or her remarks low-key enough to accompany the digestion of a meal.
- *Avoid stand-up comedy.* Many speakers treat the after-dinner speech as an opportunity to string together a series of jokes only loosely centered on a theme. However, the after-dinner speech is still a speech. If you are naturally very funny, use that skill, but in the context of a speech.

Speeches of Inspiration

While many special occasion speeches may well be inspiring, a **speech of inspiration** deliberately seeks to uplift members of the audience and to help them see things in a positive light. Sermons, commencement addresses, "pep talks," and nomination speeches are all inspirational in nature. Effective speeches of inspiration touch on deep feelings in the audience. Through emotional force, they urge us toward purer motives and harder effort and remind us of a common good.

- *Appeal to audience members' emotions (pathos).* Three means of evoking emotion are touching upon *shared values* (p. 35), using *vivid imagery* (p. 118), and telling stories (p. 55). Techniques of language, such as repetition, alliteration, and parallelism can also help transport the audience from the mundane to a loftier level (see Chapter 15).
- *Use real-life stories.* Few things move us as much as the ordinary person who achieves the extraordinary, whose struggles result in triumph over adversity and the realization of a dream.

- *Be dynamic.* If it fits your personality, use a dynamic speaking style to inspire through delivery. Combining an energetic style with a powerful message can be one of the most successful strategies for inspirational speaking.
- *Make your goal clear.* Inspirational speeches run the risk of being vague, leaving the audience unsure what the message was. Whatever you are trying to motivate your listeners to do, let them know.
- *Close with a dramatic ending.* Use a dramatic ending to inspire your audience to feel or act. Recall from Chapter 14 the various methods of concluding a speech, including a quotation, story, or call to action.

SAMPLE SPECIAL OCCASION SPEECH

Following is a eulogy for former South African president Nelson Mandela by President Barack Obama. Delivered to some 70,000 persons in attendance at the First National Bank stadium, including 100 heads of state, and broadcast to millions worldwide, Obama's speech gave praise to one of his—and the world's—greatest heroes of the twentieth century. A eulogist is charged with celebrating and commemorating the life of the deceased, and in this stirring address Obama does this with great skill.

President Obama Speaks at a Memorial Service for Nelson Mandela

December 10, 2013
Johannesburg, South Africa

Thank you. Thank you so much. Thank you. To Graça Machel and the Mandela family; to President Zuma and members of the government; to heads of states and government, past and present; distinguished guests—it is a singular honor to be with you today, to celebrate a life like no other. To the people of South Africa, people of every race and walk of life—the world thanks you for sharing Nelson Mandela with us. His struggle was your struggle. His triumph was your triumph. Your dignity and your hope found expression in his life. And your freedom, your democracy is his cherished legacy.

> Note how often Obama uses a personal pronoun—"you," "us," "we"—to create a sense of inclusion.

It is hard to eulogize any man—to capture in words not just the facts and the dates that make a life, but the essential truth of a person—their private joys and sorrows; the quiet moments and unique qualities that illuminate someone's soul. How much harder to do so for a giant of history, who moved a nation toward justice, and in the process moved billions around the world.

Born during World War I, far from the corridors of power, a boy raised herding cattle and tutored by the elders of his Thembu tribe, Madiba would emerge as the last great liberator of the twentieth century. Like Gandhi, he would lead a resistance movement—a movement that at its start had little prospect for success. Like Dr. King, he would give potent voice to the claims of the oppressed and the moral necessity of racial justice. He would endure a brutal imprisonment that began in the time of Kennedy and Khrushchev, and reached the final days of the Cold War. Emerging from prison, without the force of arms, he would—like Abraham Lincoln—hold his country together when it threatened to break apart. And like America's Founding Fathers, he would erect a constitutional order to preserve freedom for future generations—a commitment to democracy and rule of law ratified not only by his election, but by his willingness to step down from power after only one term.

Given the sweep of his life, the scope of his accomplishments, the adoration that he so rightly earned, it's tempting I think to remember Nelson Mandela as an icon, smiling and serene, detached from the tawdry affairs of lesser men. But Madiba himself strongly resisted such a lifeless portrait. Instead, Madiba insisted on sharing with us his doubts and his fears; his miscalculations along with his victories. "I am not a saint," he said, "unless you think of a saint as a sinner who keeps on trying."

It was precisely because he could admit to imperfection—because he could be so full of good humor, even mischief, despite the heavy burdens he carried—that we loved him so. He was not a bust made of marble; he was a man of flesh and blood—a son and a husband, a father and a friend. And that's why we learned so much from him, and that's why we can learn from him

---

Eulogies celebrate the positive contributions of the deceased—an easy task with Mandela.

Obama begins three successive sentences with the word "like." This rhetorical device (anaphora), lends a rhythmic quality.

Obama uses Mandela's traditional clan name, creating a deep sense of connection with the audience.

Note the many concrete nouns and verbs Obama uses to paint a vivid picture of Mandela.

still. For nothing he achieved was inevitable. In the arc of his life, we see a man who earned his place in history through struggle and shrewdness, and persistence and faith. He tells us what is possible not just in the pages of history books, but in our own lives as well.

Mandela showed us the power of action; of taking risks on behalf of our ideals. Perhaps Madiba was right that he inherited "a proud rebelliousness, a stubborn sense of fairness" from his father. And we know he shared with millions of black and colored South Africans the anger born of "a thousand slights, a thousand indignities, a thousand unremembered moments . . . a desire to fight the system that imprisoned my people," he said.

> With a person as renowned as Mandela, it's fitting to quote him.

But like other early giants of the ANC—the Sisulus and Tambos—Madiba disciplined his anger and channeled his desire to fight into organization, and platforms, and strategies for action, so men and women could stand up for their God-given dignity. Moreover, he accepted the consequences of his actions, knowing that standing up to powerful interests and injustice carries a price. "I have fought against white domination and I have fought against black domination. I've cherished the ideal of a democratic and free society in which all persons live together in harmony and [with] equal opportunities. It is an ideal which I hope to live for and to achieve. But if needs be, it is an ideal for which I am prepared to die."

Mandela taught us the power of action, but he also taught us the power of ideas; the importance of reason and arguments; the need to study not only those who you agree with, but also those who you don't agree with. He understood that

> Note again Obama's use of personal pronouns—in this case the inclusive "us."

ideas cannot be contained by prison walls, or extinguished by a sniper's bullet. He turned his trial into an indictment of apartheid because of his eloquence and his passion, but also because of his training as an advocate. He used decades in prison to sharpen his arguments, but also to spread his thirst for knowledge to others in the movement. And he learned the language and the customs of his oppressor so that one day he might better convey to them how their own freedom depends upon his.

Mandela demonstrated that action and ideas are not enough. No matter how right, they must be

The concrete verb "chiseled" produces a vivid image.

chiseled into law and institutions. He was practical, testing his beliefs against the hard surface of circumstance and history. On core principles he was unyielding, which is why he could rebuff offers of unconditional release, reminding the Apartheid regime that "prisoners cannot enter into contracts."

But as he showed in painstaking negotiations to transfer power and draft new laws, he was not afraid to compromise for the sake of a larger goal. And because he was not only a leader of a movement but a skillful politician, the Constitution that emerged was worthy of this multiracial democracy, true to his vision of laws that protect minority as well as majority rights, and the precious freedoms of every South African.

And finally, Mandela understood the ties that bind the human spirit. There is a word in South Africa— Ubuntu—a word that captures Mandela's greatest gift: his recognition that we are all bound together in ways that are invisible to the eye; that there is a oneness to humanity; that we achieve ourselves by sharing ourselves with others, and caring for those around us.

We can never know how much of this sense was innate in him, or how much was shaped in a dark and solitary cell. But we remember the gestures, large and small—introducing his jailers as honored guests at his inauguration; taking a pitch in a Springbok uniform; turning his family's heartbreak into a call to confront HIV/AIDS—that revealed the depth of his empathy and his understanding. He not only embodied Ubuntu, he taught millions to find that truth within themselves.

It took a man like Madiba to free not just the prisoner, but the jailer as well, to show that you must trust others so that they may trust you; to teach that reconciliation is not a matter of ignoring a cruel past, but a means of confronting it with inclusion and generosity and truth. He changed laws, but he also changed hearts.

For the people of South Africa, for those he inspired around the globe, Madiba's passing is rightly a time of mourning, and a time to celebrate a heroic life. But I believe it should also prompt in each of us a time for self-reflection. With honesty, regardless of our station or our circumstance, we must ask: How well have I applied his lessons in my own life? It's a question I ask myself, as a man and as a president.

We know that, like South Africa, the United States had to overcome centuries of racial subjugation. As was true here, it took sacrifice — the sacrifice of countless people, known and unknown, to see the dawn of a new day. Michelle and I are beneficiaries of that struggle. But in America, and in South Africa, and in countries all around the globe, we cannot allow our progress to cloud the fact that our work is not yet done.

The struggles that follow the victory of formal equality or universal franchise may not be as filled with drama and moral clarity as those that came before, but they are no less important. For around the world today, we still see children suffering from hunger and disease. We still see run-down schools. We still see young people without prospects for the future. Around the world today, men and women are still imprisoned for their political beliefs, and are still persecuted for what they look like, and how they worship, and who they love. That is happening today.

And so we, too, must act on behalf of justice. We, too, must act on behalf of peace. There are too many people who happily embrace Madiba's legacy of racial reconciliation, but passionately resist even modest reforms that would challenge chronic poverty and growing inequality. There are too many leaders who claim solidarity with Madiba's struggle for freedom, but do not tolerate dissent from their own people. And there are too many of us on the sidelines, comfortable in complacency or cynicism when our voices must be heard.

The questions we face today — how to promote equality and justice; how to uphold freedom and human rights; how to end conflict and sectarian war — these things do not have easy answers. But there were no easy answers in front of that child born in World War I. Nelson Mandela reminds us that it always seems impossible until it is done. South Africa shows that is true. South Africa shows we can change, that we can choose a world defined not by our differences, but by our common hopes. We can choose a world defined not by conflict, but by peace and justice and opportunity.

We will never see the likes of Nelson Mandela again. But let me say to the young people of Africa and the young people around the world — you, too, can make his life's work your own. Over thirty years ago, while still a student, I learned of Nelson Mandela and the struggles taking place in this beautiful land, and it stirred something in me. It woke me up to my responsibilities to others and to myself, and it set me on an improbable journey that finds me here today. And while I will always fall short of Madiba's example, he makes me want to be a better man. He speaks to what's best inside us.

After this great liberator is laid to rest, and when we have returned to our cities and villages and rejoined our daily routines, let us search for his strength. Let us search for his largeness of spirit somewhere inside of ourselves. And when the night grows dark, when injustice weighs heavy on our hearts, when our best-laid plans seem beyond our reach, let us think of Madiba and the words that brought him comfort within the four walls of his cell: "It matters not how straight the gate, how charged with punishments the scroll, I am the master of my fate: I am the captain of my soul."

What a magnificent soul it was. We will miss him deeply. May God bless the memory of Nelson Mandela. May God bless the people of South Africa.

As he concludes, Obama issues a final inspirational call to action.

part

Online, Group, and Business Contexts

26. **Preparing Online Presentations** 204

27. **Communicating in Groups** 210

28. **Delivering Group Presentations** 214

29. **Business and Professional Presentations** 218

CHAPTER 26

Preparing Online Presentations

As virtual communication technologies gain in sophistication and travel costs rise, the demand for people skilled in speaking in mediated environments continues to grow. So you'll want to feel confident in your ability to deliver presentations for distribution online.

◉ Apply Your Knowledge of Face-to-Face Speaking

Online presentations require the same basic elements of planning and delivery as in-person presentations. As in traditional public speaking, an online speaker will select among the three general speech purposes of informing, persuading, or marking a special occasion (see p. 49). Both kinds of speaking call for careful audience analysis, credible supporting materials, a clear organizational structure, and a natural style of delivery. And whether presenting electronically or in person, as a speaker you must continually engage the audience; when separated physically, this focus becomes all the more critical.

◉ Plan for the Unique Demands of Online Delivery

While much is similar, important differences exist between online and in-person speaking, in both the means of delivery and nature of the audience. As you plan your presentations, follow the fundamental techniques of public speaking you already know while making the necessary adjustments to transmit your message effectively online.

❷ LaunchPadSolo Go to LaunchPad Solo to watch a video of the online speech *Preventing Cyberbullying* at **macmillanhighered.com/pocketspeak5e**

Review the Equipment

Unlike in-person speeches, online presentations require some familiarity with digital communication tools. Well before your actual delivery, review the equipment you'll be using, and rehearse your presentation several times with it.

Tools used to produce and display online presentations:

- Broadband Internet connection
- Website or server for distribution to audience
- Hardware for recording audio and video (Webcam/video camera/microphone)

- Software for recording and editing audio and video (e.g., Adobe Audition)
- Video capture software (e.g., ScreenFlow, Camtasia)
- Web-based presentation software (e.g., Prezi, SlideRocket)
- Podcasting software (e.g., Propaganda, Audacity)
- Popular commercial websites (e.g., YouTube, Vimeo)
- Online conferencing tools (e.g., Glance, GoToMeeting, Yugma, Skype)

Focus on Vocal Variety

In an online presentation, the audience cannot interact with your physical presence, making your voice an even more critical conduit of communication. In place of body movement, **vocal variety**—alterations in volume, pitch, speaking rate, pauses, and pronunciation and articulation—must hold audience interest. Especially important to eliminate are vocal fillers such as "umm" and "aww." In place of these, use strategic pauses to help audience members process information.

QUICK TIP

Sounding Enthusiastic and Natural Online

Staring into a computer screen rather than listeners' eyes makes it difficult to infuse your voice with the enthusiasm and naturalness that eye contact encourages. But a lively conversational style is key for most online presentations. Consider delivering your first presentations with someone else in the room, talking to that person rather than to the screen. Alternatively, experiment with addressing your remarks to a picture, photograph, or even your own reflection in a mirror.[1]

Provide Superior Visual Aids

The audience might not see you in person, but with presentation aids you can still provide them with a compelling visual experience. Consider how you can illustrate your talking points in eye-catching text form or with photos, animations, and video clips (see Chapters 19–21).

◎ Plan for the Delivery Mode

Online presentations can be streamed in real time, or recorded for distribution later whenever an audience wants to access them. Understanding the advantages and limitations of both delivery modes can help you plan more effectively.

Real-Time Presentations

Real-time presentations connect presenter and audience live, in **synchronous communication**. Interactivity is a chief advantage of this type of presentation: Speaker and audience can respond to one another in real time even though they are not in the same location. As in traditional speaking situations, audience feedback allows you to adapt topic coverage according to audience input and questions, for example, or adjust technical issues as they occur.

A chief limitation of real-time presentations is scheduling them around conflicting time zones. The more geographically dispersed the audience, the greater the logistical challenge. As such, many speakers reserve real-time presentations for occasions when they are in time zones close to the audience.

Recorded Presentations

In a **recorded presentation**, transmission and reception occur at different times, in **asynchronous communication**. Viewers can access the presentation at their convenience, such as listening to a podcast at night.

Lack of direct interaction with the audience poses challenges, however. Without immediate feedback from the audience to enliven the presentation, you must work harder to produce something polished and engaging, especially by providing compelling content, delivery style, and presentation aids.

◉ Choose an Online Presentation Format

Online presentation formats include videos, podcasts, vodcasts, and Webinars, any of which may be streamed in real time or recorded for later delivery.

Video

Many people get their message out by presenting it visually via video: from individuals using a smartphone camera or Webcam, to professional companies sending out messages using high definition digital video cameras. With **video capture software**, such as Camtasia or Adobe Audition, you can seamlessly incorporate video clips into an online presentation.

You can also use video capture software or dedicated screencasting software to create screencasts. A **screencast** captures whatever is displayed on your computer screen, from text to slides to streaming video. Screencasts can be streamed in real time, recorded for playback, or exported to a hosting website. The screencast format is especially useful for training purposes. For example, a presentation relying on screen captures can be used to demonstrate how to create a screencast using QuickTime Player on the Mac.

Podcasts and Vodcasts

A **podcast** is a digital audio recording of a speech or presentation captured and stored in a form that is accessible via the Web. A **vodcast** (also called *vidcast* and *video podcasting*) is a podcast containing video clips.

Recording, storing, and delivering a speech via podcast requires a microphone attached to a computer; simple,

---

✓ CHECKLIST
Creating a Podcast

Most current models of desktop, laptop, and tablet computers include the basic equipment and software needed to create a podcast. The only other pieces you may need are an external microphone and audio recording software such as Audacity (http://audacity.sourceforge.net/). Then try these steps:

❏ Plan what you want to say.

❏ Seat yourself in an upright, direct position facing your computer, with the microphone no more than 8 inches from your mouth.

❏ Make sure that your external microphone is plugged into your computer, or that your built-in microphone is operational.

❏ Open your audio recording software. Be familiar with how to start, pause, and stop a recording.

❏ Activate the recording software and begin speaking into the microphone. You're now making your presentation.

❏ At the conclusion of your presentation, stop the recording.

❏ Save the new recording as an audio file, such as .mp3.

❏ Close your audio recording software and disengage the microphone.

❏ Go to the new audio file saved to your computer, and open and play it. Now you are listening to your recorded presentation.

❏ Transfer the saved file to a website, blog, or podcast hosting site.

FIGURE 26.1 Podcast Offerings from WhiteHouse.gov

cost-free digital audio recording software (e.g., Audacity); and a website to host the podcast and provide your audience with access to it. Using PowerPoint, you can use the "Record Narration" feature in the slide creation function to produce a podcast-like presentation file; the file can be used and distributed as you would any PowerPoint file, even via e-mail.

Webinars

Webinars are real-time seminars, meetings, training sessions, or other presentations that connect presenters and audiences from their computers or mobile devices.[2] Webinars typically include video capture and screencasting, as well as interactive functions such as chat and polling.

As in any speech or presentation, planning a Webinar starts with considering the audience's needs and wants. Many Webinars are *team presentations*, so use the guidelines on p. 216 during the planning stages.[3]

1. Start with a title that indicates what the Webinar will do for the audience (e.g., "How the Affordable Care Act Will Affect You").

2. Time each aspect of the Webinar and distribute the following information to each presenter:

    Introduction of speaker(s) and purpose

    Length and order of each speaker's remarks

    Length of question-and-answer session, if separate

3. Rehearse the Webinar (remotely if necessary).

4. Check meeting room for noise and visual distractions; check equipment.

5. Create a backup plan in case of technical problems.

✓ CHECKLIST
Online Presentation Planning

Keeping in mind both the fundamental guidelines for preparing and presenting an in-person speech as well as those unique considerations of online presentations, here are some additional tips to follow.[4]

❑ *Be well organized.* Offer a clear statement of purpose and preview of main points. Proceed with a solid structure that the audience can easily follow. Conclude by restating your purpose, reviewing the main points, and encouraging the audience to watch or listen for more.

❑ *Design powerful presentation aids.* For video and Webcasts, plan for meaningful graphics and images that properly convey your ideas.

❑ *Keep your audience engaged.* In real-time presentations, encourage audience interaction by incorporating chat, instant messaging, or polling features. In recorded presentations, offer an e-mail address, Weblog comment, URL, or Twitter address where audience members can submit comments and questions. Use these tools to acquire feedback from your audience, much the way you would use eye contact in a face-to-face speech or presentation.

❑ *Prepare a contingency plan in case of technology glitches.* For example, have a backup computer running simultaneously with the one used to deliver the presentation. Provide a list of FAQs or a Web page with instructions for audience members to manage technology problems.

❑ *Maintain ethical standards.* Use the same degree of decorum as you would in an in-person speech, bearing in mind that online presentations have the potential to go viral.

❑ *Get in plenty of practice time.* Rehearse, record, and listen to yourself as many times as needed.

> **QUICK TIP**
>
> **Put a Face to the Speaker(s)**
>
> To encourage a feeling of connection between yourself and the audience during a Webinar, consider displaying a photographic headshot, captioned by your name and title. A second slide might announce start and finish times; a third, a list of speech objectives.[5] During the presentation, you can alternate displays of text and graphic slides with views of your photograph (and/or other presenters) or, in some cases, side-by-side with the aids.

CHAPTER 27 ●●●●

Communicating in Groups

Most of us will spend a substantial portion of our educational and professional lives participating in **small groups** or teams (usually between three and twenty people); and many of the experiences we have as speakers—in the classroom, workforce, and in *virtual groups* online—occur in a group setting. Thus, understanding how to work cooperatively within a group setting, as described in this chapter, is a critical life skill.

◎ Focus on Goals

How well or poorly you meet the objectives of the group—whether to coordinate a team presentation or to accomplish some other purpose—is largely a function of how closely you keep sight of the group's goals and avoid behaviors that detract from these goals. Setting an *agenda* can help participants stay on track by identifying items to be accomplished during a meeting; often it will specify time limits for each item.

◎ Plan on Assuming Dual Roles

In a work group, you will generally assume a task role and a social role, and sometimes both.[1] **Task roles** are the hands-on roles that directly relate to the group's accomplishment of its objectives. Examples include *recording secretary* (takes notes) and *moderator* (facilitates discussion).

Members also adopt various **social roles** reflecting individual members' personality traits. Social roles function to help facilitate effective group interaction, such as *the harmonizer* (smoothes over tension by settling differences) and *gatekeeper* (keeps the discussion moving and gets everyone's input).

Sometimes, group members focus on individual needs irrelevant to the task at hand. **Anti-group roles** such as *floor hogger* (not allowing others to speak), *blocker* (being overly negative about group ideas; raising issues that have been settled), and *recognition seeker* (calling attention to oneself rather than to group tasks) do not further the group's goals and should be avoided.

◉ Center Disagreements around Issues

Whenever people come together to consider an important issue, conflict is inevitable. But conflict doesn't have to be destructive. In fact, the best decisions are usually those that emerge from productive conflict.[2] In *productive conflict*, group members clarify questions, challenge ideas, present counter-examples, consider worst-case scenarios, and reformulate proposals. Productive conflict centers disagreements around issues rather than personalities. Rather than wasting time arguing with one another over personal motives or perceived shortcomings, productive conflict encourages members to rigorously test and debate ideas and potential solutions.

◉ Resist Groupthink

For groups to be truly effective, its members need to form a cohesive unit with a common goal. At the same time, they must avoid **groupthink**, the tendency to minimize conflict by refusing to examine ideas critically or test solutions.[3] Groups prone to groupthink typically exhibit these behaviors:

- Participants reach a consensus and avoid conflict in order not to hurt others' feelings, but without genuinely agreeing.
- Members who do not agree with the majority feel pressured to conform.
- Disagreement, tough questions, and counterproposals are discouraged.
- More effort is spent justifying the decision than testing it.

◉ Adopt an Effective Leadership Style

When called upon to lead a group, bear in mind the four broad styles of leadership, and mix and match the *leadership styles that best suit your group's needs*.[4]

- *Directive:* Leader controls group communication by conveying specific instructions to members
- *Supportive:* Leader attends to group members' emotional needs, stressing positive relationships
- *Achievement-oriented:* Leader sets challenging goals and high standards

- *Participative:* Leader views members as equals, welcoming their opinions, summarizing points, and identifying problems that must be solved rather than dictating solutions

Whatever style or styles of leadership you adopt, remember that the most effective leaders (1) remain focused on their group's goals; (2) hold themselves and the group accountable for achieving results; (3) treat all group members in an ethical manner; and (4) inspire members to contribute their best.[5]

Set Goals

As a leader, aim to be a catalyst in setting and reaching goals in collaboration with other group members. It is the leader's responsibility to ensure that each group member can clearly identify the group's purpose(s) and goal(s).

QUICK TIP

Optimize Decision Making in Groups

Research suggests that groups can reach the best decisions by adopting two methods of argument: *devil's advocacy* (arguing for the sake of raising issues or concerns about the idea under discussion) and *dialectical inquiry* (devil's advocacy that goes a step further by proposing a countersolution to the idea).[6] Both approaches help expose underlying assumptions that may be preventing participants from making the best decision. As you lead a group, consider how you can encourage both methods of argument.

Encourage Active Participation

Groups tend to adopt solutions that receive the largest number of favorable comments, whether these comments emanate from one individual or many. If only one or two members participate, it is their input that sets the agenda, whether or not their solution is optimal.[7]

When you lead a group, take these steps to encourage group participation:

- *Directly ask members to contribute.* Sometimes one person, or a few people, dominate the discussion. Encourage others to contribute by redirecting the discussion in their direction ("Patrice, we haven't heard from you yet" or "Juan, what do you think about this?").
- *Set a positive tone.* Some people are reluctant to express their views because they fear ridicule or attack. Minimize such fears by setting a positive tone, stressing fairness, and encouraging politeness and active listening.
- *Make use of devil's advocacy and dialectical inquiry (see Quick Tip above).* Raise pertinent issues or concerns, and entertain solutions other than the one under consideration.

Use Reflective Thinking

To reach a decision or solution that all participants understand and are committed to, guide participants through the six-step process of reflective thinking shown in Figure 27.1, which is based on the work of educator John Dewey.[8]

Step 1   Identify the Problem
- What is being decided upon?

Group leader summarizes problem, ensures that all group members understand problem, and gains agreement from all members.

↓

Step 2   Conduct Research and Analysis
- What information is needed to solve the problem?
Conduct research to gather relevant information.
Ensure that all members have relevant information.

↓

Step 3   Establish Guidelines and Criteria
- Establish criteria by which proposed solutions will be judged.
Reach criteria through consensus and record criteria.

↓

Step 4   Generate Solutions
- Conduct brainstorming session.
Don't debate ideas; simply gather and record all ideas.

↓

Step 5   Select the Best Solution
- Weigh the relative merits of each idea against criteria. Select one alternative that can best fulfill criteria.
If more than one solution survives, select solution that best meets criteria.
Consider merging two solutions if both meet criteria.
If no solution survives, return to problem identification step.

↓

Step 6   Evaluate Solution
- Does the solution have any weaknesses or disadvantages?
- Does the solution resemble the criteria that were developed?
- What other criteria would have been helpful in arriving at a better solution?

FIGURE 27.1 Making Decisions in Groups: John Dewey's Six-Step Process of Reflective Thinking

CHAPTER 28

Delivering Group Presentations

Group presentations are oral presentations prepared and delivered by a group of three or more individuals. Regularly assigned in the classroom and frequently delivered in the workplace, successful group presentations require close cooperation and planning.

◉ Working in Groups

Preparing and delivering a successful group presentation depends on effective communication among members. Use the guidelines in Chapter 27 on collaborating in groups to set goals, assign roles and tasks, and manage conflict.

Analyze the Audience and Set Goals

Even if the topic is assigned and the audience consists solely of the instructor and classmates (perhaps in an online setting), consider the audience's interests and needs with respect to the topic and how you can meet them. If it is a business report or proposal, is it for an *internal* or *external* *audience*—employees or clients/customers/regulators/others of the company? Just as you would prepare an individual speech, brainstorm and set down in writing the central idea (*thesis*) and goals for the presentation.

Establish Information Needs

Gain agreement among members on the scope and type of research needed. What types of sources best suit the topic, purpose, and audience, for example, surveys, scholarly articles, government data, or online news outlets? (See Chapter 9 for more on primary and secondary sources.)

Assign Roles and Tasks

First, designate a *team leader* to help guide coordination among members, beginning with the selection of roles and tasks. Next, assign members to various aspects of the research, perhaps selecting different members to present the introduction, body of the presentation, and conclusion, or other responsibilities. Set firm time limits for each portion of the presentation.

Establish Transitions between Speakers

Work out transitions between speakers ahead of time—for example, whether a designated group member will introduce every speaker or whether each speaker will introduce the next speaker upon the close of his or her presentation. The quality of the presentation will depend in great part on smooth transitions between speakers.

Consider the Presenters' Strengths

Audiences become distracted by marked differences in style, such as hearing a captivating speaker followed by an extremely dull one. If you are concerned about an uneven delivery, consider choosing the person with the strongest presentation style and credibility level for the opening. Put the more cautious presenters in the middle of the presentation. Select another strong speaker to conclude the presentation.[1]

Coordinate the Presentation Aids

To ensure design consistency, consider assigning one person the job of coordinating templates for slides, video, and/or audio (see Chapter 20). The team can also assign a single individual the task of presenting the aids as the other team members speak. If this is done, be sure to position the person presenting the aids unobtrusively so as not to distract the audience from the speaker.

QUICK TIP

Be Mindful of Your Nonverbal Behavior

During a team presentation, the audience's eyes will fall on everyone involved, not just the person speaking. Thus any signs of disinterest or boredom by a team member will be easily noticed. Give your full attention to the other speakers on the team, and project an attitude of interest toward audience members.

Rehearse the Presentation Several Times

Together with the whole group, members should practice their portions of the presentation, *with* any presentation aids they will use, in the order they will be given in the final form. Rehearse with all group members several times, until the presentation proceeds smoothly. Assign at least one member to set up and check any equipment needed to display the aids.

◉ Presenting in Panels, Symposia, and Forums

Panels, symposia, and forums are group discussions in which multiple speakers share their expertise with an audience; forums are convened specifically to discuss issues of public interest. Members of panels, symposia, and forums often may not meet beforehand to coordinate their remarks.

✓ CHECKLIST

Group Presentation Tips

- ❏ Establish in writing the specific purpose and goals of the presentation.
- ❏ Decide on the scope and types of research needed.
- ❏ Specify each team member's responsibilities regarding content and presentation aids.
- ❏ Determine how introductions will be made—all at once at the beginning or by having each speaker introduce the next one.
- ❏ Practice introductions and transitions to create a seamless presentation.
- ❏ Establish an agreed-upon set of hand signals to indicate when a speaker is speaking too loud or soft, too slow or fast.
- ❏ Assign someone to manage the question-and-answer session.
- ❏ Rehearse the presentation with all group members and *with* presentation aids several times from start to finish.

Panel Discussions

In a **panel discussion**, a group of people (at least three, and generally not more than nine) discusses a topic in the presence of an audience. Panel discussions do not feature formally prepared speeches. Instead, they require the presence of a skilled chairperson or **moderator** to direct the discussion, who begins by describing the purpose of the panel and introducing panel members. The moderator then launches the discussion by directing a question to one or more of the participants. At the conclusion of the panel, the moderator summarizes the discussion and directs questions from the audience.

Prior to the presentation, a good moderator will circulate an agenda and list of ground rules to the participants. When preparing remarks for a panel discussion, or when preparing to serve as a moderator, consider the following:

- Who is your audience, and what do they know about the topic? What ideas can be emphasized to encourage greater understanding?
- What aspects of the topic will the other participants address? What are their areas of expertise?
- How much time is allotted for the question-and-answer session? You will need to plan accordingly.
- Which key points should be reviewed in conclusion?

Symposia and Colloquia

A **symposium** is a meeting or conference at which several speakers deliver prepared remarks on different aspects of the same topic. Symposia provide audiences with in-depth and varied perspectives on a topic. Sometimes the symposium concludes with a question-and-answer period; at other times, it is followed by a panel discussion among symposium participants. Following symposia, the presentations may be published.

When preparing a presentation for a symposium, consider the following:

- Who is your audience?
- What aspects of the topic will the other participants address?
- In what order will the speakers address the audience?
- What are your time constraints for your prepared remarks?
- Will you engage in questions and answers with the other speakers, or just with the audience?

Public Forums

A **forum** is an assembly for the discussion of issues of public interest. Public forums often are convened to help policy-makers and voters alike deliberate about key policy issues. These forums can take place in a physical space, such as a town hall, on television, or online.

Forums may feature a panel or a symposium, followed by an extensive question-and-answer period with the audience. One well-known forum is the **town hall meeting**, in which citizens deliberate on issues of importance to the community. City and state governments sponsor town hall meetings to gather citizen input about issues that affect them, using this input to formulate policy.

When participating in public forums as a member of the audience, consider the following:

- Organize your thoughts as much as possible in advance by jotting down your question or comment on a piece of paper. Use the guidelines for impromptu speaking described in Chapter 16.
- Do not duplicate someone else's questions or comments unless it adds to the discussion.
- Use no more time than necessary to make your points.
- If appropriate, include a *call to action* at the conclusion of your comments (see p. 180).

CHAPTER 29 ● ● ●●

Business and Professional Presentations

In many business and professional positions, delivering presentations is part of the job. Whether pitching a service to customers or informing managers of a project's progress, the skilled speaker will get noticed and, often, promoted.

Rather than being formal public speeches, business and professional presentations are forms of **presentational speaking**—oral presentations delivered by individuals or teams addressing people in the classroom, workplace, or other group settings (see Chapters 30–36). Presentational speaking has much in common with formal public speaking, yet important differences exist:[1]

- *Degree of formality.* Presentational speaking is *less formal* than public speaking; on a continuum, it would lie midway between public speaking at one end and conversational speaking at the other.
- *Audience factors.* Public-speaking audiences tend to be self-selected or voluntary participants, and they regard the speech as a onetime event. Attendees of oral presentations are more likely to be part of a "captive" audience, as in the workplace or classroom, and may be required to attend frequent presentations. Due to the ongoing relationship among the participants, attendees also share more information with one another than those who attend a public speech and thus can be considered to have a common knowledge base.
- *Speaker expertise.* Listeners generally assume that a public speaker has more expertise or firsthand knowledge than they do on a topic. Presentational speakers, by contrast, are more properly thought of as "first among equals."

Apart from these differences, the public speaking guidelines described throughout this *Pocket Guide* apply equally to oral presentations and public speeches.

◎ Become Familiar with Reports and Proposals

The majority of business and professional presentations (both oral and written) take the form of *reports* or *proposals*. Corporations and nonprofit, educational, and government organizations alike depend on reports and proposals, both formal and informal, to supply information and shape decisions.

A **report** is a systematic and objective description of facts and observations related to business or professional interests;

it may or may not contain recommendations. Reports without recommendations are strictly informative; those that offer analysis and recommendations combine both informative and persuasive intent.

Reports address literally thousands of different topics, audiences, and objectives; some require extensive research and offer lengthy analyses while others may simply summarize weekly changes in personnel or projects. Formats for reports vary accordingly, but many reports include the following:

1. Preview/summary of reasons for the report; including its scope, methods, and limitations; and main conclusions and recommendations
2. Discussion of the findings/presentation of evidence
3. Key conclusions drawn from evidence
4. Recommendations based on the evidence

Proposals offer ("propose") a product, procedure, or policy to a client or company and typically seek to persuade the audience to accept the speaker's recommendations. Organizations must constantly make decisions such as whether to switch to a new health plan or implement a new employee grievance procedure, and proposals offer a plan on how to proceed. Generally, proposals advocate for a specific solution, with the presenter arguing in favor of one course of action over another. Careful adaptation to the audience is therefore critical to an effective presentation (see Chapter 6).

AUDIENCE The audience for a proposal can be a single individual or large group; the individual or individuals have primary or sole decision-making responsibility. Proposals may be assigned by a superior, solicited by a potential client (by a written *request for proposal* or *"RFP"*), or offered unsolicited to either superiors or clients. Frequently, proposals incorporate or respond to information communicated in reports.

ORGANIZATION Proposals can be quite lengthy and formally organized or relatively brief and loosely structured. As in reports, individual organizations have their own templates for organizing proposals; but many proposals follow these general steps:

1. Introduce the issue.
2. State the problem.
3. Describe the method by which the problem was investigated.
4. Describe the facts learned.
5. Offer explanations and an interpretation of the findings.

Sample Types of Reports and Proposals in Business and the Professions	
Reports	Proposals
• Progress report • Audit report • Market research report • Quality testing report • Staff report • Committee report	• Sales proposal • Business plan proposal • Request for funding • Research proposal • Quality improvement proposal • Policy proposal

6. Offer recommendations, including time lines and budgets.
7. Leave them with a **call to action**, reiterating your recommendation persuasively.

Three reports and proposals typically delivered in the workplace are the *sales proposal*, *staff report*, and *progress report*. The *case study*, described at the end of this chapter, is an oral presentation assignment unique to the classroom environment. See Chapters 30–36 for a review of the *request for funding presentation* (p. 237), *policy proposal* (p. 238), and *quality improvement proposal* (p. 245).

The Sales Proposal

A **sales proposal** or **sales pitch** is a presentation that attempts to lead a potential buyer to purchase a service or a product. Successful sales pitches, which are persuasive by nature, clearly show how the product or service meets the needs of the potential buyer and demonstrate how it surpasses other options available.

AUDIENCE   The target audience for a sales presentation depends on who has the authority to make the purchase under consideration. Some sales presentations are invited by the potential buyer; others are "cold sales" in which the presenter/seller approaches a first-time potential buyer with a product or a service. In some cases the audience might be an intermediary—a firm's office manager, for example, who then makes a recommendation to the company's director.

ORGANIZATION   Plan on organizing a sales presentation as you would a persuasive speech, selecting among the motivated sequence, problem-solution/problem-cause-solution, or comparative advantages patterns (see Chapter 24). The *comparative advantage pattern* works well when the buyer must choose between competing products and seeks reassurance

QUICK TIP

Adapt the Motivated Sequence to the Selling Situation

When making a sales pitch following the motivated sequence, the extent to which you focus on each step depends on the nature of the selling situation. In cold-call sales situations, consider spending more time discovering the potential buyer's needs. For invited sales presentations, spend more time detailing the characteristics of the product and showing how it will satisfy the buyer's needs.

that the product being presented is indeed superior. The *problem-solution* or *problem-cause-solution pattern* is especially effective when selling to a buyer who needs a product to solve a problem.

Sometimes called the *basic sales technique*, the **motivated sequence**, with its focus on audience needs, offers an excellent means of appealing to buyer psychology. To use it to organize a sales presentation, do the following:

1. Draw the potential buyer's attention to the product.
2. Isolate and clarify the buyer's need for the product.
3. Describe how the product will satisfy the buyer's need.
4. Invite the buyer to purchase the product.

✓ CHECKLIST

Using Monroe's Motivated Sequence in a Sales Presentation

❑ Identify the potential buyer's needs and wants and appeal to them.

❑ Using the product's features, match its benefits to the customer's needs and wants.

❑ Stress what the product can do for the customer.

❑ Engage the customer's senses, using sight, sound, smell, and touch.

❑ Do not leave the sales encounter without making the ask.[2]

❑ Get the buyer to do something (look something up, promise to call someone, or schedule a meeting). Buyers who invest their time are more likely to invest in what you are selling.[3]

The Staff Report

A **staff report** informs managers and other employees of new developments that affect them and their work, or reports on the completion of a project or task.

AUDIENCE   The audience for a staff report is usually a group, but it can be an individual. The recipients of a staff report then use the information to implement new policy, to coordinate other plans, or to make other reports to other groups.

ORGANIZATION   Formal staff reports are typically organized as follows:

1. State the problem or question under consideration (sometimes called a "charge" to a committee or a subcommittee).
2. Provide a description of procedures and facts used to address the issue.
3. Discuss and analyze the facts that are most pertinent to the issue.
4. Provide a concluding statement.
5. Offer recommendations.

The Progress Report

A progress report is similar to a staff report, with the exception that the audience can include people *outside* the organization as well as within it. A **progress report** updates clients or principals on developments in an ongoing project. On long-term projects, progress reports may be given at designated intervals or at the time of specific task completions. On short-term projects, reports can occur daily. Progress reports have become increasingly important to managers as a means to determine the value of employees and uncover hidden costs of doing business.[4]

AUDIENCE   The audience for a progress report might be supervisors, clients, or customers; developers and investors; company officers; media representatives; or same-level co-workers. Progress reports are commonplace in staff and committee meetings in which subcommittees report on their designated tasks.

ORGANIZATION   Different audiences may want different kinds of reports, so establish expectations with your intended audience, then modify the following accordingly:

1. Briefly review progress made up to the time of the previous report.
2. Describe new developments since the previous report.
3. Describe the personnel involved and their activities.
4. Detail the time spent on tasks.
5. Explain supplies used and costs incurred.

QUICK TIP

Speak Ethically at Work

As in public speeches, the ethical standards of trustworthiness, respect, responsibility, and fairness (see Chapter 4) must infuse any workplace presentation. Such presentations should also comply with legal standards and adhere to internal rules and regulations.

6. Explain any problems and recommendations for their resolution.
7. Provide an estimate of tasks to be completed for the next reporting period.

◉ Use the Case Study to Demonstrate Critical Thinking

An exciting and effective learning tool, a **case study** documents a real (or realistic) situation, relating to business, law, medicine, science, or other discipline, which poses difficult dilemmas or problems requiring solutions. Students read a detailed account and then apply what they have studied to analyze and resolve the problems. Instructors typically ask students to report orally on the case study, either alone or in teams. Students are expected to consider the case carefully and then report on the following items:

1. Description/overview of the major issues involved in the case
2. Statement of the major problems and issues involved
3. Identification of any relevant alternatives to the case
4. Presentation of the best solutions to the case, with a brief explanation of the logic behind them
5. Recommendations for implementing the solutions, along with acknowledgment of any impediments

QUICK TIP

Build Career Skills

Approach your business presentation assignments as a way to build critically important career skills. Many prospective employers will ask about such classroom experience, and you will deliver similar presentations throughout your business career. Entry-level business and professional employees with superior oral presentation skills tend to get promoted sooner than their co-workers.

part

9

Speaking in Other College Courses

30. **Presentations Assigned across the Curriculum** 226

31. **Science and Mathematics Courses** 231

32. **Technical Courses** 235

33. **Social Science Courses** 238

34. **Arts and Humanities Courses** 240

35. **Education Courses** 243

36. **Nursing and Allied Health Courses** 245

Presentations Assigned across the Curriculum

No matter which major you select, oral presentations will be part of your academic career. Rather than being formal public speeches, classroom presentations are forms of *presentational speaking*; see p. 218 for a review of the differences between public and presentational speaking.

Chapters 31–36 describe various course-specific presentations, from the *scientific talk* to the *literature review*. This chapter contains guidelines for presentations frequently assigned across the curriculum, including the *journal article review*, *debate*, *poster presentation*, and *service learning presentation*. You often will be called upon to deliver presentations in groups, so be sure to review the guidelines on collaborating in and preparing group presentations described in Chapters 27–28.

◎ Journal Article Review

A frequent speaking assignment in many courses is the **journal article review**. A biology instructor might ask you to provide an overview of a peer-reviewed study on cell regulation, for example, or a psychology teacher might require that you talk about a study on fetal alcohol syndrome. Typically, when delivering a presentation on a journal article, your instructor will expect you to do the following:

- Identify the author's thesis or hypothesis.
- Explain the methods by which the author arrived at his or her conclusions.
- Explain the results of the study.
- Identify the author's methods and, if applicable, theoretical perspective.
- Evaluate the study's quality, originality, and validity, if applicable.
- Describe the author's sources, and evaluate their credibility.
- Show how the findings advance knowledge in the field.

◎ The Debate

Debates are a popular presentation format in many college courses, calling upon skills in persuasion (especially the reasoned use of evidence; see Chapter 24), in delivery, and in the ability to think quickly and critically. In an *academic debate*, two students or groups of students consider or argue an issue from opposing viewpoints (the *proposition side* and the *opposition side*). Generally there will be a winner and a loser, lending this form of speaking a competitive edge.

Take a Side

Opposing sides in a debate are taken by speakers in one of two formats. In the *individual debate format*, one person takes a side against another person. In the *team policy debate format*, multiple people take sides against another team, with each person on the team assuming a speaking role.

The *affirmative* side in the debate supports the topic with a *resolution*—a declarative statement asking for change or consideration of a controversial issue. "Resolved, that the United States government should provide amnesty to undocumented immigrants" is a resolution that the affirmative side must support and defend. The affirmative side tries to convince the judge/audience to accept the proposition; the *negative* side opposes the affirmative side's arguments.

Debates are characterized by refutation, in which each side attacks the arguments of the other. Refutation can be made against an opponent's claim, evidence, or reasoning, or some combination of these elements. Refutation also involves rebuilding arguments that have been refuted or attacked by the opponent. This is done by adding new evidence or attacking the opponent's reasoning or evidence.

Advance Strong Arguments

Whether you take the affirmative or negative side, your primary responsibility is to advance strong arguments in

---

QUICK TIP

Flowing the Debate

In formal debates (in which judges take notes and keep track of arguments), debaters must attack and defend each argument, but even in the less formal classroom debates, "dropping" or ignoring an argument can seriously compromise your credibility. To ensure that you respond to each of your opponent's arguments, try using a technique called "flowing the debate." Using a sheet of paper or spreadsheet, write down each of your opponent's claims, and then check it when you (or another team member) have refuted it. As much as possible, record the names and dates of your opponent's sources so that you can challenge unreliable sources and/or outdated information.

support of your position. Strong evidence and warrants (reasons) are key to arguing for or against the debate proposition or claim (see Chapter 24). Judges will also look for strong backing, qualifiers, and rebuttals. *Backing* is evidence that shows why the particular type of warrant supports the claim; the *qualifier* states the degree of probability or certainty of the claim, using words such as "most," "sometimes," or "always;" the *rebuttal* addresses counterarguments that may pertain (see Chapter 24).

◉ The Poster Presentation

Another common speaking assignment across the curriculum is the **poster presentation**, which displays information about a study, an issue, or a concept on a large (usually roughly 4 × 3 or 4 × 6 foot) poster. Poster presentations typically follow the structure of a scientific journal article, including an *abstract, introduction, description of methods, results section, conclusion,* and *references*. Presenters display their key findings on posters, arranged so session participants can examine them freely; on hand are copies of the written report, with full details of the study. The presenter is prepared to answer questions as they arise.

A good poster presenter considers his or her audience, understanding that with so much competing information, the poster must be concise, visually appealing, and focused on the most important points of the study.

When preparing the poster:

- Select a concise and informative title; make it 84-point type or larger.
- Arrange blocks of text in columns beginning from the upper left to lower right side of the poster.
- Include an *abstract* (a brief summary of the study) describing the essence of the report and how it relates to other research in the field. Offer compelling and "must know" points to hook viewers and summarize information for those who will only read the abstract.
- Ensure a logical and easy-to-follow flow from one part of the poster to another.
- Edit text to a minimum, using clear graphics wherever possible.
- Select a muted color for the poster itself, such as gray, beige, light blue, or white and use a contrasting, clear font color (usually black).
- Make sure your font size is large enough to be read comfortably from at least three feet away.
- Label and include a concise summary of each figure in a legend below each one.

- Be prepared to provide brief descriptions of your poster and to answer questions; keep your explanations short.[1]

Address your audience while presenting and explain your research without reading verbatim from the poster; if needed, prepare a speaking outline (see Chapter 13). Rehearse your poster presentation as you would any other speech.

◎ The Service Learning Presentation

Many courses offer the opportunity to engage in service learning projects, in which students learn about and help address a need or problem in a community agency or nonprofit organization, such as may exist in a mental-health facility, an economic development agency, or antipoverty organization. Typically, the **service learning presentation** describes the student's participation in the project and includes the following information:

1. Description of the service task.
   a. What organization, group, or agency did your project serve?
   b. What is the issue, and how did you address it?
2. Description of what the service task taught you about those you served.
   a. How were they affected by the problem or issue?
   b. How did your solution help them? What differences did you observe?
3. Explanation of how the service task and outcome related to your service learning course.
   a. What course concepts, principles, or theory relate to your service project, and how?
   b. What observations give you evidence that the principles apply to your project?
4. Application of what was learned to future understanding and practice.
   a. How was your understanding of the course subject improved or expanded?
   b. How was your interest in or motivation for working in this capacity affected by the project?
   c. What do you most want to tell others about the experience and how it could affect them?

◎ Presenting to Different Audiences

In the workplace, presentations may be delivered to fellow workers, colleagues, managers, clients, or others. Knowing this, instructors may ask that you tailor your oral presentations

to a mock (practice) on-the-job audience, with your classmates serving as stand-ins. The types of audiences you will
likely address on the job include the **expert or insider audience**, **colleagues within the field**, the **lay audience**, and the
mixed audience. The checklist below offers guidelines on
addressing the mixed audience.

Types of Audiences in the Working World	
Type of Audience	Characteristics
Expert or insider audience	People who have intimate knowledge of the topic, issue, product, or idea being discussed (e.g., an investment analyst presents a financial plan to a group of portfolio managers).
Colleagues within the field	People who share the speaker's knowledge of the general field under question (e.g., psychology or computer science), but who may not be familiar with the specific topic under discussion (e.g., short-term memory or voice recognition systems, respectively).
Lay audience	People who have no specialized knowledge of the field related to the speaker's topic or of the topic itself (e.g., a city engineer describes failure of water treatment system to the finance department).
Mixed audience	An audience composed of a combination of people—some with expert knowledge of the field and topic and others with no specialized knowledge. This is perhaps the most difficult audience to satisfy (e.g., an attending surgeon describes experimental cancer treatment to a hospital board comprised of medical professionals, financial supporters, and administrative personnel).

✅ CHECKLIST

Tips on Presenting to a Mixed Audience

- ❏ Research the audience and gear your talk to the appropriate level of knowledge and interests.

- ❏ Avoid technical or specialized terms and explain any that you must use.

- ❏ Carefully construct the introduction and clearly identify the central idea and main points of the talk. If possible, present as a compelling "story" listeners can learn about if they stay the course.

- ❏ Alert the audience to the order of your coverage: "I will first focus on the big picture and on marketing/sales issues. I will then present design specifications and data analysis." In this way, each audience segment will know what to expect and when.

- ❏ Devote half to two-thirds of your time to an introduction or overview of your subject and save the highly technical material for the remaining time.[2]

- ❏ Include everyone. Try to address different levels of knowledge and different perspectives in turn.

- ❏ Be clear about the level at which you are speaking: "I am going to present the primary results of this project with minimal detailed information, but I'm happy to review the statistics or experimental results in more detail following the presentation."

- ❏ Be alert to audience reactions. If you notice that your listeners are experiencing discomfort, consider stopping and asking for feedback about what they want. You might then change course and opt for a more in-depth, high-level approach, depending on what they say.

CHAPTER 31 ●●●●

Science and Mathematics Courses

The purpose of most science and math presentations is to inform the audience of the results of original or replicated research or problem solving. Instructors and classmates want to know the processes by which you arrived at your experimental results. For example, your biology instructor may assign an oral report on the extent to which you were able to replicate an experiment on cell mitosis. A math instructor may ask you to apply a concept to an experiment or an issue facing the field. A key challenge of these presentations is communicating complex information to audiences with varying levels of knowledge.

◉ Preparing Effective Presentations in Science and Mathematics

Science and mathematics instructors, and employers and colleagues on the job, will expect your presentations to be grounded in the scientific method. Credible presentations must clearly and compellingly illustrate the nature of the research question—describe the methods used in gathering and analyzing data, and explain the results. Well-executed presentation aids, from slides to equations drawn on a whiteboard, are critical to scientific and mathematical presentations, and instructors generally require them (see Chapters 19–21).

Scientific and mathematical presentations need not be dry and merely factual. Experimentation is a process of discovery, and the fits and starts that often accompany its completion can make for compelling stories during your talk.

Typically, instructors will expect you to do the following in a scientific or mathematics presentation:

- Use observation, proofs, and experiments as support for your points.
- Be selective in your focus on details, highlighting critical information but not overwhelming listeners with information they can refer to in the written paper.
- Use analogies to build on prior knowledge and demonstrate underlying causes (see Chapter 22 for guidelines on explaining difficult concepts).
- Use aids to illustrate important concepts.

◎ Research Presentation

In the **research presentation** (also called the **scientific talk** or *oral scientific presentation*), you describe research you conducted, either alone or as part of a team. You may deliver this information as a stand-alone oral presentation or as a poster session (see pp. 228–29).

A research presentation usually follows the standard model used in scientific investigation and includes the following elements:

1. *An introduction* describing the research question and the scope and objective of the study.

2. *A description of methods* used to investigate the research question, including where it took place and the conditions under which it was carried out.

3. *The results of the study* summarizing key results and highlighting insights regarding the questions/hypotheses investigated; this is the "body" of the presentation.

4. *A conclusion* (or "discussion"), in which the speaker interprets the data or results and discusses their significance. As in any speech, the conclusion should link back to the introduction, reiterating the research question and highlighting the key findings.

✓ CHECKLIST
Focusing Your Scientific Talk

- ❑ State the research question accurately and in a way that will motivate listeners to pay attention.
- ❑ Clearly state the hypothesis to the research question.
- ❑ Describe the study's research design and rationales.
- ❑ Describe the methods used to obtain the results and why you used them.
- ❑ Explain and evaluate the results of the study (i.e., the data).
- ❑ Address the significance of the study.

◎ Methods/Procedure Presentation

The **methods/procedure presentation** describes how an experimental or a mathematical process works and under what conditions it can be used. This is generally a ten- to fifteen-minute individual presentation. In a theoretical math class, for example, your assignment might be to describe an approach to solving a problem, such as the Baum-Welch algorithm, including examples of how this approach has been used, either inappropriately or appropriately. This type of presentation generally does the following:

1. Identifies the conditions under which the process should be used
2. Offers a detailed description of the process (at times including a demonstration)
3. Discusses the benefits and shortcomings of the process

QUICK TIP

Clue the Audience in Quickly

As in any kind of speech, if you lose the audience in the introduction of your scientific presentation, chances are slim that you'll regain their attention. Listeners want to know what the point of the talk is about (e.g., what key question did you investigate), so make certain that you communicate it in the first few minutes of your scientific talk. Follow this by telling the audience why you believe the research is important and why solving the problem is relevant.

Field Study Presentation

A **field study presentation** describes research conducted in natural settings, using methods such as direct observation, surveys, and interviews. For example, a biology major might research links between soil erosion and hiking activity in a public park, or an environmental studies major might describe animal behavior in an oil spill. Field study presentations may be assigned as individual, team, or poster-session presentations. Whatever the topic under investigation and methods of data collection, field study presentations address the following:

1. Overview and scope of the field research (e.g., if explaining animal behavior in an oil spill, describe the prevalence of oil spills and the effects on environment and wildlife)
2. Description of the site (e.g., describe the habitat before and after the spill, noting ecological interactions)
3. Methods used in the research (e.g., participant observation, type of sample collection, measurement techniques) (e.g., how were the behaviors observed? Who provided the observations? When and for how long?)[1]

4. Interpretation/analysis of the data

5. Future directions for the research

✓ CHECKLIST

Steps in Preparing a Focused Scientific Presentation

❏ Create an informative title that describes the research.

❏ Place your presentation in the context of a major scientific principle.

❏ Focus on a single issue and adjust it to the interests and knowledge level of your audience.

❏ Identify the underlying question you will address, divide it into subquestions, and answer each question.

❏ Follow a logical line of thought.

❏ Explain scientific concepts unambiguously, with a minimum of jargon.

❏ Use analogies to increase understanding.

❏ End with a clearly formulated conclusion related to your chosen scientific principle.[2]

CHAPTER 32 ●●●●

Technical Courses

Oral presentations in technical courses often focus on the design of a product or system, whether it is a set of plans for a building, a prototype robot, or an innovative computer circuit design. Technical presentations include *reports* and *proposals* that provide instructions, advocate a product or service, update progress, make recommendations, or request funding. (See Chapter 29 on reports and proposals and the

---

QUICK TIP

What Are the Technical Disciplines?

Technical disciplines include, but are not limited to, the STEM fields (science, technology, engineering, and math) as well as the design-oriented disciplines of graphic design, architecture, and industrial design.

progress report; see this chapter for requests for funding.) Assignments in engineering, architecture, and other technical courses also typically include the *design review,* described below.

◉ Preparing Effective Technical Presentations

The technical presenter faces the challenge of scaling complex information and processes to audience members with differing levels of technical expertise. Carefully conceived presentation aids—including diagrams, prototypes, drawings, computer simulations, design specifications, and spreadsheets—are key to the technical presentation, yet the aids must not overwhelm it. Presentations are often delivered in teams, so close coordination among members is essential (see Chapter 28).

Typically, people who attend technical presentations possess a range of technical knowledge, and effective technical speakers gear the presentation to the appropriate level for the audience (see Chapter 30), using accessible language, avoiding jargon (see Chapter 15), and offering analogies to clarify hard-to-understand concepts and processes (see Chapter 22).

Both informative and persuasive strategies come into play in technical presentations, and the best technical presenters know how to appeal to their audiences' needs and motivations to gain agreement for a proposal or design [1] (see p. 168).

Effective technical presentations sell ideas. The technical presenter must persuade clients, managers, or classmates that a design, an idea, or a product is a good one. As one instructor notes, "You can never assume that your product or design will just sell—*you* have to do that."[2]

Effective technical presentations are also detailed and specific and use numbers as evidence. Instead of offering general, sweeping statements, they provide hard data and clearly stated experimental results.

◉ Engineering Design Review

The **engineering design review** explains problem-solving steps in devising a product or system in response to an identified need. Virtually all capstone engineering courses require that students prepare design reviews, which are generally informative in nature, although their purpose may include convincing the audience that the design decisions are sound. (In varying formats, design reviews are also assigned in basic science and mathematics courses.) Design reviews may incorporate a **prototype** (model) demonstration and are usually

> **QUICK TIP**
>
> **Avoid These Technical Presentation Pitfalls**
> Professionals working in technical fields point to three
> major obstacles to designing and delivering a successful
> technical presentation: (1) too much information crammed
> into aids and failure to construct and practice with them
> early in the process, (2) insufficient preparation and prac-
> tice with fellow team members, and (3) failure to select an
> appropriate organization and structure for the presentation.[3]
> Bearing these pitfalls in mind during preparation will set
> you on a winning path.

delivered as team presentations. Design reviews typically
include the following:

1. Identification of problem to be solved/need to be met
   and overview of objectives
2. Description of design concept and specifications
3. Discussion of why the proposed design will solve the
   problem
4. Discussion of any experimental testing that has been
   completed on the design
5. Discussion of future plans and unresolved problems
6. Discussion of schedule, budget, and marketing issues

Architecture Design Review

The **architecture design review** combines two functions: It
enables the audience to visualize the design, and it sells it.
Using a narrative structure, in which you tell the "story" of
the design, combined in places with a *spatial organizational
pattern*, in which you arrange main points in order of physical proximity of the design (see Chapter 12), can help you do
this. At a minimum, architecture design reviews typically
cover:

1. Background on the site
2. Discussion of the design concept
3. Description and interpretation of the design

Request for Funding

In the **request for funding presentation**, a team member or
the entire team provides evidence that a project, a proposal,
or a design idea is worth funding. Requests for funding,
which are persuasive in nature, cover the following ground:

1. Overview of customer specifications and needs
2. Analysis of the market and its needs
3. Overview of the design idea or project and how it meets those needs
4. Projected costs for the project
5. Specific reasons why the project should be funded

CHAPTER 33 ●●●●

Social Science Courses

Students in such social sciences as psychology, sociology, political science, economics, anthropology, and communication learn to evaluate and conduct both *qualitative research*, in which the emphasis is on observing, describing, and interpreting behavior, as well as *quantitative research*, in which the emphasis is on statistical measurement. Often the focus of inquiry is explaining or predicting human behavior or social forces, answering questions such as what, how, and why?[1]

Oral presentation assignments in social science courses frequently include the *review-of-the-literature presentation*, *theoretical research presentation*, *program evaluation presentation*, and *policy proposal*. Other commonly assigned presentations are described elsewhere in this guide: see the *poster presentation* (p. 228), *scientific research ("scientific talk") presentation* (p. 233), *methods/procedure presentation* (p. 233), *field study presentation* (p. 234), *evidence-based practice presentation* (p. 246), and *case study presentation* (p. 246).

◉ Preparing Effective Presentations in the Social Sciences

Good social scientific presentations clearly explain the research question, refer to current research, support arguments with evidence, use theory to build explanations, and use timely data.

- *Illustrate the research question.* Pay special attention to illustrating the nature of the research question and the methods used to investigate it.
- *Refer to current research.* Credible social scientific presentations refer to recent findings in the field. Instructors are more likely to accept experimental evidence if it is replicable over time and is supported by current research.
- *Use theory to build explanations.* Theory is central to social scientific research, informing the types of questions asked, the research methods used, and means by which

evidence is interpreted. Thus your discussion of the research should reflect the theoretical framework within which the research was conducted.[2]

- *Support arguments with evidence.* Each of your assertions or claims must be accompanied by evidence for or against it and which can be used by others to evaluate the claims.

◎ Review of the Literature Presentation

Frequently, instructors ask students to summarize and evaluate the existing research related to a given topic. A communications student, for example, might review the literature on gender bias in the hiring of journalists. After considering the key studies related to the topic, the student would describe the conclusions uncovered by the research and suggest directions for future work. A **review-of-the-literature presentation** typically includes the following:

1. Statement of the topic under review
2. Description of the available research, including specific points of agreement and disagreement among sources
3. Evaluation of the strengths and weaknesses of the research, including the methodology used and whether findings can be generalized to other studies
4. Conclusions that can be drawn from the research
5. Suggested directions for future study

When including a literature review in conjunction *with your own research study*, follow these broad guidelines:

1. Introduce your topic.
2. Review the literature pertinent to your topic.
3. State your research question or hypothesis and describe how it relates to the literature.
4. Discuss your research methods.
5. Discuss your results, including shortcomings and implications for future research.

QUICK TIP

Narrow Your Topic

Since most of your social scientific presentations will be relatively brief, make sure to sufficiently narrow your topic or research question and scale your findings to fit the time allotted (see Chapter 7). For example, rather than selecting an overly broad topic such as "substance abuse," consider "frequency of alcohol-related deaths among U.S. college students in year X."

◉ Program Evaluation Presentation

In addition to explaining social phenomena, social scientists often measure the effectiveness of programs developed to address these issues. Instructors may ask you to evaluate a program or policy, perhaps one you observed in a service learning assignment. Typically, the **program evaluation presentation** includes the following:

1. Explanation of the program's mission
2. Description of the program's accomplishments
3. Discussion of how the accomplishments were measured (e.g., the evaluation methods and questions), including any problems in collecting and/or assessing the evaluation research
4. Conclusions regarding how well or poorly the program has met its stated objectives

◉ Policy Proposal Presentation

As well as evaluating programs and policies, you may be asked to recommend a course of action on an issue or a problem. A **policy proposal presentation** typically includes the following:

1. Definition and background review of the current policy and its shortcomings
2. Discussion of alternatives to policy, including the pros and cons of each
3. Recommendation of a specific policy with clear argument for why this option is better than each of the alternatives
4. Application of forecasting methods to show likely results of the recommended policy
5. Plan for implementation of the recommendations
6. Discussion of future needs or parameters to monitor and evaluate the policy option.

CHAPTER 34 ● ●●

Arts and Humanities Courses

Speaking assignments in arts and humanities courses often require that you analyze and interpret the meaning of a particular idea, event, person, story, or artifact. Instructors expect that these interpretations will be grounded in the conventions of the field and build on the research within it. An instructor of literature may ask you to explain the theme of a novel or a poem, for example, or an art history professor may ask you to identify the various artistic and historical influences on a sculpture or a painting. Some presentations may be performative in nature, with students expressing artistic content. Assignments include summaries of works, presentations of interpretation and analysis, presentations that compare and contrast an idea, an event, or a work, and individual and team debates (see pp. 226–28).

QUICK TIP

Disciplines in the Arts and Humanities

What fields are included in the arts and humanities? Typically included are English, literature, history, religion, philosophy, foreign languages, art history, theater, and music.

◎ Preparing Effective Arts and Humanities Presentations

Good presentations in the arts and humanities help audiences understand and put into context the meaning of original works or scholarship. Working from within the conventions of the discipline, the presenter identifies the work's key themes and the means by which the author or creator communicates them. Instructors will expect you to investigate the following:

- What is the thesis or central message in the text or work?
- What questions/issues/themes does the author address?
- How does the author or creator organize or structure the work?
- Who is the audience for the work?
- What influences or sources inform the work?

◎ Presentations of Interpretation and Analysis

Often in the arts and humanities, instructors assign presentations requiring students to interpret the relevance of a historical or a contemporary person or event; a genre or school of philosophical thought; or a piece of literature, music, or art. Instructors look to students to think of topics in new ways by providing original interpretations. A presentation on the historical significance of Reconstruction after the Civil War of 1861–1865, for example, will be more effective if you offer a new way of viewing the topic rather than reiterating what other people have said or what is already generally accepted knowledge. A debate on two philosophical ideas will be most effective when you assert issues and arguments that are different from those that the audience has thought of before. The more original the interpretation (while remaining logical and supported by evidence), the more compelling the presentation will be for the audience.

◎ Presentations That Compare and Contrast

A common assignment in the arts and humanities is to *compare and contrast* events, stories, people, or artifacts in order to highlight similarities or differences. For example, you might compare two works of literature from different time periods or two historical figures or works of art. These presentations may be informative or persuasive; if the latter, the student will argue in favor of one figure or period over another. Presentations that compare and contrast include the following elements:

1. *Thesis statement* outlining the connection between the events, stories, people, or artifacts
2. *Discussion of main points*, including several examples that highlight similarities and differences
3. *Concluding evaluative statement* about the comparison (e.g., if the presentation is persuasive, why one piece of literature was more effective than another; if informative, a restatement of similarities and differences)

◎ Debates

Often, students will engage in debates on opposing ideas, historical figures, or philosophical positions. In a history class, students might argue whether women in sixteenth-

---

QUICK TIP

Be Prepared to Lead a Discussion

Many students taking arts and humanities courses will research a question and then lead a classroom discussion on it. For example, a student of literature may lead a discussion on Anton Chekhov's play *The Cherry Orchard*. The speaker would be expected to provide a synopsis of the plot, theme, and characters and offer an analysis of the play's meaning. For directions on leading a discussion, see p. 245.

century Western Europe experienced a Renaissance. The speaker must present a brief assertion (two to three minutes) about the topic; the opposing speaker then responds with a position. Whatever side of an issue you address, prepare a well-composed argument with strong supporting evidence (see pp. 226–28).

CHAPTER 35 ●●●●

Education Courses

In education courses (including subfields such as *curriculum* and *instruction*, *physical education*, *secondary* and *elementary education*, and *education administration*), the most common speaking assignments focus on teaching and related instructional tasks, such as giving a lecture or demonstrating an activity. In a mathematics education course, you may give a mini-lecture on a particular geometric theorem. In a learning-styles course, you may tailor an activity to a variety of different learners.

◎ Preparing Effective Education Presentations

Good presentations in education are marked by clear organization, integration of the material into the broader course content, two-way communication, and student-friendly supporting material. Above all, effective educational presentations succeed in fostering understanding:

- *Use a learning framework.* Select one or more cognitive learning frameworks, such as the Bloom or Marazano taxonomy, and frame the information accordingly.
- *Organize material logically.* Presentations in education must be tightly organized so that the audience can easily access information. The simpler the organizational structure, the better (see Chapters 12 and 24). Use organizing devices such as preview statements, internal summaries, and transitions to help listeners follow ideas in a lecture, for example.
- *Integrate discussion to overall course content.* Describe how the lecture for the day relates to the previous day's lecture, and articulate learning objectives for the presentation. In a discussion or group activity, make clear connections between students' comments and other topics that have been raised or will be raised later in the course.

- *Tailor examples and evidence to the audience.* Use familiar examples and evidence that the audience can grasp easily. Don't support an idea with a statistical proof, for example, unless students are trained in statistics. Using familiar examples will enhance learning (see section on analogies in Chapter 24); try to choose examples that are close to the students' experiences.

◉ Delivering a Lecture

A **lecture** is an informational speech for an audience of student learners. Standard lectures range from thirty minutes to one hour in length; a *mini-lecture* generally lasts about ten to fifteen minutes. Typically, lectures include the following:

1. A clear introduction of the topic (see Chapter 14)
2. Statement of the central idea of the lecture
3. Statement of the connection to previous topics covered
4. Discussion of the main points
5. Summary of the lecture and preview of the next assigned topic
6. Question-and-answer period

QUICK TIP

Focus on Interactive Learning

Good lecturers actively engage students in the learning process, pausing to pose questions about the topic, allowing time for discussion, and incorporating short activities into the mix.[1] Rather than delivering a monologue, they encourage student participation.

◉ Facilitating a Group Activity

In the **group activity presentation**, you describe an activity to be completed following a lecture. Typically this short presentation includes the following:

1. A brief review of the main idea of the lecture
2. An explanation of the goal of the activity
3. Directions on carrying out the activity
4. A preview of what students will gain from the activity and what the discussion following it will cover

◎ Facilitating a Classroom Discussion

In a **classroom discussion**, you will lead a discussion following a lecture, offering brief remarks and then guiding the discussion as it proceeds.

1. Begin by outlining critical points to be covered.
2. Prepare several general guiding questions to launch the discussion.
3. Prepare relevant questions and examples for use during the discussion.

CHAPTER 36 ● ●●●

Nursing and Allied Health Courses

Speaking assignments in nursing and allied health courses—physical therapy, occupational therapy, radiology, pharmacy, and other areas of health care—range from the *service learning presentation, poster presentation*, and *review of academic articles* (see Chapter 30 for detailed guidelines) to the *evidence-based practice presentation, clinical case study, quality improvement proposal, case conference*, and *shift report* (see this chapter).[1] Students are assigned a mix of individual and group presentations (see Chapter 28).

◎ Preparing Effective Presentations in Nursing and Allied Health Courses

Good presentations in health-related courses accurately communicate scientific knowledge while reviewing the patient's clinical status and potential treatment options. The presenter will support any assertions and recommendations with relevant scientific literature supporting evidence-based clinical practice. Instructors will expect you to do the following:

1. Use evidence-based guidelines.
2. Demonstrate a solid grasp of the relevant scientific data.
3. Organize the presentation in order of severity of patient problems.
4. Present the patient as well as the illness. That is, remember that the patient is not merely a collection of symptoms, but a human being, so present him or her as such.
5. Include only essential facts, but be prepared to answer any questions about all aspects of the patient and care.

◉ Evidence-Based Practice Presentation

The **evidence-based practice (EBP) presentation** reviews scientific literature on a clinical problem, critically evaluates the findings, and suggests best practices for standards of care. To fulfill these criteria, EBP presentations do the following:

1. Define the research problem (e.g., the clinical issue).
2. Critically review the scientific literature on a practice related to the clinical issue, describing method/design, sample size, and reliability.
3. Discuss the strength of the evidence and indicate whether or not the practice should be adopted into clinical practice.[2]

◉ Clinical Case Study Presentation

A **clinical case study** is a detailed analysis of a person or group with a particular disease or condition. Clinical case studies inform medical teams or other audiences about the following:

1. Overview of patient information (presentation and background)
2. Description of pre-treatment workup, including results
3. Review of treatment options/plan of care
4. Outcome of treatment plan
5. Surveillance plan (follow-up patient care based on evidence-based practice)

◉ Quality Improvement Proposal

In the **quality improvement proposal**, the speaker recommends the adoption of a new (or modified) health practice or policy, such as introducing an improved treatment regimen at a burn center. This report (sometimes assigned as part of a capstone course) addresses the following:

1. Review of existing practice
2. Description of proposed quality improvement
3. Review of the scientific literature on the proposed practice
4. Plan of action for implementation

◉ Treatment Plan Reports

The ability to communicate information about patients or clients is important for all health care providers. Either individually or as part of a health care team, people in the helping professions routinely report patients' conditions and outline plans of treatment to other health care providers. One form of treatment plan report, called the **case conference**, includes the following:

1. Description of patient status
2. Explanation of the disease process
3. Steps in the treatment regimen
4. Goals for patient and family
5. Plans for patient's care at home
6. Review of financial needs
7. Assessment of resources available

The **shift report** is a concise overview of the patient's status and needs, delivered to the oncoming caregiver. It includes the following information:

1. Patient name, location, and reason for care
2. Current physical status
3. Day on clinical pathway for particular diagnosis
4. Pertinent psychosocial data, including plans for discharge and involvement of caregivers
5. Care needs (physical, hygiene, activity, medication, nutritional)

Appendices

A.   Citation Guidelines   250

B.   Question-and-Answer Sessions   263

C.   Preparing for Mediated
     Communication   264

D.   Tips for Non-Native Speakers
     of English   266

APPENDIX A ●●●●

Citation Guidelines

Instructors will often require that you include a bibliography of sources with your speech (see Chapters 4 and 9). You can document sources by following documentation systems such as *Chicago,* APA, MLA, CSE, and IEEE.

◉ *Chicago* Documentation

Two widely used systems of documentation are outlined in *The Chicago Manual of Style*, Sixteenth Edition (2010). The first, typically used by public speakers in a variety of disciplines, provides for bibliographic citations in endnotes or footnotes. This method is illustrated below. The second form employs an author-date system: Sources are cited in the text with full bibliographic information given in a concluding list of references. For information about the author-date system — and more general information about *Chicago*-style documentation — consult the *Chicago Manual,* Chapters 14 and 15.

1. BOOK BY A SINGLE AUTHOR Give the author's full name followed by a comma. Then italicize the book's title. In parentheses, give the city of publication followed by a colon, the publisher's name followed by a comma, and publication date. Place a comma after the closing parenthesis; then give page numbers from which your paraphrase or quotation is taken.

> 1. Eric Alterman, *What Liberal Media? The Truth about Bias and the News* (New York: Basic Books, 2003), 180–85.

2. BOOK BY MULTIPLE AUTHORS

> 2. Bill Kovach and Tom Rosenstiel, *The Elements of Journalism: What Newspeople Should Know and the Public Should Expect*, rev. ed. (New York: Three Rivers Press, 2007), 57–58.

3. EDITED WORK AND WORK WITHIN AN EDITED COLLECTION

> 3. Joseph B. Atkins, ed., *The Mission: Journalism, Ethics, and the World* (Ames: Iowa State University Press, 2002), 150–57.

> 3. Jonathan Dube, "Writing News Online," in *Shop Talk and War Stories: American Journalists Examine Their Profession*, ed. Jan Winburn (Boston: Bedford/ St. Martin's, 2003), 202.

4. ENCYCLOPEDIA OR DICTIONARY After the title of the work, add "s.v." (Latin *sub verbo,* "under the word") and the term you looked up. If the citation is from an online reference work, add the URL (Internet address) and the publication date or date of last revision; if neither is available, use your access date.

    4. *Encyclopedia Britannica Online,* s.v. "Yellow Journalism," accessed October 17, 2007, http://www.britannica.com/eb/article-9077903/yellow-journalism.

5. ARTICLE IN A MAGAZINE

    5. John Leo, "With Bias toward All," *U.S. News & World Report,* March 18, 2002, 8.

6. ARTICLE IN A JOURNAL

Give the author's full name, the title of the article in quotation marks, the title of the journal in italics, the volume and issue numbers, the year of publication in parentheses followed by a colon, and the pages used. If the journal article was found online, list the URL or use the DOI (digital object identifier) instead of the URL if one is available. It is not necessary to include page numbers for articles accessed online.

    6. Tom Goldstein, "Wanted: More Outspoken Views; Coverage of the Press Is Up, but Criticism Is Down," *Columbia Journalism Review* 40, no. 4 (2001): 144–45.

    6. Bree Nordenson, "Vanity Fire," *Columbia Journalism Review* 45, no. 5 (2007), http://www.cjr.org/profile/vanity_fire.php.

7. ARTICLE IN A NEWSPAPER

    7. Felicity Barringer, "Sports Reporting: Rules on Rumors," *New York Times,* February 18, 2002, sec. C.

8. WEBSITE

Give the name of the author (if not available, use the name of the site sponsor); the title of the page, in quotation marks, followed by a comma; the title of the website (if the site is an online publication, place the title in italics); the sponsor of the site, if different from the name of the site or name of the author; the date of publication or modification (if no date is provided, or if your instructor requests it, include the date accessed, preceded by the word "accessed"); and the URL.

    8. FAIR (Fairness & Accuracy in Reporting), "Challenging Hate Radio: A Guide for Activists," accessed February 9, 2012, http://www.fair.org/index.php?page=112.

9. E-MAIL MESSAGE

    9. Grace Talusan, e-mail message to author, March 20, 2011.

10. ELECTRONIC MAILING LIST

10. Ola Seifert to Society of Professional Journalists mailing list, August 23, 2002, http://f05n16.cac.psu .edu.

11. BLOG POST

11. Brian Stetler, "Study: Some Viewers Were Misinformed by TV News," *Media Decoder* (blog), *New York Times,* December 17, 2010, http://mediadecoder .blogs.nytimes.com.

12. ARTICLE IN AN ELECTRONIC DATABASE Provide the DOI (if available), or the name of the database and the document number.

12. Mark J. Miller, "Tough Calls: Deciding When a Suicide Is Newsworthy and What Details to Include Are among Journalism's More Sensitive Decisions," *American Journalism Review* 24, no. 10 (2002): 43, Expanded Academic ASAP (A95153129).

13. GOVERNMENT DOCUMENT

13. U.S. Congress, *Electronic Freedom of Information Amendments of 1996* (Washington, D.C.: GPO, 1996), 22.

14. PERSONAL COMMUNICATION

14. Soo Jin Oh, letter to author, August 13, 2005.

15. INTERVIEW

15. Walter Cronkite, interview by Daniel Schorr, *Frontline,* PBS, April 2, 1996.

16. VIDEO RECORDING

16. *All the President's Men,* directed by Alan J. Pakula (1976; Burbank, CA: Warner Home Video, 1998), VHS.

17. SOUND RECORDING

17. Noam Chomsky, *The Emerging Framework of World Power,* read by the author (AK Press, 2003), compact disc.

17. Antonio Vivaldi, *The Four Seasons,* Boston Symphony Orchestra, conducted by Seiji Ozawa, Telarc 80070, compact disc.

◉ APA Documentation

Most disciplines in the social sciences—psychology, anthropology, sociology, political science, education, and economics—use the author-date system of documentation established by the American Psychological Association (APA). This citation style highlights dates of publication because the currency of published material is of primary importance in these fields.

In the author-date system, use an author or organization's name in a signal phrase or parenthetical reference within the main text to cite a source.

For example, you could cite Example 1 in this section with the author's name in a signal phrase as follows:

> Nakazawa (2009) states that stress hormones like cortisol can dramatically alter how immune cells work.

or with a parenthetical reference as follows:

> Stress hormones such as cortisol travel to the immune system and can dramatically alter how immune cells work (Nakazawa, 2009).

Each in-text citation refers to an alphabetical references list that you must create.

For more information about APA format, see the *Publication Manual of the American Psychological Association,* Sixth Edition (2010). The manual advises users to omit retrieval dates for content that is unlikely to change, such as published journal articles, and to omit the database from which material is retrieved as long as an identifier such as a URL (Internet address) or DOI (digital object identifier) is included.

The numbered entries that follow introduce and explain some conventions of this citation style using examples related to the topic of stress management. Note that in the titles of books and articles, only the first word of the title and subtitle and proper nouns are capitalized.

1. BOOK BY A SINGLE AUTHOR Begin with the author's last name and initials, followed by the date of publication in parentheses. Next, italicize the book's title, and end with the place of publication, including city and state or country, and the publisher.

Nakazawa, D. J. (2009). *The autoimmune epidemic.* New York, NY: Simon & Schuster.

2. BOOK BY MULTIPLE AUTHORS OR EDITORS

Williams, S., & Cooper, L. (2002). *Managing workplace stress: A best practice blueprint.* New York, NY: Wiley.

3. ARTICLE IN A REFERENCE WORK If an online edition of the reference work is cited, give the retrieval date and the URL. Omit end punctuation after the URL.

Beins, B. C. (2010). Barnum effect. In I. B. Weiner & W. E. Craighead (Eds.), *The Corsini encyclopedia of psychology* (4th ed., Vol. 4, pp. 203–204). Hoboken, NJ: Wiley.

Biofeedback. (2007). In *Encyclopaedia Britannica online.* Retrieved from http://www.britannica.com/EBchecked/topic/65856/biofeedback

4. GOVERNMENT DOCUMENT

U.S. Department of Health and Human Services. (1997). *Violence in the workplace: Guidelines for understanding and response.* Washington, DC: Government Printing Office.

5. JOURNAL ARTICLE

Begin with the author's last name and initials followed by the date of publication in parentheses. Next, list the title of the article and italicize the title of the journal in which it is printed. Then give the volume number, italicized, and the issue number in parentheses if the journal is paginated by issue. End with the inclusive page numbers of the article. For an article found online, if a DOI number is given, add "doi:" and the number after the publication information. Otherwise, add "Retrieved from" and the URL of the journal home page. Omit the end period after a DOI or URL.

Dollard, M. F., & Metzer, J. C. (1999). Psychological research, practice, and production: The occupational stress problem. *International Journal of Stress Management, 6*(4), 241–253.

Christian, M. S., Bradley, J. C., Wallace, J. C., & Burke, M. J. (2009, September). Workplace safety: A meta-analysis of the roles of person and situation factors. *Journal of Applied Psychology, 94,* 1103–1127. doi:10.1037/a0016172

6. MAGAZINE ARTICLE

Cobb, K. (2002, July 20). Sleepy heads: Low fuel may drive brain's need to sleep. *Science News, 162,* 38.

7. NEWSPAPER ARTICLE

Zimmerman, E. (2010, December 19). Learning to tame your office anxiety. *The New York Times,* p. BU8.

Zimmerman, E. (2010, December 19). Learning to tame your office anxiety. *The New York Times.* Retrieved from http://www.nytimes.com

8. UNSIGNED NEWSPAPER ARTICLE

Stress less: It's time to wrap it up. (2002, December 18). *Houston Chronicle,* p. A1.

9. DOCUMENT FROM A WEBSITE

List the author, the date of publication (use "n.d." if there is no date), the title of the document, italicized, the words "Retrieved from," and the URL for the document. If there is no author, begin the entry with the document title. Do not include a retrieval date unless the content is likely to change. Omit punctuation at the end of the URL.

Centers for Disease Control and Prevention. (1999). *Stress . . . at work* (NIOSH Publication No. 99-101). Retrieved from http://www.cdc.gov/niosh/docs/99-101

10. PERSONAL WEBSITE Simply note the site in your speech:

Dr. Wesley Sime's stress management page is an excellent resource (http://www.unl.edu/stress/mgmt/).

11. ELECTRONIC MAILING LIST, NEWSGROUP, ONLINE FORUM, OR DISCUSSION GROUP MESSAGE

Lippin, R. (2008, November 2). Re: The relation between work-related psychosocial factors and the development of depression [Electronic mailing list message]. Retrieved from Occupational & Environmental Medicine Mailing List, http://lists.unc.edu/read/archive?id=4872034

Dimitrakov, J. (2001, February 21). Re: Immune effects of psychological stress [Online discussion group message]. Retrieved from http://groups.google.com/groups?q=stress&start=40&hl=en&lr=&ie=UTF-8&selm=3A9ABDE4%40MailAndNews.com&rnum=44

12. BLOG POST

Lippin, R. (2007, July 31). US corporate EAP programs: Oversight, Orwellian or Soviet psychiatry redux? [Web log post]. Retrieved from http://medicalcrises.blogspot.com/2007/07/us-corporate-eap-programs-oversight.html

13. E-MAIL MESSAGE Simply note the message in your speech:

An e-mail message from the staff of AltaVista clarifies this point (D. Emanuel, personal communication, May 12, 2005).

14. MATERIAL FROM AN ONLINE DATABASE

Waring, T. (2002). Stress management: A balanced life is good for business. *Law Society Journal, 40,* 66–68. Retrieved from http://www.lawsociety.com.au

15. ABSTRACT FROM AN INFORMATION SERVICE OR ONLINE DATABASE Begin the entry with the publication information as for a print article. End the entry with "Abstract retrieved" followed by the URL of the database or the name of the database and any identifying number.

Viswesvaran, C., Sanchez, J., & Fisher, J. (1999). The role of social support in the process of work stress: A meta-analysis. *Journal of Vocational Behavior, 54,* 314–334. Abstract retrieved from ERIC database. (EJ581024)

16. PERSONAL INTERVIEW Simply note the interview in your speech:

> During her interview, Senator Cole revealed her enthusiasm for the new state-funded stress management center (M. Cole, personal communication, October 7, 2005).

◉ MLA Documentation

Created by the Modern Language Association, MLA documentation style is fully outlined in the *MLA Handbook for Writers of Research Papers,* Seventh Edition (2009). Disciplines that use MLA style include English literature, the humanities, and various foreign languages.

In MLA format, you document materials from other sources with in-text citations that incorporate signal phrases and parenthetical references.

For example, you could cite Example 1 in this section with the author's name in a signal phrase as follows:

> Berg notes that "'Chicano' is the term made popular by the Mexican American civil rights movement in the 1960s and 1970s" (6).

Or with a parenthetical reference as follows:

> The term "Chicano" was "made popular by the Mexican American civil rights movement in the 1960s and 1970s" (Berg 6).

Each in-text citation refers to an alphabetical works-cited list that you must create.

The sample citations given here all relate to a single topic: film appreciation and criticism.

1. BOOK BY A SINGLE AUTHOR Citations for most books are arranged as follows: (1) the author's name, last name first; (2) the title and subtitle, italicized; and (3) the city of publication, an abbreviated form of the publisher's name, and the date. Each of these three pieces of information is followed by a period and one space. End the citation with the medium of publication (Print) and a period.

Berg, Charles Ramírez. *Latino Images in Film: Stereotypes, Subversion, and Resistance.* Austin: U of Texas P, 2002. Print.

2. BOOK BY MULTIPLE AUTHORS OR EDITORS Give the first author's name, last name first; then list the name(s) of the other author(s) in regular order with a comma between authors and the word *and* before the last one. The final name in a list of editors is followed by a comma and "ed." or "eds."

Grieveson, Lee, and Haidee Wasson, eds. *Inventing Film Studies*. Durham: Duke UP, 2008. Print.

3. ARTICLE IN A REFERENCE WORK If the citation is to an online version of the work, give the author, article title, and name of the website. Then add the publisher or sponsor of the site, the date of publication or last update, the medium (Web), and the date you accessed the work (day, month, year). End with a period.

Katz, Ephraim. "Film Noir." *The Film Encyclopedia*. 6th ed. 2008. Print.

"Auteur Theory." *Encyclopaedia Britannica Online*. Encyclopaedia Britannica, 2007. Web. 22 Oct. 2007.

4. GOVERNMENT DOCUMENT

United States. Cong. House. Committee on the Judiciary. *National Film Preservation Act of 1996*. 104th Cong., 2nd sess. H. Rept. 104–558. Washington: GPO, 1996. Print.

United States. Cong. House. Committee on House Administration. *Library of Congress Sound Recording and Film Preservation Programs Reauthorization Act of 2008*. 110th Cong., 2nd sess. H. Rept. 110–683. *GPOAccess, Congressional Reports*. Web. 15 Jan. 2012.

5. MAGAZINE ARTICLE If you are citing the article from an online edition of the magazine, after the title of the article, add the name of the website in italics, followed by a period. Then add the publisher or sponsor of the site, the date of publication, the medium (Web), and the date you accessed the article.

Ansen, David. "Shock and Yawn." *Newsweek* 26 Oct. 2009: 48. Print.

Horn, Robert. "From Bangkok to Cannes, Thai Political Tensions Remain." *Time*. Time, 24 May 2010. Web. 3 Nov. 2010.

6. JOURNAL ARTICLE If an article is accessed online through a database service, after the publication information, add the name of the database in italics, followed by a period. Then give the medium (Web) and your date of access. End with a period.

Skrebels, Paul. "*All Night Long*: Jazzing around with Othello." *Literature/Film Quarterly* 36.2 (2008): 147–56. Print.

Holcomb, Mark. "A Classic Revisited: *To Kill a Mockingbird*." *Film Quarterly* 55.4 (2002): 34–40. *Academic OneFile*. Web. 22 Oct. 2011.

7. NEWSPAPER ARTICLE If you are citing a newspaper article found online, after the title of the article, give the name of the newspaper's website followed by a period. Then specify the publisher or sponsor of the site, the date of publication, the medium consulted (Web), and the date you accessed the article.

Peers, Martin. "HBO Could Draw True Blood Online." *Wall Street Journal* 23 Oct. 2010: B16+. Print.

Dargis, Manohla. "Unblinking Eye, Visual Diary: Warhol's Films." *New York Times*. New York Times, 21 Oct. 2007. Web. 30 Oct. 2007.

8. NEWSPAPER EDITORIAL

"Avatars Don't Smoke." Editorial. *New York Times* 8 Jan. 2010: A26. Print.

9. ONLINE SCHOLARLY PROJECT OR REFERENCE DATABASE

"Origins of American Animation." *American Memory*. Lib. of Cong. 31 Mar. 1999. Web. 26 June 2011.

10. PERSONAL OR COMMERCIAL WEBSITE

Last, Kimberly. *007*. Kimberly Last, n.d. Web. 18 Oct. 2007.

"American Beauty." *Crazy for Cinema*. N.p., n.d. Web. 24 Oct. 2011.

11. POSTING OR COMMENT ON A BLOG Give the author's name; the title of the post or comment in quotation marks (if there is no title, use the description "blog post" or "blog comment"); the title of the blog, italicized; the sponsor of the blog (if there is none, use "N.p."); the date of the most recent update; the medium (Web); and the date of access.

Scola, Nancy. "And the White House Tweets Back." *techPresident*. Personal Democracy Forum, 5 May 2009. Web. 5 May 2009.

12. ARTICLE IN AN ONLINE PERIODICAL

Williams, Mary Elizabeth. "The NC-17 Rating's Perverse Failure." *Salon.* Salon Media Group, 8 Dec. 2010. Web. 11 Jan. 2012.

13. POSTING TO A DISCUSSION GROUP

Granger, Susan. "Review of *The Cider House Rules.*" *Rotten Tomatoes.* IGN Entertainment, 30 Mar. 2000. Web. 2 Oct. 2011.

14. E-MAIL MESSAGE

Boothe, Jeanna. "Re: Top 100 Movies." Message to the author. 16 Feb. 2012. E-mail.

15. SINGLE-ISSUE CD-ROM, DISKETTE, OR MAGNETIC TAPE

"Pulp Fiction." *Blockbuster Movie Trivia.* 3rd ed. New York: Random, 1998. CD-ROM.

16. WORK OF ART OR PHOTOGRAPH

Christenberry, William. *Coleman's Café.* 1971. Ektacolor Brownie Print. Hunter Museum of Art, Chattanooga.

17. INTERVIEW

Sanderson, Andrew. Telephone interview. 12 June 2011.

◎ CSE Documentation

The CSE (Council of Science Editors) style is most frequently used in the fields of biology and environmental science. The current CSE style guide is *Scientific Style and Format: The CSE Manual for Authors, Editors, and Publishers,* Seventh Edition (2006). Publishers and instructors who require the CSE style do so in three possible formats: a citation-sequence superscript format, a name-year format, or a citation-name format, which combines aspects of the other two systems.

- Citation-sequence superscript format: Use superscript numbers for in-text references. In the references list, number and arrange the references in the sequence in which they are first cited in the speech.
- Name-year format: Use the name and year, in parentheses, for the in-text reference. In the references list, give the references, unnumbered, in alphabetical order.
- Citation-name format: Use superscript numbers for in-text references. In the references list, arrange the references in alphabetical order and number the list sequentially.

In the following examples, all of which refer to environmental issues, you will see that the citation-sequence format calls for listing the date after the publisher's name in references for books and after the name of the periodical in references for articles. The name-year format calls for listing the date immediately after the author's name in any kind of reference. Notice also the absence of a comma after the author's last name, the absence of a period after an initial, and the absence of italics in titles of books or journals.

1. BOOK BY ONE AUTHOR Be sure to list the total number of pages in the book.

Citation-Sequence and Citation-Name

[1] Houghton JT. Global warming: the complete briefing. 4th ed. Cambridge (UK): Cambridge University Press; 2009. 456 p.

Name-Year

Houghton JT. 2009. Global warming: the complete briefing. 4th ed. Cambridge (UK): Cambridge University Press. 456 p.

2. BOOK BY TWO OR MORE AUTHORS

Citation-Sequence and Citation-Name

[2] Harf JE, Lombardi MO. Taking sides: clashing views on global issues. 6th ed. New York: McGraw-Hill; 2010. 432 p.

Name-Year

Harf JE, Lombardi MO. 2010. Taking sides: clashing views on global issues. 6th ed. New York: McGraw-Hill. 432 p.

3. JOURNAL ARTICLE If citing a journal on the Internet, add the medium, date cited, and the URL. Also give the DOI code if available. Omit end punctuation after a URL or DOI.

Citation-Sequence and Citation-Name

[3] Brussard PF, Tull JC. Conservation biology and four types of advocacy. Conserv Biol. 2007; 21(1):21–24.

[3] Brussard PF, Tull JC. Conservation biology and four types of advocacy. Conserv Biol. [Internet]. 2007 [cited 2010 Oct 22]; 21(1):21–24. Available from: http://www.blackwell-synergy .com/toc/cbi/21/1 doi:10.1111/j.1523-1739.2006.00640.x

Name-Year

Brussard PF, Tull JC. 2007. Conservation biology and four types of advocacy. Conserv Biol. 21(1):21–24.

Brussard PF, Tull JC. 2007. Conservation biology and four types of advocacy. Conserv Biol [Internet]. [cited

2010 Oct 22]; 21(1):21–24. Available from: http://www
.blackwell-synergy.com/toc/cbi/21/1 doi:10.1111/ j.1523
-1739.2006.00640.x

4. MAGAZINE ARTICLE

Citation-Sequence and Citation-Name

[4] Sheppard K. Bad breakup: why BP doesn't have to tell the EPA—or the public—what's in its toxic dispersants. Mother Jones. 2010 Sep-Oct:41.

Name-Year

Sheppard K. 2010 Sep-Oct. Bad breakup: why BP doesn't have to tell the EPA—or the public—what's in its toxic dispersants. Mother Jones. 41.

5. NEWSPAPER ARTICLE

Citation-Sequence and Citation-Name

[5] Zeller T Jr. Negotiators at climate talks face deep set of fault lines. New York Times. 2009 Dec 6; Sect. WK:3 (col. 1).

Name-Year

Zeller T Jr. 2009 Dec 6. Negotiators at climate talks face deep set of fault lines. New York Times. Sect. WK:3 (col. 1).

6. WEBSITE For material found on a website, give the author's name (if any) and the title of the material, followed by "Internet" in brackets. Add the place of publication, the publisher, date of publication, followed by the date of citation in brackets. Add "Available from:" and the URL.

Citation-Sequence and Citation-Name

[6] Coastal Programs: The Barnegat Bay Estuary Program [Internet]. Trenton (NJ): Department of Environmental Protection, Division of Watershed Management. c1996-2004 [updated 2010 Feb 18; cited 2011 Oct 23]. Available from: http://www.nj.gov/dep/watershedmgt/bbep.htm

Name-Year

Coastal Programs: The Barnegat Bay Estuary Program [Internet]. c1996-2004. Trenton (NJ): Department of Environmental Protection, Division of Watershed Management. [updated 2010 Feb 18; cited 2011 Oct 23]. Available from: http://www.nj.gov/dep/watershedmgt /bbep.htm

7. E-MAIL MESSAGE CSE recommends mentioning personal communications in text, but not listing them in the list of references. An explanation of the material should go in the "Notes."

> . . . (2012 e-mail from Maura O'Brien to me; unreferenced, see "Notes").

8. E-MAIL DISCUSSION LIST OR NEWSGROUP MESSAGE

> [8] Affleck-Asch W. Lawncare methods causing heavy damage to environment [discussion list on the Internet]. 2004 Aug 17, 2:30 pm [cited 2011 Dec 2]. [about 10 paragraphs]. Available from: http://www.mail-archive.com/ecofem%40csf .colorado.edu

◉ IEEE Documentation

The Institute of Electrical and Electronics Engineers (IEEE) style requires that references appear at the end of the text, not in alphabetical order but in the order in which the references are cited in the text or speech. A bracketed reference number beginning with *B* precedes each entry. For more information on IEEE documentation, check the *IEEE Standards Style Manual* online at **https://development.standards .ieee.org/myproject/Public/mytools/draft/styleman.pdf**.

1. BOOK

[B1] Thomas, R. E., Albert, R. J., and Toussaint G. J., *The Analysis and Design of Linear Circuits,* 6th ed. Hoboken, NJ: Wiley, 2009, p. 652.

2. PERIODICAL

[B2] Melfi, M., Evon, S., and McElveen R.,"Induction versus permanent magnet motors," *IEEE Industry Applications Magazine,* vol. 15, no. 6, pp. 28–35, Nov./Dec. 2009. doi: 10.1109/MIAS.2009.934443

3. WEB PAGE

[B3] National Academy of Engineering,"Lasers and fiber optics timeline," *Greatest Engineering Achievements of the 20th Century,* 2010.*

*Available at **www.greatachievements.org**.

APPENDIX B ●●●●

Question-and-Answer Sessions

Deftly fielding questions is a final critical component of making a speech or a presentation. As the last step in preparing your speech, anticipate and prepare for questions the audience is likely to pose to you. Write these questions down, and practice answering them. Spend time preparing an answer to the most difficult question that you are likely to face. The confidence you will gain from smoothly handling a difficult question should spill over to other questions.[1]

◉ Protocol during the Session

As a matter of courtesy, call on audience members in the order in which they raise their hands. Consider the following guidelines:

- *Repeat or paraphrase the question* ("The question is 'Did the mayor really vote against . . .'"). This will ensure that you've heard it correctly, that others in the audience know what you are responding to, and that you have time to reflect upon and formulate an answer. Note that there are a few exceptions to repeating the question, especially when the question is hostile. One expert suggests that you should always repeat the question when speaking to a large group; when you're in a small group or a training seminar, however, doing so isn't necessary.[2]

- *Initially make eye contact with the questioner; then move your gaze to other audience members.* This makes all audience members feel as though you are responding not only to the questioner but to them as well.

- *Remember your listening skills.* Give questioners your full attention, and don't interrupt them.

- *Don't be afraid to pause while formulating an answer.* Many speakers feel they must feed the audience instantaneous responses; this belief sometimes causes them to say things that they later regret. This is especially the case in media interviews (see Appendix C). Pauses that seem long to you may not appear lengthy to listeners.

- *Keep answers concise.* The question-and-answer session is not the time to launch into a lengthy treatise on your favorite aspect of a topic.

◉ Handling Hostile and Otherwise Troubling Questions

When handling hostile questions, do not get defensive. Doing so will damage your credibility and only encourage the other person. Maintain an attitude of respect, and stay cool and in control. Attempt to defuse the hostile questioner with respect and goodwill. Similarly, never give the impression that you think a question is stupid or irrelevant, even if it clearly is.

- *Do not repeat or paraphrase a hostile question.* This only lends the question more credibility than it is worth. Instead, try to rephrase it more positively[3] (e.g., in response to the question "Didn't your department botch the handling of product X?" you might respond, "The question was 'Why did product X experience a difficult market entry?' To that I would say that . . .").
- *If someone asks you a seemingly stupid question, do not point that out.* Instead, respond graciously.[4]

◉ Ending the Session

Never end a question-and-answer session abruptly. As time runs out, alert the audience that you will take one or two more questions and then must end. The session represents one final opportunity to reinforce your message, so take the opportunity to do so. As you summarize your message, thank your listeners for their time. Leave an air of goodwill behind you.

APPENDIX C ●●●●●

Preparing for Mediated Communication

The underlying principles described throughout this guide will stand you in good stead as you prepare to communicate online, as discussed in Chapter 26, or on television or radio. These speaking situations do present some unique challenges, however.

◉ Speaking on Television

On television, you are at the mercy of reporters and producers who will edit your remarks to fit their time frame. Therefore, before your televised appearance, find out as much as you can about the speech situation—for example, how long you will be on camera and whether the show will be aired live or taped. You may need to convey your message in *sound bite* form—succinct statements that summarize your key points in twenty seconds or less.

Eye Contact, Body Movements, and Voice

Knowing where to direct your gaze is critical in televised appearances, as is controlling body movement and voice. The following are some guidelines:

- Don't play to the camera. In a one-on-one interview, focus on the interviewer. Do not look up or down or tilt your head sideways; these movements will make you look uncertain or evasive.[1]
- If there is an audience, treat the camera as just another audience member, glancing at it only as often as you would at any other individual during your remarks.
- If there is only the camera, direct your gaze at it as you speak.
- Keep your posture erect.
- Exaggerate your gestures slightly.
- Project your voice, and avoid speaking in a monotone.

Dress and Makeup

To compensate for the glare of studio lights and distortions caused by the camera, give careful consideration to dress and grooming:

- Choose dark rather than light-colored clothing. Dark colors such as blue, gray, green, and brown photograph better than lighter shades.
- Avoid stark white, because it produces glare.
- Avoid plaids, dots, and other busy patterns because they tend to jump around on the screen.
- Avoid glittering jewelry, including tie bars.
- Wear a little more makeup than usual because bright studio lights tend to make you look washed out.

◎ Speaking on Radio: The Media Interview

The following are guidelines for preparing for media interviews on the radio. These same guidelines can be applied to the television interview.

- Know the audience and the focus of the program. What subjects does the broadcast cover? How long will the interview be? Will it be in real-time or recorded?
- Brush up on background information, and have your facts ready. Assume that the audience knows little or nothing about the subject matter.
- Use the interviewer's name during the interview.
- Prepare a speaking outline on notecards for the interview. Remember that the microphone will pick up the sound of papers being shuffled.

- Remember that taped interviews may be edited. Make key points in short sentences, and repeat them using different words.[2] Think in terms of sound bites.
- Anticipate questions that might arise, and decide how you will answer them.
- Use transition points to acknowledge the interviewer's questions and to bridge your key message points, such as "I am not familiar with that, but what I can tell you is . . ."; "You raise an interesting question, but I think the more important matter is. . . ."[3]
- Avoid the phrase "No comment." It will only exaggerate a point you are trying to minimize. Instead, say "I am not at liberty to comment/discuss. . . ."

APPENDIX D ●●●●

Tips for Non-Native Speakers of English

In addition to the normal fear of being at center stage, non-native speakers of English face the burden of worrying about delivering a speech in a non-native language. If English is your first language, remind yourself of how difficult it would be for you to deliver a speech in another language. As you listen to a non-native speaker, place yourself in his or her shoes. If necessary, politely ask questions for clarification.

If you are a non-native speaker of English, think about public speaking as an opportunity to learn more about the English language and how to use it. As you listen to your classmates' speeches, for example, you will gain exposure to spoken English. Practicing your speech will give you time to work on any accent features you want to improve.[1] Research shows that thinking positively about preparing speeches actually *reduces anxiety* and helps you prepare a better speech. So tell yourself that by studying public speaking you will find many good opportunities to improve your English and become a better communicator of English. In addition, by spending time writing and outlining your speech, you will gain confidence in your written language skills. Here are a few tips to get you started:

- *Take your time and speak slowly.* This will give your listeners time to get used to your voice and to focus on your message.
- *Identify English words that you have trouble saying.* Practice saying these words five times. Pause. Then say the words

again five times. Progress slowly until the word becomes easier to pronounce.

- *Avoid using language that you don't really have to use, such as jargon* (see Chapter 15). Learn to use a thesaurus to find synonyms—words that mean the same thing—that are simpler and easier to pronounce.
- *Offer words from your native language to emphasize your points.* This will help the audience to better appreciate your native language and accent. For example, the Spanish word *corazón* has a lyrical quality that makes it sound much better than its English counterpart, "heart." Capitalize on the beauty of your native language.

Learn by Listening

Listening is the key to learning a language. Using textbooks to study usage and grammar is important, but it is through spoken language—hearing it and speaking it—that we gain fluency.

Listening to the speeches of colleagues or classmates, as well as those broadcast by television channels such as C-Span, can help you hone the skills you need to become a better speaker. Nearly all college libraries own many DVDs and other recorded materials made specifically for ESL (English as a second language) speakers such as yourself, and the reference librarian will be happy to locate them for you. The Internet also offers many helpful listening resources. Among the many sites you can find is the *Talking Merriam Webster English Dictionary* (at **www.webster.com/**). This online dictionary allows you to hear the correct pronunciations of words.

Broaden Your Listeners' Perspectives

Consider sharing a personal experience with the audience. Stories from other lands and other ways of life often fascinate listeners. Unique cultural traditions, eyewitness accounts of newsworthy events, or tales passed down orally from one generation to the next are just some of the possibilities. Depending on the goal of your speech, you can use your experiences as supporting material for a related topic or as the topic itself.

Record Yourself Practicing

Most experts recommend that you prepare for delivering your first speech (as well as for subsequent speeches) by practicing with a video or an audio recorder.[2] Non-native speakers may wish to pay added attention to pronunciation and articulation as they play back the recorded speech. *Pronunciation* is the correct formation of word sounds. *Articulation* is the clarity or forcefulness with which the sounds are made, regardless of whether they are pronounced correctly. It is important to pay attention to and work on both areas.

Because languages vary in the specific sounds they use and the way these sounds are produced by the vocal cords, each of us will speak a non-native language a bit differently than do native speakers. That is, we all speak with some sort of accent. This should not concern you in and of itself. What is important is identifying which specific features of your pronunciation, if any, seriously interfere with your ability to make yourself understandable. Listening to your speech on a video or an audio recording, perhaps in the presence of a native speaker, will allow you to identify trouble spots. Once you have identified which words you tend to mispronounce, you can work to correct the problem. If possible, try to arrange an appointment with an instructor to help you identify key linguistic issues in your speech practice recording. If instructors are unavailable, try asking a fellow student.

◎ Use Vocal Variety

Non-native speakers may be accustomed to patterns of vocal variety—volume, pitch, rate, and pauses—that are different from a native English speaker. The pronunciation of English depends on learning how to combine a series of about forty basic sounds (fifteen vowels and twenty-five consonants) that together serve to distinguish English words from one another. Correct pronunciation also requires that the speaker learn proper word stress, rhythm, and intonation or pitch.[3] As you practice your speeches, pay particular attention to these facets of delivery. Seek feedback from others, including your teacher, making sure that your goal of shared meaning can be met when you do deliver your speech.

QUICK TIP

Check for Correct Articulation

As you listen to your recording, watch also for your articulation of words. ESL students whose first languages don't differentiate between the */sh/* sound and its close cousin */ch/*, for example, may say "share" when they mean "chair" or "shoes" when they mean "choose."[4] It is important therefore that you also check to make sure that you are using the correct meaning of the words you have selected for your speech.

◉ **Improve Intelligibility of Speech**

Virtually everyone who learns to speak another language will speak that language with an accent. What steps can you take to ensure understanding?

In the long term, interacting with native speakers in every-day life will help enormously. With immersion, non-native speakers can begin to stop translating things word for word and start thinking in English. Using a video or an audio recorder and practicing your speech in front of others are also very important.

But what if your experience with English is limited and you must nonetheless give an oral presentation? Robert Anholt, a scientist and the author of *Dazzle 'Em with Style: The Art of Oral Scientific Presentation,* suggests the following:

- Practice the presentation often, preferably with a friend who is a native English speaker.
- Learn the presentation almost by heart.
- Create strong presentation aids that will convey most of the story by themselves.[5]

Glossary ● ●●●

abstract language Language that is general or nonspecific.

active listening Listening that is focused and purposeful.

ad hominem fallacy A logical fallacy that targets the person instead of the issue at hand in an attempt to discredit an opponent's argument. See also *logical fallacy*.

after-dinner speech A speech that is likely to occur before, after, or during a formal dinner; a breakfast or lunch seminar; or other type of business, professional, or civic meeting.

agora In ancient Greece, a public square or marketplace. See also *forum* and *public forum*.

alliteration The repetition of the same sounds, usually initial consonants, in two or more neighboring words or syllables.

analogy An extended metaphor or simile that compares an unfamiliar concept or process with a more familiar one in order to help the listener understand the one that is unfamiliar. See also *figure of speech*.

anecdote A brief story of interesting and often humorous incidents based on real life.

anti-group roles Disruptive roles such as "floor hogger" and "blocker" that detract from a group's roles and so should be avoided.

antithesis A rhetorical device in which two ideas are set off in balanced (parallel) opposition to each other.

anxiety stop-time technique A technique for dealing with pre-performance anxiety by allowing anxiety to present itself for a few minutes and then declaring time for confidence to step in to help complete practicing a speech.

architecture design review An oral presentation that enables the audience to visualize and judge the feasibility and appeal of an architectural design.

argument A stated position, with support, for or against an idea or issue; contains the core elements of claim, evidence, and warrants.

articulation The clarity or forcefulness with which sounds are made, regardless of whether they are pronounced correctly.

asynchronous communication Communication in which interaction between speaker and receiver does not occur simultaneously. See also *recorded presentation*.

attitudes Our general evaluations of people, ideas, objects, or events.

audience analysis The process of gathering and analyzing information about audience members' psychological and demographic attributes and motivations in order to develop speeches that will be meaningful to them.

audience-centered perspective Speaker focus on the needs, attitudes, and values of the audience.

authoritative warrant A line of reasoning based on the credibility or trustworthiness of the source. See also *warrant*.

average Data calculated on the basis of typical characteristics.

bandwagoning A fallacy of reasoning that uses (unsubstantiated) general opinion as its (false) basis. See also *logical fallacy*.

begging the question A fallacy of reasoning in which what is stated cannot help but be true, even though no evidence has been presented. See also *logical fallacy*.

beliefs The ways in which people perceive reality or determine the very existence or validity of something.

body (of speech) The part of the speech in which the speaker develops the main points intended to fulfill the speech's purpose.

body language Facial expressions, eye behavior, gestures, and general body movements during the delivery of a speech.

brainstorming A problem-solving technique that involves the spontaneous generation of ideas through word association, topic mapping, and other means.

brief example A single illustration of an idea, item, or event being described.

call to action A challenge to audience members to act in response to a speech; placed at the conclusion of a persuasive speech.

canned speech A speech used repeatedly and without sufficient adaptation to the rhetorical speech situation.

canons of rhetoric A classical approach to speechmaking in which the speaker divides the process into five parts: invention, arrangement, style, memory, and delivery.

captive audience An audience required to attend a speech. See also *voluntary audience*.

case conference An oral report prepared by health care professionals evaluating a patient's condition and outlining a treatment plan.

case study A detailed illustration of a real (or realistic) situation, relating to business, law, or other disciplines, which poses dilemmas or problems requiring solutions.

categorical pattern See *topical pattern*.

causal (cause-effect) pattern A pattern of organizing speech points in order of causes and of effects, or vice versa.

causal reasoning A line of reasoning ("warrant") offering a cause-and-effect relationship as proof of a claim.

central processing A mode of processing a persuasive message that involves thinking critically about the contents of the message and the strength and quality of the speaker's arguments. See also *peripheral processing* and *elaboration likelihood model of persuasion (ELM)*

channel The medium through which the speaker sends a message, such as sound waves, air waves, electronic devices, and so forth.

chart A visual representation of data and its relationship to other data in meaningful form, such as flow charts, organization charts, and tabular charts (tables).

cherry-picking Selectively presenting only those facts and statistics that buttress one's point of view while ignoring competing data.

chronological pattern A pattern of organizing speech points in a natural sequential order; used when describing a series of events in time or when the topic develops in line with a set pattern of actions or tasks.

civic-mindedness Caring about your community, in word and deed; one of five "ethical ground rules" in public speaking. See also *trustworthiness, respect, responsibility,* and *fairness.*

claim The declaration of a state of affairs in which a speaker attempts to prove something by providing evidence and reasoning.

claim of fact An argument that focuses on whether something is or is not true or whether something will or will not happen.

claim of policy An argument that recommends that a specific course of action be taken, or approved, by an audience.

claim of value An argument that addresses issues of judgment.

classroom discussion presentation Oral presentation in which the speaker presents a brief overview of the topic under discussion and introduces a series of questions to guide students through the topic.

cliché An overused phrase such as "burning the midnight oil" or "works like a dog."

clinical case study A presentation providing medical personnel with a detailed analysis of a person or group with a particular disease or condition and reviews plans for treatment.

closed-ended question A structured question designed to elicit a small range of specific answers supplied by the interviewer.

co-culture A community of people whose perceptions and beliefs differ significantly from those of other groups within the larger culture.

code-switching The selective use of dialect within a speech.

colleagues within the field audience Those persons in an audience who share the speaker's knowledge of the general field under question but who may not be familiar with the specific topic under discussion.

colloquial expression An informal expression characterized by regional variations of speech.

common knowledge Information that is likely to be known by many people and is therefore in the public domain and does not need attribution.

comparative advantage pattern A pattern of organizing speech points so that the speaker's viewpoint or proposal is shown to be superior to one or more alternative viewpoints or proposals.

conclusion (of speech) The part of the speech in which the speaker reiterates the speech thesis, summarizes main points, and leaves the audience with something to think about and possibly act upon.

concrete language Nouns and verbs that convey specific (as opposed to abstract) meaning.

connotative meaning Meaning derived from the individual associations that different people bring to bear on a word. See also *denotative meaning*.

coordinate points Speech points given the same weight in an outline and aligned with one another; thus Main Point II is coordinate with Main Point I. See also *subordinate points*.

coordination and subordination Logical alignment of speech points in an outline relative to their importance to one another. Coordinate ideas receive equal weight; subordinate ideas receive relatively less weight than coordinate ideas and are placed below them.

copyright A legal protection afforded original creators of literary or artistic works.

Creative Commons An organization that allows creators of works to decide how they want other people to use their copyrighted works.

cultural values Dominant values in a given culture. See also *values*.

decoding The part of the communication process in which receivers decode the message. See also *encoding*.

deductive reasoning Reasoning from a general condition to a specific instance. See also *inductive reasoning*.

deep Web The large portion of the Web that general search engines cannot access because the information is licensed and/or fee-based.

defensive listening A poor listening behavior in which the listener reacts defensively to a speaker's message.

definition by example Defining something by providing an example of it.

definition by negation Defining something by explaining what it is not.

definition by synonym Defining something by comparing it with another term that has an equivalent meaning. For example: "A friend is a comrade, or a buddy."

definition by word origin (etymology) Defining something by providing an account of a word's history.

delivery (of speech) The vocal and nonverbal behavior that a speaker uses in a public speech; one of the five *canons of rhetoric*.

delivery cues Brief reminder notes or prompts placed in the speaking outline that can refer to transitions, timing, speaking rate and volume, presentation aids, quotations, statistics, and difficult-to-pronounce or remember names or words.

demographics Statistical characteristics of a given population considered in analysis of audience members; typically includes age, gender, ethnic or cultural background, socioeconomic status (including income, occupation, and education), and religious and political affiliation; other factors such as group membership, geographic location, and disability may also be important to consider.

denotative meaning The literal or dictionary definition of a word. See also *connotative meaning*.

dialect A distinctive way of speaking associated with a particular region or social group.

dialogic communication Sharing ideas through civil discourse.

digital storytelling Using multimedia to tell a story about yourself or others with resonance for the audience.

dignity The feeling that one is worthy, honored, or respected as a person; audience members want to feel that the speaker accords them dignity.

direct quotation Statement made verbatim—word for word—by someone else. Direct quotations should always be acknowledged in a speech.

disinformation The deliberate falsification of information.

dyadic communication Communication between two people, as in a conversation.

either-or fallacy A fallacious argument stated in terms of two alternatives only, even though there are multiple ways of viewing the issue. See also *logical fallacy*.

effective delivery Skillful application of natural conversational behavior to a speech in a way that is relaxed, enthusiastic, and direct.

elaboration likelihood model of persuasion (ELM) A model of persuasion that states that people process persuasive messages by one of two routes—either central or peripheral processing—depending on factors such as their degree of involvement in the message.

encoding The process of organizing a message, choosing words and sentence structure, and verbalizing the message. See also *decoding*.

engineering design review An oral presentation that enables the audience to visualize and judge the feasibility and appeal of an engineering design project.

epiphora (or "epistrophe") A rhetorical device in which the speaker repeats a word or phrase at the end of successive statements.

ethics The rules or standards of moral conduct. In public speaking, the responsibilities speakers have toward their audience and themselves and that listeners have toward speakers.

ethos The Greek word for "character." According to classical rhetoricians such as Aristotle, audiences listen to and trust speakers if they exhibit competence (as demonstrated by the speaker's grasp of the subject matter) and good moral character. See also *logos* and *pathos*.

eulogy A speech whose purpose is to celebrate and commemorate the life of someone while consoling those who are left behind.

evidence Supporting material that provides grounds for belief. See also *claim* and *warrant*.

evidence-based practice (EBP) presentation A presentation that reviews the scientific literature on a clinical problem, critically evaluates the findings, and suggests best practices for standards of care.

example (as form of support) An illustration whose purpose is to aid understanding by making ideas more concrete and by clarifying and amplifying meaning.

expert or insider audience An audience of persons with an intimate knowledge of the topic, issue, product, or idea being discussed.

expert testimony Any findings, eyewitness accounts, or opinions by professionals who are trained to evaluate or report on a given topic; a form of supporting material.

extemporaneous speech A type of speaking that falls somewhere between impromptu and manuscript (written) or memorized delivery. Speakers delivering an extemporaneous speech prepare well and practice in advance, and instead of memorizing or writing the speech word for word, speak from an outline of key words and phrases.

extended example Multifaceted illustration of the idea, item, or event being described, thereby getting the point across and reiterating it effectively.

facts Documented occurrences, including actual events, dates, times, places, and people involved; a form of supporting material in a speech.

fairness The act of making a genuine effort to see all sides of an issue; being open-minded; one of five "ethical ground rules" in public speaking. See also *trustworthiness, respect, responsibility,* and *civic-mindedness.*

fair use doctrine Legal guidelines permitting the limited use of copyrighted works without permission for various purposes.

faulty analogy An inaccurate or misleading comparison suggesting that because two things are similar in some ways, they are necessarily similar in others.

feedback Audience response to a message, which can be conveyed both verbally and nonverbally. Feedback from the audience often indicates whether a speaker's message has been understood and well or poorly received.

field study presentation An oral presentation describing research conducted in natural settings, using methods such as direct observation, surveys, and interviews.

"fighting words" Speech that provokes people to violence.

"fight-or-flight" response The body's automatic response to threatening or fear-inducing events.

figures of speech Expressions, such as metaphors, similes, and analogies, in which words are used in a nonliteral fashion and make striking comparisons to help listeners visualize, identify with, and understand the speaker's ideas.

First Amendment The amendment to the U.S. Constitution that guarantees freedom of speech, with important caveats for ethical public speakers to consider. ("Congress shall make no law abridging the freedom of speech.")

fixed-alternative question A closed-ended question that contains a limited choice of answers, such as "Yes," "No," or "Sometimes."

flip chart A large (27–34 inch) pad of paper on which a speaker can illustrate speech points.

flowchart A diagram that shows step-by-step the progression through a procedure, relationship, or process.

forum In ancient Rome, a public space in which people gathered to deliberate about the issues of the day. In modern terms, an assembly for the discussion of issues of public interest. See also *agora* and *public forum*.

free speech The right to be free from unreasonable constraints on expression; a legal rather than ethical right.

frequency A count of the number of times something occurs.

full-sentence transition A signal to listeners, in the form of a declarative sentence, that the speaker is turning to another topic.

gender Social or psychological sense of self as male or female.

general speech purpose A statement of the broad speech purpose that answers the question, "Why am I speaking on this topic for this particular audience and occasion?" Usually the general speech purpose is to inform, to persuade, or to celebrate or commemorate a special occasion. See also *specific speech purpose*.

generational identity Collective cultural identity of a generation or cohort.

graph A graphical representation of numerical data. Speakers use graphs to neatly illustrate relationships among components or units and demonstrate trends. Four major types of graphs are line graphs, bar graphs, pie graphs, and pictograms.

group activity presentation An oral presentation that introduces students to an activity and provides them with clear directions for its completion.

group presentation A type of oral presentation prepared and delivered by a group of three or more people.

groupthink The tendency of a group to accept information and ideas without subjecting them to critical analysis.

handout Printed material that conveys information that is either impractical to give to the audience in another manner or intended to be kept by audience members after a presentation.

hasty generalization A fallacy of reasoning in which a speaker attempts to support a claim by asserting that a particular piece of evidence (an isolated instance) is true for all conditions concerned.

hate speech Any offensive communication—verbal or nonverbal—directed against people's race, ethnicity, religion, gender, disability, or other characteristics.

hearing The physiological, largely passive process of perceiving sound. See also *listening*.

heckler's veto Speech meant to drown out a speaker's message; such speech silences freedom of expression.

hierarchy of needs A classic model of human action developed by Abraham Maslow built on the principle that people are motivated to act first on the basis of their elemental needs.

hypothetical example An illustration of something that could happen in the future if certain events were to occur.

identification A feeling of commonality with another. Effective speakers attempt to foster a sense of identification between themselves and audience members.

imagery Colorful and concrete words and figures of speech that appeal to the senses. See also *analogy, metaphor*, and *simile*.

inductive reasoning Reasoning from specific instances to a general condition. See also *deductive reasoning*.

information Data set in a context for relevance.

informative speech Speech providing new information, new insights, or new ways of thinking about a topic. The general purpose of informative speaking is to increase the audience's understanding and awareness of a topic.

integrity The quality of being incorruptible; the unwillingness to compromise for the sake of personal expediency; a component of *ethos* or *speaker credibility*.

internal preview An extended transition that alerts audience members to ensuing speech content.

internal summary An extended transition used within the body of a speech that summarizes important ideas before proceeding to another speech point.

intonation The rising and falling of voice pitch across phrases and sentences.

introduction (of speech) The first part of a speech, in which the speaker establishes the speech purpose and its relevance to the audience and previews the topic and main points.

invective Abusive, accusatory, and attacking speech.

jargon Specialized terminology developed within a given endeavor or field of study and which must be translated for lay audiences.

journal article review A presentation (or written report) that reviews and critically assesses the article's ideas for an audience of knowledgeable persons in the discipline.

key-word outline The briefest form of outline; uses the smallest possible units of understanding associated with a specific point to outline the main and supporting points.

lavaliere microphone A microphone that attaches to a lapel or a collar.

lay audience An audience of persons lacking specialized knowledge of the general field related to the speaker's topic and of the topic itself.

lay testimony Firsthand findings, accounts, or opinions from nonexperts such as eyewitnesses.

lazy speech A poor speech habit in which the speaker fails to properly articulate words.

learning styles Preferred ways of processing information; one learning theory model suggests visual, aural, read/write, and kinesthetic modes of learning.

lecture An informational speech to an audience of student learners.

library portal A vetted entry point to a large collection of research and reference information

listening The conscious act of receiving, comprehending, interpreting, and responding to messages. See also *hearing*.

logical fallacy A statement that is based on an invalid or a deceptive line of reasoning. See also *ad hominem fallacy, bandwagoning, begging the question, either-or fallacy, hasty generalization, non sequitur,* and *slippery slope.*

logos The Greek rhetorician Aristotle used this term to refer to persuasive appeals to reason and logic.

main points Statements that express the key ideas and major themes of a speech. Their function is to make claims in support of the thesis statement.

malapropism The inadvertent use of a word or phrase in place of one that sounds like it.

mass communication Communication that occurs between a speaker and a large audience of unknown people. The receivers of the message are not present with the speaker or are part of such an immense crowd that there can be little or no interaction between speaker and listener. Television, radio news broadcasts, and mass rallies are examples of mass communication.

mean The sum of the scores divided by the number of scores; the arithmetic (or computed) average.

median A type of average that represents the center-most score in a distribution; the point above and below which 50 percent of the scores fall.

message The content of the communication process—thoughts and ideas put into meaningful expressions. A message can be expressed both verbally (through the sentences and points of a speech) and nonverbally (through eye contact, vocal behavior, and gestures).

metaphor A figure of speech used to make implicit comparisons without the use of "like" or "as" (e.g., "Love is a rose").

methods/procedure presentation An oral presentation describing and sometimes demonstrating an experimental or a mathematical process, including the conditions under which it can be applied; frequently delivered in scientific and mathematics related fields.

mind mapping See *topic mapping*.

misinformation Information that is false.

mixed audience An audience composed of a combination of persons—some with expert knowledge of the field and topic and others with no specialized knowledge.

mixed metaphor A comparison that juxtaposes two unlike, often clichéd, expressions, such as "He went off the deep end like a bull in a china shop."

mode A type of average that represents the most frequently occurring score(s) in a distribution.

model A three-dimensional, scale-size representation of an object such as a building.

moderator A person who presides over a discussion or meeting.

motivated sequence pattern An organizational pattern for a persuasive speech based on a five-step process developed by Alan Monroe that begins with arousing attention and ends with calling for action.

motivational warrant A line of reasoning that appeals to the needs, desires, emotions, and values of audience members as the basis for accepting evidence in support of a claim.

mumbling Slurring words together at low volume and pitch so they are barely audible.

narrative A story based on personal experiences or imaginary incidents. See also *story*.

narrative pattern A pattern of organizing speech points so that the speech unfolds as a story, with characters, plot, and setting. In practice, this pattern often is combined with other organizational patterns.

noise Anything that interferes with the communication process between a speaker and an audience so that the message cannot be understood; source may be external (in the environment) or internal (psychological or physical factors).

non sequitur ("does not follow") A fallacy of reasoning in which the conclusion does not connect to the reasoning. See also *logical fallacy*.

nonverbal communication Communication other than the spoken word; includes body language, voice, and appearance.

nonverbal immediacy Acts that create the perception of psychological closeness between the speaker and audience members.

one-sided message In persuasive speaking, a message that does not mention opposing claims. See also *two-sided message.*

online presentation A presentation delivered over any distance via the Internet; can include both real-time and recorded presentations.

open-ended question A survey or interview question designed to allow respondents to elaborate as much as they want.

oral citation A speaker's oral acknowledgement of the source of speech material that is derived from other people's ideas.

oral style The specific word choice, sentence structure, and rhetorical devices (techniques of language) that speakers use to express their ideas.

oratory In classical terms, the art of public speaking.

outline An organizing device that separates main and supporting points—the major speech claims and the evidence to support them—into larger and smaller divisions and subdivisions.

panel discussion A type of oral presentation in which a group of persons (at least three, and generally not more than nine) discusses a topic in the presence of an audience and under the direction of a moderator.

parallelism The arrangement of words, phrases, or sentences in similar grammatical and stylistic form. Parallel structure can help the speaker emphasize important ideas in the speech.

paraphrase A restatement of someone else's statements or written work that alters the form or phrasing but not the substance of that person's ideas.

pathos The Greek rhetorician Aristotle used this term for persuasive appeals to emotion.

pauses Strategic elements of a speech used to enhance meaning by providing a type of punctuation, emphasizing a point, drawing attention to a key thought, or just allowing listeners a moment to contemplate what is being said.

percentage The quantified portion of a whole.

performance anxiety A feeling of anxiety that occurs the moment one begins to perform.

peripheral processing A mode of processing a persuasive message that does not consider the quality of the speaker's message, but is influenced by such non-content issues as the speaker's appearance or reputation, certain slogans or one-liners, or obvious attempts to manipulate emotions. Peripheral processing of messages occurs when people lack the motivation or the ability to pay close attention to the issues. See also *elaboration likelihood model of persuasion (ELM)* and *central processing.*

persuasive speech Speech whose general purpose is to effect some degree of change in the audience's beliefs, attitudes, values, or behavior.

phrase outline A delivery outline that uses a partial construction of the sentence form of each point, instead of using complete sentences that present the precise wording for each point.

pitch The range of sounds from high to low (or vice versa) determined by the number of vibrations per unit of time; the more vibrations per unit (also called *frequency*), the higher the pitch, and vice versa.

plagiarism The act of using other people's ideas or words without acknowledging the source.

podcast A digital audio recording of a presentation captured and stored in a form accessible via the Internet.

policy proposal presentation An oral presentation that offers recommendations for solving a problem or addressing an issue.

poster presentation A visual presentation on a poster, arranged on a freestanding board, containing a display summarizing a study or an issue for viewing by participants at professional conferences. The speaker prepares brief remarks and remains on hand to answer questions as needed.

preparation anxiety A form of public speaking anxiety (PSA) that arises when the speaker begins to prepare for a speech, at which point he or she might feel overwhelmed at the amount of time and planning required. See also *performance anxiety*.

pre-performance anxiety A form of public speaking anxiety (PSA) that occurs when a speaker begins to rehearse a speech.

pre-preparation anxiety A form of public speaking anxiety (PSA) that arises when a speaker learns he or she must give a speech.

presentation aids Objects, models, pictures, graphs, charts, video, audio, or multimedia used alone or in combination to illustrate speech points.

presentational speaking A form of speaking in which individuals or groups deliver reports addressing colleagues, clients, or customers within a business or professional environment.

preview statement Statement included in the introduction of a speech in which the speaker identifies the main speech points.

primary source Firsthand accounts or direct evidence of the information involved. See also *secondary source*.

problem-cause-solution pattern of arrangement A pattern of organizing speech points so that they demonstrate (1) the nature of the problem, (2) reasons for the problem, and (3) proposed solution(s).

problem-solution pattern A pattern of organizing speech points so that they demonstrate the nature and significance of a problem first, and then provide justification for a proposed solution.

program evaluation presentation A report on a program's mission with a description of its accomplishments and how they were measured, and conclusions on how well or poorly the program has met its stated objectives.

progress report A report that updates clients or principals on developments in an ongoing project.

pronunciation The correct formation of word sounds.

prop Any live or inanimate object used by a speaker as a presentation aid.

propaganda Information represented in such a way as to provoke a desired response.

proposal A type of business or professional presentation in which the speaker provides information needed for decisions related to modifying or adopting a product, procedure, or policy.

prototype A model of a design.

public discourse Open conversation or discussion in a public forum.

public forum Any space (physical or virtual) in which people gather to voice their ideas about public issues.

public speaking A type of communication in which a speaker delivers a message with a specific purpose to an audience of people who are present during the delivery of the speech. Public speaking always includes a speaker who has a reason for speaking, an audience that gives the speaker its attention, and a message that is meant to accomplish a purpose.

public-speaking anxiety (PSA) Fear or anxiety associated with a speaker's actual or anticipated communication to an audience.

quality improvement proposal A report that recommends the adoption of a new (or modified) health practice or policy.

real-time presentation A presentation broadcast at the time of delivery; real-time presentations connect the presenter and the audience live and at the same time. See also *synchronous communication*.

reasoning Drawing inferences or conclusions from evidence.

reasoning by analogy Comparing two similar cases to imply that what is true in one case is true in the other. See also *warrant by analogy*.

receiver The recipient(s) of a source's message.

reckless disregard for the truth A quality of statements made with the awareness that they are false; this form of speech is illegal. See also *slander*.

recorded presentation A presentation in which speaker and audience are separated by time and space and the presentation is stored and played back from a digital medium. See also *asynchronous communication*.

refutation pattern A pattern of organizing speech points in which each main point addresses and then refutes an opposing claim to a speaker's position.

report An oral or written presentation providing systematic and objective description of facts and observations related to business or professional interests.

request for funding presentation A type of oral presentation providing evidence that a project, proposal, or design idea is worth funding; frequently delivered in technical fields such as engineering, computer science, and architecture.

research presentation (scientific talk) A type of oral presentation following the model used in scientific investigations, including an introduction, description of methods, results, and conclusion.

respect To feel or show deferential regard; one of five "ethical ground rules" in public speaking. See also *trustworthiness, responsibility, fairness,* and *civic-mindedness.*

responsibility A charge, trust, or duty for which one is accountable; one of five "ethical ground rules" in public speaking. See also *trustworthiness, respect, fairness,* and *civic-mindedness.*

review-of-the-literature presentation A type of oral presentation in which the speaker reviews the body of research related to a given topic or issue and offers conclusions about the topic based on this research; frequently delivered in social scientific fields.

rhetoric The practice of oratory, or public speaking. More broadly, a term with multiple meanings, all of which relate to aspects of human communication.

rhetorical device A technique of language to achieve a desired effect.

rhetorical question A question that does not invite actual responses but is used to make the listener or the audience anticipate answers from the speaker.

rhetorical situation The circumstances that call for a public response and for the speech itself; in broad terms, consideration of the audience, occasion, and overall speech context when planning a speech.

roast A humorous tribute to a person; one in which a series of speakers jokingly poke fun at the individual being honored.

roman numeral outline An outline format in which main points are enumerated with roman numerals (I, II, III); supporting points with capital letters (A, B, C); third-level points with Arabic numerals (1, 2, 3); and fourth-level points with lowercase letters (a, b, c).

sales proposal (sales pitch) A type of oral presentation that attempts to lead a potential buyer to purchase a service or product described by the presenter.

scale question A closed-ended question that measures the respondent's level of agreement or disagreement with specific issues.

scanning A technique for creating eye contact with audiences; the speaker moves his or her gaze across an audience from one listener to another and from one section to another, pausing to gaze briefly at each individual.

screencast An online presentation that relies on software that captures whatever is displayed on a computer, from text to slides to streaming video.

scientific talk See *research presentation*.

secondary source Information gathered by others; can include published facts and statistics, texts, documents, and any other information not originally collected and generated by the researcher. See also *primary source*.

selective perception A psychological principle that posits that listeners pay attention selectively to certain messages and ignore others.

sentence outline An outline in which each main and supporting point is stated in sentence form and in precisely the way the speaker wants to express the idea; generally used for working outlines.

service learning presentation Presentation in which students report on how they helped to address a need or problem in a community agency or nonprofit organization.

shift report Oral report by a health care worker that concisely relays patient status and needs to incoming caregivers.

simile A figure of speech used to compare one thing with another by using the words "like" or "as" (e.g., "He works like a dog"). See also *figure of speech*.

six-by-six rule Rule of design that suggests using no more than six words per line and six lines or bullet points per slide or other visual aid.

slander Defamatory speech.

slippery slope A fallacy of reasoning in which one instance of an event is offered as leading to a series of events or actions. See also *logical fallacy*.

small group A collection of between three and twenty people.

small group communication Communication involving a small number of people who can see and speak directly with one another, as in a business meeting.

social roles In groups, roles that help facilitate effective group interaction, such as the "harmonizer" and the "gatekeeper." See also *task roles*.

socioeconomic status (SES) A cluster of demographic characteristics of audience members, including income, occupation, and education.

source The source, or sender, who creates the message.

source credibility The level of trust audience members place in a source's credentials and track record for providing accurate information.

source qualifier A brief description of the source's qualifications.

spatial pattern A pattern of organizing main points in order of their physical proximity or direction relative to each other; used when the purpose of a speech is to describe or explain the physical arrangement of a place, a scene, or an object.

speaker credibility The quality that reveals that a speaker has a good grasp of the subject, displays sound reasoning skills, is honest and nonmanipulative, and is genuinely interested in the welfare of audience members; a modern version of ethos.

speaking from manuscript A type of delivery in which the speaker reads the speech verbatim—that is, from prepared written text that contains the entire speech, word for word.

speaking from memory A type of delivery in which the speaker puts the entire speech, word for word, into writing and then commits it to memory.

speaking outline A delivery outline to be used when practicing and actually presenting a speech.

speaking rate The pace at which a speech is delivered. The typical public speech occurs at a rate slightly less than 120 words per minute.

special occasion speech A speech whose general purpose is to entertain, celebrate, commemorate, inspire, or set a social agenda.

specific speech purpose A statement of precisely what the speaker wants the audience to gain from the speech;

need not be articulated in the speech itself but should be firmly set in the speaker's mind. See also *general speech purpose*.

speech of acceptance A speech made in response to receiving an award. Its purpose is to express gratitude for the honor bestowed on the speaker.

speech of inspiration A speech whose purpose is to inspire or motivate the audience to consider positively, reflect on, and sometimes even to act on the speaker's words.

speech of introduction A short speech whose purpose is to prepare or "warm up" audience members for the speaker and to motivate them to listen to what the speaker has to say.

speech of presentation A speech whose purpose is twofold: to communicate the meaning of the award and to explain why the recipient is receiving it.

staff report A presentation that informs managers and other employees of new developments relating to personnel that affect them and their work.

statistics Quantified evidence; data that measure the size or magnitude of something, demonstrate trends, or show relationships with the purpose of summarizing information, demonstrating proof, and making points memorable.

story An account of events. See also *narrative*.

subordinate points Speech points subordinate to others that are thus given relatively less weight. In an outline, they are indicated by their indentation below the more important points.

substantive warrant A line of reasoning in which the speaker justifies the link between claim and evidence by targeting the audience's faith in the speaker's factual evidence; this appeal is based on logos, or the audience's rational thinking on a matter.

supporting points Information (examples, narratives, testimony, and facts and statistics) that clarifies, elaborates, and verifies the speaker's main points.

syllogism A set of propositions to be proved, that lead to a conclusion; a three-part argument that consists of a general case or major premise, a specific case or minor premise, and a conclusion. See also *deductive reasoning*.

symposium A formal meeting at which several speakers deliver short speeches on different aspects of the same topic.

synchronous communication Communication in which people exchange messages simultaneously, in real time. See also *real-time presentation*.

table A systematic grouping of data or other information in column form.

talking head A speaker who remains static, standing stiffly behind a podium, and so resembles a televised shot of a speaker's head and shoulders.

target audience Those individuals within the broader audience who are most likely to be influenced in the direction the speaker seeks.

task roles Types of roles that directly relate to the accomplishment of the objectives and missions of a group. Examples include "recording secretary" and "moderator." See also *social roles*.

testimony Firsthand findings, eyewitness accounts, and opinions by people, both lay (nonexpert) and expert.

thesis statement The central idea of a speech, which serves to connect all the parts of the speech in a single line. The main points, supporting material, and conclusion all relate to the thesis.

toast A brief tribute to a person or an event being celebrated.

topical pattern (categorical pattern) A pattern of organizing main points as subtopics or categories of the speech topic.

topic (mind) mapping A brainstorming technique in which words are laid out in diagram form to show categorical relationships among them; useful for selecting and narrowing a speech topic.

town hall meeting A public forum in which citizens deliberate on issues of importance to the community.

transitions Words, phrases, or sentences that tie speech ideas together and enable a speaker to move smoothly from one point to the next.

trustworthiness The quality of displaying both honesty and dependability; one of five "ethical ground rules" in public speaking. See also *respect, responsibility, fairness,* and *civic-mindedness.*

two-sided message In persuasive speaking, a message that mentions opposing points of view and refutes them. See also *one-sided message.*

values Our most enduring judgments about what is good and bad in life, as shaped by our culture and our unique experiences within it.

video capture software Software used to incorporate video clips into an online presentation.

visualization An exercise for building confidence in which the speaker, while preparing for the speech, closes his or her eyes and envisions a series of positive feelings and reactions that will occur on the day of the speech.

vocal fillers Unnecessary and undesirable sounds or words used by a speaker to cover pauses in a speech or conversation. Examples include "uh," "hmm," "you know," "I mean," and "it's like."

vocal variety The variation of volume, pitch, rate, and pauses to create an effective delivery.

vodcast A podcast with video clips. See also *podcast*.

voice A feature of verbs in written and spoken text that indicates the subject's relationship to the action; verbs can be either active or passive.

volume The relative loudness of a speaker's voice while giving a speech.

voluntary audience As opposed to a captive audience, an audience whose members have chosen to attend.

warrant A line of reasoning that justifies the link between a claim and evidence in the minds of the audience. See also *reasoning*.

warrant ("reasoning") by analogy A line of reasoning in which the speaker justifies the link between claim and evidence by comparing two similar cases and implying that what is true for one case is true for the other.

warrant ("reasoning") by cause A line of reasoning in which the speaker justifies the link between claim and evidence by providing a cause-effect relationship as proof of the claim.

Webinar Real-time presentations, including training sessions, seminars, and other presentations that connect presenters and listeners through their computers or mobile devices, regardless of where they are in the world.

word association A brainstorming technique in which one writes down ideas as they come to mind, beginning with a single word.

working outline A preparation or rough outline using full sentences in which the speaker firms up and organizes main points and develops supporting points to substantiate them.

Notes ●●●●

CHAPTER 1

1. "Why Warren Buffett's Most Valuable Skill Wasn't from a Diploma," Fox on Stocks, December 19, 2012, accessed August 13, 2013 at **www.foxonstocks.com/why-warrenbuffetts-most-valuable0skill-wasn't-from-a-diploma/**.

2. "It Takes More than a Major: Employer Priorities for College Learning and Student Success," Hart Research Associates (on behalf of The Association of American Colleges and Universities), April 10, 2013, **www.aacu.org/leap/documents/2013_EmployerSurvey.pdf**.

3. "Youth Voting/Political Participation," Center for Information and Research on Civic Learning and Engagement (CIRCLE), accessed August 26, 2013, **www.civicyouth.org/ ResearchTopics/research-topics/political-participation-and-voting/**; "Voter Turnout," FairVote/Center for Voting and Democracy, accessed August 26, 2013, **www.fairvote.org/voter-turnout#.Uhtfvhbt7Q0**.

4. For a discussion of Daniel Yankelovich's three-step process by which public judgments occur, see Yankelovich, *Coming to Public Judgment: Making Democracy Work in a Complex World* (Syracuse, NY: Syracuse University Press, 1991).

5. For a discussion of conversation stoppers and rules of engagement, see W. Barnett Pearce, "Toward a National Conversation about Public Issues," in *The Changing Conversation in America: Lectures from the Smithsonian,* eds. William F. Eadie and Paul E. Nelson (Thousand Oaks, CA: Sage, 2002), 16.

6. Robert Perrin, "The Speaking-Writing Connection: Enhancing the Symbiotic Relationship," *Contemporary Education* 65 (1994): 62–64.

7. Kristine Bruss, "Writing for the Ear: Strengthening Oral Style in Manuscript Speeches," *Communication Teacher* 26, no. 2 (April 2012): 76–81.

8. Lloyd F. Bitzer, "The Rhetorical Situation," *Philosophy and Rhetoric* (Winter 1968): 1–14.

CHAPTER 3

1. Graham D. Bodie, "A Racing Heart, Rattling Knees, and Ruminative Thoughts: Defining, Explaining, and Treating Public Speaking Anxiety," *Communication Education* 59 (2010): 70–105.

2. Ralph Behnke and Chris R. Sawyer, "Milestones of Anticipatory Public Speaking Anxiety," *Communication Education* 48 (April 1999): 165–72.

3. Christine Kane, "Overcoming Stage Fright — Here's What to Do," *Christinekane* (blog), April 24, 2007, **http://christinekane.com/blog/overcoming-stage-fright-heres-what-to-do/**.

4. Behnke and Sawyer, "Milestones of Anticipatory Public Speaking Anxiety."

5. David-Paul Pertaub, Mel Slater, and Chris Barker, "An Experiment on Public Speaking Anxiety in Response to Three Different Types of Virtual Audience," *Presence: Teleoperators and Virtual Environments* 11 (2002): 670–78.

6. Joe Ayres, "Coping with Speech Anxiety: The Power of Positive Thinking," *Communication Education* 37 (1988): 289–96; Joe Ayres, "An Examination of the Impact of Anticipated Communication and Communication Apprehension on Negative Thinking, Task-Relevant Thinking, and Recall," *Communication Research Reports* 9 (1992): 3–11.

7. Pamela J. Feldman, Sheldon Cohen, Natalie Hamrick, and Stephen J. Lepore, "Psychological Stress, Appraisal, Emotion, and Cardiovascular Response in a Public Speaking Task," *Psychology and Health* 19 (2004): 353–68; Senqi Hu and Juong-Min Romans-Kroll, "Effects of Positive Attitude toward Giving a Speech on Cardiovascular and Subjective Fear

Responses during Speech on Anxious Subjects," *Perceptual and Motor Skills* 81 (1995): 609–10.

8. Elizabeth Quinn, "Visualization in Sport: Imagery Can Improve Performance," About.com: Sports Medicine, accessed August 29, 2007, **http://sportsmedicine.about.com/cs/sport_psych/a/aa091700a.htm**; Joe Ayres and Tim Hopf, "Visualization: Is It More Than Extra Attention?" *Communication Education* 38 (1989): 1–5; Joe Ayers and Tim Hopf, *Coping with Speech Anxiety* (Norwood, NJ: Ablex, 1993).

9. Joe Ayres, Chia-Fang "Sandy" Hsu, and Tim Hopf, "Does Exposure to Visualization Alter Speech Preparation Processes?" *Communication Research Reports* 17 (2000): 366–74.

10. Ayres and Hopf, "Visualization," 2–3.

11. Herbert Benson and Miriam Z. Klipper, *The Relaxation Response* (New York: HarperCollins, 2000).

12. Laurie Schloff and Marcia Yudkin, *Smart Speaking* (New York: Plume, 1991), 91–92.

13. Lars-Gunnar Lundh, Britta Berg, Helena Johansson, Linda Kjellén Nilsson, Jenny Sandberg, and Anna Segerstedt, "Social Anxiety Is Associated with a Negatively Distorted Perception of One's Own Voice," *Cognitive Behavior Therapy* 31 (2002): 25–30.

CHAPTER 4

1. *Oxford English Dictionary Online*, s.v. "responsibility," accessed June 17, 2013, **www.oed.com/view/Entry/163862?redirectedFrom=responsibility**.

2. Richard L. Johannesen, Kathleen S. Valde, and Karen E. Whedbee, *Ethics in Human Communication* (Long Grove, IL: Waveland Press, 2007).

3. Cited in Edward P. J. Corbett, *Classical Rhetoric for the Modern Student* (New York: Oxford University Press, 1990).

4. Shalom H. Schwartz, "An Overview of the Schwartz Theory of Basic Values," *Online Readings in Psychology and Culture* 2, no. 1 (2012), **http://dx.doi.org/10.9707/2307-0919.1116**.

5. Pew Center for People & the Press, "Trends in American Values: 1987–2012," June 4, 2012, **www.people-press.org/files/legacy-pdf/06-04-12%20Values%20Release.pdf**.

6. Douglas M. Fraleigh and Joseph S. Tuman, *Freedom of Speech in the Marketplace of Ideas* (New York: Bedford/St. Martin's, 1997).

7. W. Gudykunst, S. Ting-Toomey, S. Suweeks, and L. Stewart, *Building Bridges: Interpersonal Skills for a Changing World* (Boston: Houghton Mifflin, 1995), 92.

8. Michael Josephson, *Making Ethical Decisions: The Six Pillars of Character* (Josephson Institute of Ethics, 2002).

9. Ibid.

10. Ibid.

11. Rebecca Moore Howard, "A Plagiarism Pentimento," *Journal of Teaching Writing* 11 (1993): 233.

12. Francie Diep, "Fast Facts about the Japan Earthquake and Tsunami," *Scientific American*, March 14, 2011, **www.scientificamerican.com/article.cfm?id=fast-facts-japan**.

13. U.S. Copyright Office Web site, accessed June 19, 2014, **www.copyright.gov**.

14. U.S. Copyright Office, "Fair Use," accessed July 1, 2013, **www.copyright.gov/fls/fl102.html**.

CHAPTER 5

1. "An ILA Definition of Listening," *Listening Post* 53, no. 1 (1995): 4–5.

2. Laura A. Janusik and Andrew D. Wolvin, "24 Hours in a Day: Listening Update to the Time Studies," *23* (2009): 104–20; see also Richard Eman-

uel, Jim Adams, Kim Baker, E. K. Daufin, Coke Ellington, Elizabeth Fitts et al.,"How College Students Spend Their Time Communicating," *International Journal of Listening* 22 (2008): 13–28.

3. Ibid.

4. Avraham N. Kluger and Keren Zaidel, "Are Listeners Perceived as Leaders?" *International Journal of Listening* 27, no. 2 (2013): 73–84; S. A. Welch and William T. Mickelson, "A Listening Competence Comparison of Working Professionals," *International Journal of Listening* 27, no. 2 (2013): 85–99.

5. Albert H. Hastorf and Hadley Cantril, "They Saw a Game: A Case Study," *Journal of Abnormal and Social Psychology* 49, no. 1 (1954): 129–34; Gordon W. Allport, and Lee J. Postman, "The Basic Psychology of Rumor," *Transactions of the New York Academy of Sciences* 8 (1945): 61–81.

6. Christian Kiewitz, James B. Weaver III, Hans-Bernd Brosius, and Gabriel Weimann, "Cultural Differences in Listening Style Preferences: A Comparison of Young Adults in Germany, Israel, and the United States," *International Journal of Public Opinion Research* 9, no. 3 (1997): 233–47, **search.proquest.com/docview/60068159?accountid=10965**; M. Imhof and L. A. Janusik, "Development and Validation of the Imhof-Janusik Listening Concepts Inventory to Measure Listening Conceptualization Differences between Cultures," *Journal of Intercultural Communication Research* 35, no. 2 (2006): 79–98.

7. Ibid.

8. Thomas E. Anastasi Jr., *Listen! Techniques for Improving Communication Skills* (Boston: CBI Publishing, 1982).

9. Ronald D. Gordon, "Communication, Dialogue, and Transformation," *Human Communication* 9, no. 1 (2006): 17–30.

10. James Floyd, "Provocation: Dialogic Listening as Reachable Goal," *International Journal of Listening* 24 (2010): 170–73.

CHAPTER 6

1. Pablo Briñol and Richard E. Petty, "The History of Attitudes and Persuasion Research," in *Handbook of the History of Social Psychology*, eds. Arie Kruglanski and Wolfgang Stroebe (New York: Psychology Press, 2011).

2. Richard E. Petty and John T. Cacioppo, *Attitudes and Persuasion: Classic and Contemporary Approaches* (Dubuque, IA: Wm. C. Brown, 1981); M. Fishbein and I. Ajzen, *Belief, Attitude, Intention, and Behavior: An Introduction to Theory and Research* (Reading, MA: Addison-Wesley, 1975); I. Ajzen and M. Fishbein, "The Influence of Attitudes on Behavior," in *The Handbook of Attitudes*, eds. Dolores Albarracín, Blair T. Johnson, and Mark P. Zanna (Mahwah, NJ: Erlbaum, 2005), 173–221.

3. Richard E. Petty, S. Christian Wheeler, and Zakary L. Tormala, "Persuasion and Attitude Change," in *Handbook of Psychology, Personality, and Social Psychology*, Vol. 5, eds. Theodore Millon, Melvin Lerner, and Irving B. Weiner (New York: John Wiley & Sons, 2003).

4. *The Stanford Encyclopedia of Philosophy*, s.v. "Belief," Winter 2011 edition, **http://plato.stanford.edu/archives/win2011/entries/belief/**.

5. "Human Values and Nature's Future: Americans' Attitudes on Biological Diversity," BlueStem Communications, accessed January 22, 2014, **http://bluestemcommunications.org/changing-behaviors-not-minds-a-communications-workshop/**.

6. Herbert Simon, *Persuasion in Society*, 2nd ed. (New York: Routledge, 2011).

7. Ibid.

8. Kenneth Burke, *A Rhetoric of Motives* (Berkeley, CA: University of California Press, 1969).

9. See, for example, "Millennials, Gen X and Baby Boomers: Who's Working at Your Company and What Do They Think about Ethics?" Ethics

Resource Center, 2009 National Business Ethics Survey Supplemental Research Brief, http://ethics.org/files/u5/Gen-Diff.pdf; Dennis McCafferty, "Workforce Preview: What to Expect from Gen Z," *Baseline Magazine*, April 4, 2013, **www.baselinemag.com/it-management/slideshows /workforce-preview-what-to-expect-from-gen-z**; "Generations in the Workplace in the United States and Canada," Catalyst, May 1, 2012, **www.catalyst.org/knowledge/generations-workplace-united-states -canada**.

10. Jere R. Behrman and Nevzer Stacey, eds., *The Social Benefits of Education* (Ann Arbor: University of Michigan Press, 2000).

11. Pew Forum on Religion & Public Life, "U.S. Religious Landscape Survey: Religious Affiliation," February 1, 2008, **www.pewforum.org/2008 /02/01/u-s-religious-landscape-survey-religious-affiliation/**.

12. Daniel Canary and Kathryn Dindia, eds., *Sex Differences and Similarities in Communication,* 2nd ed. (Mahwah, NJ: Erlbaum, 2006).

13. Matthew W. Brault, "Americans with Disabilities: 2010," Current Population Reports, U.S. Census Bureau; accessed January 22, 2014, **www .census.gov/content/dam/Census/library/publications/2012/demo /p70-131.pdf**.

14. U.S. Census Bureau, "U.S. Census Quick Facts," accessed December 12, 2014, **http://quickfacts.census.gov/qfd/states/00000.html**; U.S. Census Bureau, "New Census Bureau Interactive Map Shows Languages Spoken in America," August 6, 2013, **www.census.gov/newsroom /press-releases/2013/cb13-143.html**.

15. Inter-University Consortium for Political and Social Research, "World Values Survey, 1981–1984 and 1990–1993" (Irvine, CA: Social Science Data Archives, University Libraries, University of California, 1997). The 1990 World Values Survey covers four Asian countries (China, India, Japan, and South Korea) and eighteen Western countries.

16. Rushworth M. Kidder, *Shared Values for a Troubled World: Conversations with Men and Women of Conscience* (San Francisco: Jossey-Bass, 1994).

CHAPTER 8

1. Richard F. Corlin, "The Coming Golden Age of Medicine," *Vital Speeches of the Day* 68, no. 18 (2002).

2. Jonathan Drori, "Every Pollen Grain Has a Story," Filmed February 2010, TED video, 7:12, **www.ted.com/talks/jonathan_drori_every_pollen _grain_has_a_story.html**.

3. Quoted in Katharine Q. Seelye, "Congressman Offers Bill to Ban Cloning of Humans," *New York Times*, March 6, 1997, sec. A.

4. Mark Turner, *The Literary Mind* (New York: Oxford University Press, 1996).

5. Melinda French Gates, "Raising the Bar on College Completion," Keynote Address, American Association of Community Colleges, April 20, 2010, **www.gatesfoundation.org/media-center/speeches/2010/04 /raising-the-bar-on-college-completion**.

6. Robert Lehrman, *The Political Speechwriter's Companion: A Guide for Writers and Speakers* (Washington, DC: CQ Press, 2010), quoted in Steven D. Cohen, "The Art of Public Narrative: Teaching Students How to Construct Memorable Anecdotes," *Communication Teacher* 25, no. 4, (2011): 197–204, doi: 10.1080/17404622.2011.601726.

7. Jim Carrey, Commencement Address, Maharishi University of Management, May 24, 2014, **www.mum.edu/whats-happening/graduation -2014/full-jim-carrey-address-video-and-transcript/**.

8. Derek P. Ellerman, "Testimony to Subcommittee on Human Rights and Wellness, Committee on Government Reform," U.S. House of Representatives, July 8, 2004, **www.polarisproject.org/what-we-do/policy**

-advocacy/national-policy/congressional-testimony/congressional
-testimony-2004-derek-ellerman.

9. Yaacov Schul and Ruth Mayo, "Two Sources Are Better Than One: The Effects of Ignoring One Message on Using a Different Message from the Same Source," *Journal of Experimental Social Psychology* 35 (1999): 327–45; Mike Allen, Rebecca Bruflat, Renée Fucilla, Michael Kramer, Steve McKellips, Daniel J. Ryan et al., "Testing the Persuasiveness of Evidence: Combining Narrative and Statistical Forms," *Communication Research Reports* 17 (2000): 331–36, cited in R. A. Reynolds and J. L. Reynolds, "Evidence," in *The Persuasion Handbook: Developments in Theory and Practice*, eds. James P. Dillard and Michael. Pfau (Thousand Oaks, CA: Sage, 2002), 427–44, doi: 10.4135/9781412976046.n22.

10. Rodney A. Reynolds and J. Lynn Reynolds, "Evidence," in *The Persuasion Handbook: Developments in Theory and Practice*, eds. James P. Dillard and Michael Pfau (Thousand Oaks, CA: Sage, 2002), 427–44, doi: 10.4135/9781412976046.n22.

11. "A380," Airbus, accessed July 7, 2013, **www.airbus.com/aircraft families/passengeraircraft/a380family/**.

12. Cited in American Lung Association, *State of Tobacco Control 2014*, January 22, 2014, **www.stateoftobaccocontrol.org**.

13. "State and County QuickFacts," U.S. Census Bureau, accessed July 7, 2013, last revised January 6, 2014, **http://quickfacts.census.gov/qfd /states/08000.html**.

14. "State Unemployment Rates Decline in May 2013," National Conference of State Legislatures, January 28, 2014, **www.ncsl.org/issues -research/labor/state-unemploymentupdate.aspx**.

15. "Statistics and Facts about Facebook," Statista.com, February 11, 2015, **www.statista.com/topics/751/facebook/**.

16. Chuck Marr and Chye-Ching Huang, "Tax Foundation Figures Do Not Represent Typical Households' Tax Burdens," Center on Budget and Policy Priorities, April 2, 2013, **www.cbpp.org/cms/index.cfm?fa =view&id=3946**.

17. Roger Pielke Jr., "The Cherry Pick," Ogmius: Newsletter for the Center for Science and Technology Research 8 (2004), **http://sciencepolicy .colorado.edu/ogmius/archives/issue_8/intro.html**.

CHAPTER 9

1. Steve Coffman, "So What Now: The Future for Librarians," *Online Searcher*, January/February 2013, **www.infotoday.com/OnlineSearcher /Articles/Features/So-Now-What-The-Future-for-Librarians-86856 .shtml**.

2. Elizabeth E. Kirk, "Information and Its Counterfeits," Sheridan Libraries of Johns Hopkins University, 2001, **www.library.jhu.edu/researchhelp /general/evaluating/counterfeit.html**.

3. Gregory Ferenstein, "Jimmy Wales, Wikipedia Go to College," *Fast Company*, July 6, 2011, **www.fastcompany.com/1765182/jimmy-wales -wikipedia-go-college**.

CHAPTER 10

1. Ralph Underwager and Hollida Wakefield, "The Taint Hearing," paper presented at the 13th Annual Symposium in Forensic Psychology, Vancouver, BC, April 17, 1997, **www.ipt-forensics.com/journal/volume10 /j10_7.htm#en0**.

2. Institute for Writing and Rhetoric, "Sources and Citation at Dartmouth College," produced by the Committee on Sources, May 2008, **https:// writing-speech.dartmouth.edu/learning/materials/sources-and -citations-dartmouth**.

CHAPTER 11

1. Gordon H. Bower, "Organizational Factors in Memory," *Cognitive Psychology* 1 (1970): 18–46.

2. Hermann Ebbinghaus, *On Memory: A Contribution to Experimental Psychology* (New York: Teachers College, 1813); Murray Glanzer and Anita R. Cunitz, "Two Storage Mechanisms in Free Recall," *Journal of Verbal Learning and Verbal Behavior* 5 (1966): 351–60.

3. Ernest Thompson, "An Experimental Investigation of the Relative Effectiveness of Organization Structure in Oral Communication," *Southern Speech Journal* 26 (1960): 59–69; C. Spicer and R. E. Bassett, "The Effects of Organization on Learning from an Informative Message," *Southern Speech Journal* 41 (1976): 290–99.

4. Raymond G. Smith, "Effects of Speech Organization upon Attitudes of College Students," *Speech Monographs* 18 (1951): 292–301.

5. Harry Sharp Jr. and Thomas McClung, "Effects of Organization on the Speaker's Ethos," *Speech Monographs* 33 (1966): 182ff; Eldon E. Baker, "The Immediate Effects of Perceived Speaker Disorganization on Speaker Credibility and Audience Attitude Change in Persuasive Speaking," *Western Speech* 29 (1965): 148–61.

CHAPTER 12

1. Raymond G. Smith, "Effects of Speech Organization upon Attitudes of College Students," *Speech Monographs* 18 (1951): 547–49; Ernest Thompson, "An Experimental Investigation of the Relative Effectiveness of Organizational Structure in Oral Communication," *Southern Speech Journal* 26 (1960): 59–69.

2. "Life on the Internet Timeline," Public Broadcasting System, accessed April 3, 2000, **www.pbs.org/internet/timeline/index.html**.

CHAPTER 13

1. Mark B. McClellan, Fifth annual David A. Winston lecture, National Press Club, Washington, DC, October 20, 2003, **www.fda.gov/news events/speeches/speecharchives/ucm053609.htm**.

CHAPTER 14

1. Jeremey Donovan, *How to Deliver a TED Talk* (CreateSpace Independent Publishing Platform, 2012).

2. William Safire, *Lend Me Your Ears: Great Speeches in History* (New York: Norton, 1992), 676.

3. Bas Andeweg and Jap de Jong, "May I Have Your Attention? Exordial Techniques in Informative Oral Presentations," *Technical Communication Quarterly* 7, no. 3 (Summer 1998): 271–84.

4. Nancy Duarte, *Harvard Business Review Guide to Persuasive Presentations* (Boston: Harvard Business Review Press, 2012).

5. James Oliver, "Teach Every Child about Food," Filmed February 2010, TED video, 21:53, **www.ted.com/talks/jamie_oliver**.

6. Marvin Runyon, "No One Moves the Mail Like the U.S. Postal Service," *Vital Speeches of the Day* 61, no. 2 (1994): 52–55.

7. Robert L. Darbelnet, "U.S. Roads and Bridges: Highway Funding at a Crossroads," *Vital Speeches of the Day* 63, no. 12 (1997): 379.

8. Holger Kluge, "Reflections on Diversity," *Vital Speeches of the Day* 63, no. 6 (1997): 171–72.

9. Elpidio Villarreal, "Choosing the Right Path," *Vital Speeches of the Day* 72, no. 26 (2007): 784–86.

10. Hillary Rodham Clinton, "Women's Rights Are Human Rights," speech delivered to the United Nations Fourth World Conference on Women, Beijing, China, September 5, 1995.

CHAPTER 15

1. Kristine Bruss, "Writing for the Ear: Strengthening Oral Style in Manuscript Speeches," *Communication Teacher*, 26, no. 2 (April 2012): 76–81.

2. Peggy Noonan, *Simply Speaking: How to Communicate Your Ideas with Style, Substance, and Clarity* (New York: Regan Books, 1998), 51.

3. Dan Hooley, "The Lessons of the Ring," *Vital Speeches of the Day* 70, no. 20 (2004): 660–63.

4. Sheryl Sandberg, "Why We Have Too Few Women Leaders," Filmed December 2010, TED video, 14:58, **www.ted.com/talks/sheryl _sandberg_why_we_have_too_few_women_leaders.html**.

5. Susan T. Fiske and Shelley E. Taylor, "Vivid Information Is More Easily Recalled Than Dull or Pallid Stimuli," *Social Cognition,* 2nd ed. (New York: McGraw Hill), quoted in Jennifer Jerit and Jason Barabas, "Bankrupt Rhetoric: How Misleading Information Affects Knowledge about Social Security," *Public Opinion Quarterly* 70, no. 3 (2006): 278–304.

6. Loren J. Naidoo and Robert G. Lord, "Speech Imagery and Perceptions of Charisma: The Mediating Role of Positive Affect," *Leadership Quarterly* 19, no. 3 (2008): 283–96.

7. Ibid; phrase taken from President Franklin Delano Roosevelt's 1933 inaugural address.

8. L. Clemetson and J. Gordon-Thomas, "Our House Is on Fire," *Newsweek*, June 11, 2001, 50.

9. Andrew C. Billings, "Beyond the Ebonics Debate: Attitudes about Black and Standard American English," *Journal of Black Studies* 36 (2005): 68–81.

10. Sylvie Dubois, "Sounding Cajun: The Rhetorical Use of Dialect in Speech and Writing," *American Speech* 77, no. 3 (2002): 264–87.

11. Gloria Anzaldúa, "Entering into the Serpent," in *The St. Martin's Handbook,* eds. Andrea Lunsford and Robert Connors, 3rd ed. (New York: St. Martin's Press, 1995), 25.

12. P. H. Matthews, *The Concise Oxford Dictionary of Linguistics* (New York: Oxford University Press, 1997).

13. Cited in William Safire, *Lend Me Your Ears: Great Speeches in History* (New York: Norton, 1992), 22.

14. "Barack Obama's New Hampshire Primary Speech," *New York Times,* January 8, 2008, **www.nytimes.com/2008/01/08/us/politics/08text -obama.html?r=0**.

CHAPTER 16

1. James A. Winans, *Public Speaking* (New York: Century, 1925). Professor Winans was among the first Americans to contribute significantly to the study of rhetoric. His explanation of delivery is considered by many to be the best coverage of the topic in the English language. His perspective infuses this chapter.

CHAPTER 17

1. MaryAnn Cunningham Florez, "Improving Adult ESL Learners' Pronunciation Skills," National Clearinghouse for ESL Literacy Education, 1998, accessed July 16, 2005, **www.cal.org/caela/esl_resources/digests /Pronun.html**.

2. Susan Berkley, "Microphone Tips," *Great Speaking* 4, no. 7 (2002), accessed July 16, 2005, **www.antion.com/ezine/v4n7.txt**.

CHAPTER 18

1. C. F. Bond and the Global Deception Research Team, "A World of Lies," *Journal of Cross-Cultural Psychology* 37 (2006): 60–74; Timothy R. Levine, Kelli Jean K. Asada, and Hee Sun Park, "The Lying Chicken

and the Gaze Avoidant Egg: Eye Contact, Deception, and Causal Order," *Southern Communication Journal* 71 (2006): 401–11.

2. Robert Rivlin and Karen Gravelle, *Deciphering the Senses: The Expanding World of Human Perception* (New York: Simon & Schuster, 1998), 98; see also Anne Warfield, "Do You Speak Body Language?" *Training & Development* 55, no. 4 (2001): 60.

3. Eva Krumburger, "Effects of Dynamic Attributes of Smiles in Human and Synthetic Faces: A Simulated Job Interview Setting," *Journal of Nonverbal Behavior* 33 (2009): 1–15.

4. Alissa Melinger and Willem M. Levelt, "Gesture and the Communicative Intention of the Speaker," *Gesture* 4 (2004): 119–41.

5. Mike Allen, Paul L. Witt, and Lawrence R. Wheeless, "The Role of Teacher Immediacy as a Motivational Factor in Student Learning: Using Meta-Analysis to Test a Causal Model," *Communication Education* 55, no. 6 (2006): 21–31.

CHAPTER 19

1. Richard E. Mayer, *The Multimedia Principle* (New York: Cambridge University Press, 2001).

2. See discussion of the redundancy effect in Richard E. Mayer, ed., *The Cambridge Handbook of Multimedia Learning* (New York: Cambridge University Press, 2005).

3. Gary Jones, "Message First: Using Films to Power the Point," *Business Communication Quarterly* 67, no. 1 (2004): 88–91.

4. Kulwadee M. Axtell, "The Effect of Presentation Software on Classroom Verbal Interaction and on Student Retention of Higher Education Lecture Content," *Journal of Technology in Teaching and Learning* 4, no. 1 (2008): 21–23.

CHAPTER 20

1. Nancy Duarte, "Avoiding the Road to Powerpoint Hell," *Wall Street Journal,* January 22, 2011, **www.wsj.com**.

2. Ibid.

3. Ibid.

4. Edward Tufte, *The Visual Display of Quantitative Information* (Cheshire, CT: Graphics Press, 2001); Edward Tufte, "PowerPoint Is Evil," *Wired* 11 (2003), **www.wired.com/wired/archive/11.09/ppt2_pr.html**.

5. Ronald Larson, "Slide Composition for Electronic Presentations," *Journal of Educational Computing Research,* 31, no. 1 (2004): 61–76.

CHAPTER 21

1. D. Cyphert, "Presentation Technology in the Age of Electronic Eloquence: From Visual Aid to Visual Rhetoric," *Communication Education* 56, no. 2 (2007): 168–92; D. Cyphert, "The Problem of PowerPoint: Visual Aid or Visual Rhetoric?" *Business Communication Quarterly* 67, no. 1 (2004): 80–84.

2. J. Thomas, "PowerPoint Is Not the Problem with Presentations Today," March 21, 2010, *Presentation Advisors,* **http://blog.presentationadvisors .com/presentationadvisors/2010/03/powerpoint-is-not-the-problem -with-presentations.html**.

CHAPTER 22

1. Katherine E. Rowan subdivides informative communication into informatory discourse, in which the primary aim is to represent reality by increasing an audience's awareness of some phenomenon; and explanatory discourse, with the aim to represent reality by deepening understanding. See Katherine E. Rowan, "Informing and Explaining Skills:

Theory and Research on Informative Communication," in *Handbook of Communication and Social Interaction Skills*, eds. John O. Greene and Brant R. Burleson, (Mahwah, NJ: Erlbaum, 2003), 403–38.

2. Tina Blythe et al., *The Teaching for Understanding Guide* (Hoboken, NJ: Jossey-Bass, 1997); Kenneth D. Frandsen and Donald A. Clement, "The Functions of Human Communication in Informing: Communicating and Processing Information," in *Handbook of Rhetorical and Communication Theory*, eds. Carroll C. Arnold and John Waite Bowers (Needham, MA: Allyn & Bacon, 1984), 334.

3. Vickie K. Sullivan, "Public Speaking: The Secret Weapon in Career Development," *USA Today*, May 2005, 24.

4. Nick Morgan, "Two Rules for a Successful Presentation," *Harvard Business Review* Blog ("Communication"), May 14, 2010, **hbr.org/2010/05 /two-rules-for-a-successful-pre**; Harry E. Chambers, *Effective Communication Skills for Scientific and Technical Professionals* (Cambridge, MA: Perseus Publishing, 2001).

5. Howard K. Battles and Charles Packard, *Words and Sentences*, bk. 6 (Lexington, MA: Ginn & Company, 1984), 459.

CHAPTER 23

1. Carolyn W. Sherif, Muzafer Sherif, and Roger E. Nebergall, *Attitude and Attitude Change: The Social Judgment-Involvement Approach* (Philadelphia: W. B. Saunders, 1965).

2. W. Hart, Dolores Albarracín, A. H. Eagly, I. Brechan, M. J. Lindberg, and L. Merrill, "Feeling Validated versus Being Correct: A Meta-Analysis of Selective Exposure to Information," *Psychological Bulletin* 135 (2009): 555–88.

3. Russel H. Fazio, "How Do Attitudes Guide Behavior?" in *The Handbook of Motivation and Cognition: Foundations of Social Behavior*, eds. Richard M. Sorrentino and E. Tory Higgins (New York: Guilford Press, 1986).

4. With thanks to Carolyn Clark, Salt Lake Community College, for this comment.

5. Winston Churchill, "We Shall Fight on the Beaches," speech delivered to the House of Commons, June 4, 1940, The Churchill Centre and Museum at the Churchill War Rooms, **www.winstonchurchill.org/learn /speeches/speeches-of-winston-churchill/128-we-shall-fight-on -the-beaches**.

6. John S. Nelson, "Emotions as Reasons in Public Arguments," *Poroi* 4, no. 1 (2005): 1–26, doi: 10.13008/2151-2957.1028.

7. For good reviews of the literature on source credibility in general, see Richard M. Perloff, *The Dynamics of Persuasion* (Hillsdale, NJ: Erlbaum, 1993); and Dominic A. Infante, Andrew S. Rancer, and Deanna F. Womack, *Building Communication Theory*, 4th ed. (Prospect Heights, IL: Waveland Press, 2003).

8. Joseph R. Priester and Richard E. Petty, "Source Attributions and Persuasion: Perceived Honesty as a Determinant of Message Scrutiny," *Personality and Social Psychology Bulletin* 21 (1995): 637–54.

9. For an extensive review of the history of the field of communication from the classical period to the present era, see Infante, Rancer, and Womack, *Building Communication Theory*.

10. Ojenike Bolatito, "Linkage between Persuasion Principles and Advertising," *New Media and Mass Communication* 8 (2012): 7–11.

11. Susan T. Fiske, "Core Social Motivations: Views from the Couch, Consciousness, Classroom, Computers, and Collectives," in *Handbook of Motivation Science*, eds. James Y. Shah and Wendi L. Garner (New York: Guilford Press, 2008).

12. Susan T. Fiske, *Social Beings: A Core Motives Approach to Social Psychology* (New York: Wiley, 2004).

13. Richard Petty and John T. Cacioppo, "The Elaboration Likelihood Model of Persuasion," in *Advances in Experimental Social Psychology*, ed. L. Berkowitz (San Diego, CA: Academic Press, 1986), vol. 19: 123–205; Richard Petty and Duane T. Wegener, "Matching versus Mismatching Attitude Functions: Implications for Scrutiny of Persuasive Messages," *Personality and Social Psychology Bulletin* 24 (1998): 227–40.

CHAPTER 24

1. The model of argument presented here follows Stephen Toulmin, *The Uses of Argument* (New York: Cambridge University Press, 1958), as described in James C. McCroskey, *An Introduction to Rhetorical Communication,* 6th ed. (Englewood Cliffs, NJ: Prentice Hall, 1993).

2. Annette T. Rottenberg and Donna Haisty Winchell, *Elements of Argument*, 10th ed. (New York: Bedford/St. Martin's, 2012), 24–25.

3. Ibid.

4. Austin J. Freeley, *Argumentation and Debate*, 8th ed. (Belmont, CA: Wadsworth, 1993), 158.

5. Mike Allen, "Comparing the Persuasive Effectiveness of One- and Two-Sided Messages," in *Persuasion: Advances through Meta-Analysis*, ed. Mike Allen and Raymond W. Preiss (Cresskill, NJ: Hampton Press, 1998), 87–98.

6. James C. McCroskey, *An Introduction to Rhetorical Communication*, 9th ed. (Englewood Cliffs, NJ: Prentice Hall, 2005).

7. Herbert W. Simons, *Persuasion in Society*, 2nd ed. (New York: Routledge, 2011).

8. S. Morris Engel, *With Good Reason: An Introduction to Informal Fallacies*, 6th ed. (Boston: Bedford/St. Martin's, 2000), 191.

9. Alan H. Monroe, *Principles and Types of Speeches* (Chicago: Scott, Foresman, 1935).

10. C. Ilie, "Strategies of Refutation by Definition: A Pragma-Rhetorical Approach to Refutations in a Public Speech," in *Pondering on Problems of Argumentation: Twenty Essays on Theoretical Issues*, ed. F. H. van Eemeren and B. Garssen (New York: Springer Science+Business Media, 2009), doi: 10.1007/978-1-4020-9165-0_4.

CHAPTER 25

1. Roger E. Axtell, *Do's and Taboos of Public Speaking: How to Get Those Butterflies Flying in Formation* (New York: Wiley, 1992), 150.

2. Barack Obama, "Remarks by the President at White House Correspondents' Dinner," May 3, 2014, **www.whitehouse.gov/the-press -office/2014/05/03/remarks-president-white-house-correspondents -dinner**.

CHAPTER 26

1. Sheri Jeavons, "Webinars That Wow: How to Deliver a Dynamic Webinar," Webinar hosted by Citrix GoToMeeting, December, 12 2011.

2. Kami Griffiths and Chris Peters, "10 Steps for Planning a Successful Webinar," TechSoup, January 27, 2009, **www.techsoup.org/learning center/training/page/1252.cfm**; Chris Peters and Kami Griffiths, "10 Steps for Planning a Successful Webinar," TechSoup, January 31, 2012, **www.techsoup.org/support/articles-and-how-tos/10-steps-for -planning-a-successful-webinar**.

3. Ken Molay, "Best Practices for Webinars," Adobe Connect, **http://www images.adobe.com/www.adobe.com/content/dam/Adobe/en /products/adobeconnect/pdfs/web-conferencing-best-practices -webinars-wp.pdf**.

4. Patricia Fripp, "15 Tips for Webinars: How to Add Impact When You Present Online," eLearn Magazine, July 7, 2009, **elearnmag.acm.org /featured.cfm?aid=1595445**.

5. Ibid.

CHAPTER 27

1. Discussion of group roles based on Dan O'Hair and Mary Wiemann, *Real Communication*, 3rd ed. (New York: Bedford/St. Martin's, 2015), 265; C. M. Anderson, B. L. Riddle, and M. M. Martin, "Socialization in Groups," in *Handbook of Group Communication Theory and Research*, ed. Lawrence R. Frey, Dennis S. Gouran, and Marshall Scott Poole (Thousand Oaks, CA: Sage, 1999), 139–63; A. J. Salazar, "An Analysis of the Development and Evolution of Roles in the Small Group," *Small Group Research* 27 (1996): 475–503; K. D. Benne and P. Sheats, "Functional Roles of Group Members," *Journal of Social Issues* 4 (1948): 41–49.

2. W. Park, "A Comprehensive Empirical Investigation of the Relationships among Variables of the Groupthink Model," *Journal of Organizational Behavior* 21 (2000): 874–87; D. T. Miller and K. R. Morrison, "Expressing Deviant Opinions: Believing You Are in the Majority Helps," *Journal of Experimental Social Psychology* 45, no. 4 (2009): 740–47.

3. Irving Lester Janis, *Groupthink: Psychological Studies of Policy Decisions and Fiascoes* (Berkeley: University of California Press, 1982).

4. C. Pavitt, "Theorizing about the Group Communication-Leadership Relationship," in *Handbook of Group Communication Theory and Research,* ed. Frey, Gouran, and Poole, 313–334 ; D. S. Gouran, "Communication Skills for Group Decision Making," in *Handbook of Communication and Social Interaction Skills,* ed. J. O. Greene and B. R. Burleson (Mahwah, NJ: Erlbaum, 2003), 835–870.

5. Ibid.

6. Charles R. Schwenk, *Organizational Behavior and Human Decision Processes* 47, no. 1 (October 1990): 161–76.

7. L. Richard Hoffman and Norman R. F. Maier, "Valence in the Adoption of Solutions by Problem-Solving Groups: Concept, Method, and Results," *Journal of Abnormal and Social Psychology* 69 (1964): 264–71.

8. John Dewey, *How We Think* (Boston: D.C. Heath, 1950).

CHAPTER 28

1. Lin Kroeger, *The Complete Idiot's Guide to Successful Business Presentation* (New York: Alpha Books, 1997), 113.

CHAPTER 29

1. For a review, see Priscilla S. Rogers, "Distinguishing Public and Presentational Speaking," *Management Communication Quarterly* 2 (1988): 102–15; Frank E. X. Dance, "What Do You Mean 'Presentational' Speaking?" *Management Communication Quarterly* 1 (1987): 270–81.

2. Stephen Shiffman, "Ten Tips Guaranteed to Improve Sales," *American Salesman* 55 (2010): 28–30.

3. Ibid.

4. Sharon Cunningham, "Progress Reports," *Best's Review* (November 2010): 54.

CHAPTER 30

1. Several points derived from Robert Anholt, *Dazzle 'Em with Style: The Art of Oral Scientific Presentation,* 2nd ed. (New York: Academic Press, 2010).

2. Office of Naval Research, "Tips for Preparing and Delivering Scientific Talks and Using Visual Aids," modified January 1, 2001, **www.au.af.mil /au/awc/awcgate/navy/onr_navyspeakingtips.pdf**.

CHAPTER 31

1. With thanks to Professor Calvin Young, Fullerton College, for his input.
2. Robert Anholt, *Dazzle 'Em with Style: The Art of Oral Scientific Presentation*, 2nd ed. (New York: Academic Press, 2005).

CHAPTER 32

1. Deanna P. Daniels, "Communicating across the Curriculum and in the Disciplines: Speaking in Engineering," *Communication Education* 51 (July 2002): 3.
2. Deanna P. Dannels, "Features of Success in Engineering Design Presentations: A Call for Relational Genre Knowledge," *Journal of Business and Technical Communication* 23, no. 4 (2009): 399-427, doi: 10.1177/1050651909338790.
3. H. J. Scheiber, "The Nature of Oral Presentations: A Survey of Scientific, Technical, and Managerial Presentations," *IPCC 92 Santa Fe. Crossing Frontiers. Conference Record* (September 29–October 3, 1992): 95–98, doi: 10.1109/IPCC.1992.672998.

CHAPTER 33

1. James M. Henslin, *Sociology: A Down-to-Earth Approach,* 12th ed. (Boston: Pearson, 2013).
2. Peter Redman and Wendy Maples, *Good Essay Writing: A Social Sciences Guide,* 4th ed. (Thousand Oaks, CA: Sage, 2011).

CHAPTER 35

1. Rick Sullivan and Noel McIntosh, "Delivering Effective Lectures," ReproLinePlus December 2014, **www.reproline.jhu.edu/english/6read/6training/lecture/delivering_lecture.htm**.

CHAPTER 36

1. With thanks to Patricia Gowland, RN, MSN, OCN, CCRC, Executive Director of Cancer Research and Patient Navigation, Vanguard Health, Chicago, and Associate Director of Clinical Research, University of Illinois at Chicago Cancer Center, for her expert counsel and review of presentation types.
2. J. M. Brown and N. A. Schmidt, "Strategies for Making Oral Presentations about Clinical Issues: Part I. At the Workplace," *Journal of Continuing Education in Nursing* 40, no. 4 (2009): 152–53, accessed January 19, 2012, CINAHL with Full Text, EBSCOhost.

APPENDIX B

1. Patricia Nelson, "Handling Questions and Answers," Toastmasters International, Edmonton and Area, revised November 3, 1999, **www.ecn.ab.ca/toast/qa.html**.
2. Diane DiResta, *Knockout Presentations: How to Deliver Your Message with Power, Punch, and Pizzazz* (Worcester, MA: Chandler House Press, 1998), 236.
3. Ibid., 237.
4. Lillian Wilder, *Talk Your Way to Success* (New York: Eastside Publishing, 1986), 279.

APPENDIX C

1. Patricia Nelson, "Handling Questions and Answers," Toastmasters International, Edmonton and Area, revised November 3, 1999, **www.ecn.ab.ca/toast/qa.html**.
2. Daria Price Bowman, *Presentations: Proven Techniques for Creating Presentations that Get Results* (Holbrook, MA: Adams Media, 1998), 177.

3. Oklahoma Society of CPAs (OSCPA), "Tips for Successful Media Interviewing," accessed June 10, 2006, **www.oscpa.com/Content/page757**.

APPENDIX D

1. E. Flege, J. M. Munro, and I. R. A. McKay, "Factors Affecting Strength of Perceived Foreign Accent in a Second Language," *Journal of the Acoustical Society of America* 97 (1995): 312.
2. The content in this section is based on Robbin Crabtree and Robert Weissberg, *ESL Students in the Public Speaking Classroom*, 2nd ed. (Boston: Bedford/St. Martin's, 2003), 23.
3. M. C. Florez, "Improving Adult ESL Learners' Pronunciation Skills," *National Clearinghouse for ESL Literacy Education*, 1998, **www.cal.org/NCLE/DIGESTS/Pronun.htm**.
4. Ibid.
5. Robert Anholt, *Dazzle 'Em with Style: The Art of Oral Scientific Presentation* (New York: W. H. Freeman, 1994), 156.

Index ● ● ● ●

abstract, in poster presentation, 228

abstract language, 118

academic articles, review of, 239

academic debate, 226–27

acceptance, speeches of, 193–94

action step, in motivated sequence, 186

active listening, 29, 30–31

active voice, 120–21

affirmative side, in debate, 227

after-dinner speeches, 196

agenda, for group communication, 210

Agnew, Spiro, 123

agora (public square), 4. *See also* forum.

alliteration, 122–23

American Psychological Association. *See* APA documentation system

analogy(ies), 119–20
    in informative speech, 160–61
    reasoning by, 180
    warrant by, 178

anaphora, 122

anecdotes, 55–56

anti-group roles, 211

antithesis, 123

anxiety
    confidence-boosting strategies for minimizing, 16–18
    feedback and, 19–20
    movement for minimizing, 19
    points of onset of, 15–16
    relaxation for minimizing, 18–19
    sources of, 14–15
    stop-time technique for, 15–16

APA documentation system, 252–56

architecture design review, 237

argument(s)
    addressing other side of, 180–82
    claims in, 175
    defined, 171
    in debates, 227–28
    dialectical inquiry, 212
    in persuasive speeches, 174–75

Aristotle, 4, 20, 169–71, 177
    persuasive appeals, and, 169–71

Armstrong, Neil, 123

arrangement, as canon of rhetoric, 4. *See also* organization of speech

articles. *See also* citations; documentation systems
    recording and citing, 73

articulation, 132–33
    by non-native English speakers, 269

arts and humanities courses, presentations in, 240–43

asynchronous communication, 206

attention step, in motivated sequence, 186

attire, appropriate in speeches. *See* dress (attire)

attitudes, of audience, 34

attitude scales (scale questions), 43

audience. *See also* audience analysis
    age and, 37–38
    attitudes toward topic and, 34
    captive, 37
    central processing by, 173, 174
    common ground with, 111
    cultural differences in, 38, 40–42
    demographics of, 9, 37–40
    engagement with, 126
    inclusion of, 6
    income, of audience, 38–39
    interviews and surveys of, 42–44
    mixed, 230
    motivation of, 171–74
    peripheral processing by, 173–74
    persuasive strategies for different types of, 181–82
    psychology of, 34–37
    respecting values of, 21
    target, 37
    types of, 181–82
    types in workplace, 231
    voluntary, 37

audience analysis
    definition of, 9, 34
    demographics and, 37–40
    for group presentations, 214
    perception of sources in, 72

audience-centered perspective, 34

audio clips, 141, 143, 151

averages, statistical, 58

balance, in organization, 84

bar graphs, 140–41, 142

basic sales technique, 221

beliefs, of audience, 34

Bing, 48

blogs
as information sources, 67, 70
oral citations of, 76

body language
and delivery of speech, 134–36
online, 205
on television, 265

body of speech, 11, 12, 80

boldface, in presentation aids, 147

books, citation of, 73. *See also* citations; documentation systems

brainstorming, 47–48, 49

breathing
anxiety management and, 18–19
voice projection and, 130

Buffet, Warren, on public speaking, 2

business and professional presentations, 218–23

call to action, 115–16, 180

canned speeches, 196

canons of rhetoric, 4

captive audience, 37

careers, public speaking in, 2–3

Carrey, Jim, 56

case conference, in nursing and allied health courses, 247

case study
in classroom assignments, 223
clinical, 246

categorical pattern of arrangement, 93–94

causal (cause-effect) pattern of arrangement, 90–92

causal reasoning, 180

cause, warrant by, 178

celebration, special occasion speeches of, 192

central idea (thesis statement), 10, 50–51, 54

"chartjunk," 146

charts, as presentation aid, 141

cherry-picking, 59

Chicago Manual of Style documentation system, 250–52

chronological pattern of arrangement, 89–90

Churchill, Winston, and use of pathos, 170

Cicero, Marcus Tullius, 4

citations. *See also* documentation systems; specific systems
in oral delivery, 24–26, 59, 70–72
mechanical delivery of, 72
sample of, 72–73, 76–77
reasons for using, 70

claims, 175–76
in argument, 175
types of, 175–76

clichés, 119

Clinton, Hillary Rodham, 115–16

closed-end questions, 42–43

co-culture, of audience, 38

code-switching, 120

coherence, of organization, 84

colloquial expressions, 121

color
in presentation aids, 147
subjective interpretations of, 148

commemoration, special occasion speeches of, 192

common knowledge, 24–25

communication
asynchronous, 206
dialogic, 32
in groups, 210–13
in informative speech, 159–61
mediated, 265–66
nonverbal. *See* body language
process of, 7–8
public speaking as form of, 6–8
synchronous, 206
types of, 6–7

community service learning project, 229

comparative advantage pattern of arrangement, 186–87

conclusion, of speech 11, 12, 80, 114–16

concrete language, 118–20

confidence
in public speaking, 126
strategies for boosting, 16–18

conflict, in group communication, 211

connectives. *See* transition(s)

connotative meaning, 121

context, of speech, 8, 44

coordinate points, 11, 12, 82

coordination, in outlines, 82–83

copyright, 27, 154

Corlin, Richard F., 54
Council of Science Editors. *See* CSE documentation system
counterarguments, 180–82
CQ Researcher, 45
Creative Commons, 27
credibility
    of sources, 21, 71–72, 74–75
    of speaker, 23, 112, 170–71
    of statistics, 59
    of testimony, 56
    words for, 120–21
critical audience, 181
cross-cultural values, 41–42
CSE documentation system, 259–62
cultural background, of audience, 38, 40–42
cultural sensitivity
    in language, 121
    in listening, 29
culture, of audience, 41, 174
current events, 45

Darbelnet, Robert L., 113
data. *See* information
database
    of general search engines, 48
    subject-specific, 48
debates, 226–28, 242–43
decision making, in groups, 212
declarative sentence, main point as, 81
decoding, in communication model, 7
deductive reasoning, 178–79
deep (invisible) Web, 61
defamatory speech (slander), 22
defensive listening, 30
definition, in informative speech, 159
delivery cues, 104
delivery of speech
    body language and, 134–36
    definition of, 4
    effective, 126
    methods of, 126–29
    nonverbal, 13
    online, 204–5
    planning and practicing for, 13, 137
    speaking outline for, 13, 95, 104–8
    voice control in, 129–34
demographics, audience, 9, 37–40
demonstration, in informative speech, 159

denotative meaning, 121
derivative works, copyright and, 27
description, in informative speech, 159
devil's advocacy argument, 212
Dewey, John, six-step reflective thinking process of, 213
diagram, 140
dialect, 133–34
dialectical inquiry, 212
dialogic communication, 32
Diep, Francie, 25
digital collections, 64. *See also* library portals
digital images, 151
digital projectors, 143
digital storytelling, 143
dignity, as foundation of ethical speech, 23
directness, 126
directories, on Web
direct quotation, 25, 26
disability, of audience members, 40
disinformation, 62, 63
displays, methods of, 143–44
distractions
    listening and, 29–30
    during speech delivery, 8
diversity. *See* cultural background, of audience
DLP projectors, 143
documentation systems
    APA, 252–56
    Chicago Manual of Style, 250–52
    CSE, 259–62
    IEEE, 262
    MLA, 256–59
Dominque, Zachary, 97, 105
dress (attire), on television, 265–66
Drori, Jonathan, 54–55
dyadic communication, 6

education courses, presentations in, 243–45
education level, of audience, 39
Ehlers, Vernon, 55
elaboration likelihood model of persuasion, 173–74
    central processing of information, 173
    peripheral processing, by audience, 173–74
    peripheral processing of information, 173

electronic resources. *See* sources, print and online
emotions, in persuasive speech, 169–70
encoding, 7
engagement with audience, 126
engineering design review, 236–37
English language. *See* language; non-native speakers of English
entertainment, speeches of, 192
enthusiasm, 126
epiphora (epistrophe), 122
equipment, for online presentations, 204–5
ESL. *See* non-native speakers of English
ethics
    in business presentation, 223
    definition of, 20
    ethos of speaker and, 20–21
    fair use, copyright, and, 27
    free speech rights and, 22
    ground rules of, 23–24
    plagiarism and, 24–26
    positive public discourse and, 21
    in public speaking, 20–27
    respect for listeners' values and, 21
    statistics and, 59
ethnic background, of audience, 38, 40–42
ethos, 20,
    as classical persuasive appeal, 170–71
eulogy(ies), 195
    sample of, 197–202
evidence
    in arguments, 175
    evaluation of, 31–32
    in persuasive speech, 176–77
evidence-based practice (EBP) presentation, 246
example, definition by, 159
examples, 54–55
    brief, 54
    extended, 54
expertise, of speaker, 45, 64, 176–77
expert testimony, 56, 77
explanation, in informative speech, 160
extemporaneous speaking, 128
external evidence, 176. *See also* secondary sources

eye contact
    key-word outlines for, 97
    during speeches, 135
    on television, 265

facial expressions, of speaker, 134–35
facts, 56–57. *See also* citations; documentation systems
    claims of, 175
fair use, 27
    Creative Commons licensing for, 27
    for presentation software materials, 154
fallacies, in reasoning, 183–84
false dichotomy, 183
faulty analogy, 120
feedback
    constructive and compassionate, 32
    definition of, 7
    for improvement of speeches, 19–20
feedback loop, 32
field study presentation, 234–35
"fighting words," 22
"fight-or-flight" response, 18
figures of speech, 119
First Amendment, 22
fixed-alternative questions, 43
flip charts, 143
flowcharts, 141, 142
flowing the debate, 227
fonts, for presentation aids, 146–47
forum, 5, 217. *See also* agora
fragments. *See* sentence fragments
free speech, rights of, 22
frequency, statistical, 57
full-sentence transitions, 85

Gates, Melinda French, 55
gender, of audience, 39–40
gender-neutral language, 121
general speech purpose, 9, 48–49
generational identity, 37–38
gestures, 135–36
goals. *See* purpose of speech
Google, 48, 61
graphs, 140–41, 142
group presentations, 214–17
groups
    active participation in, 212
    audience affiliation with, 40
    communication in, 210–13
    decision making in, 212

Dewey's six-step reflective
thinking process for, 213
presentation to, 214–17
groupthink, 211

Hahn, Jacob, 188–91
handouts, 144
hasty generalization fallacy, 179,
184
hate speech, 22
health courses, presentations in,
245–47
hearing, *vs.* listening, 28
heckler's veto, 22
hierarchy of needs (Maslow),
172–73
Hofstede, Geert, 41–42
hostile audience, 181
humanities courses, presentations in, 240–43
humor
in after-dinner speeches,
196
in introduction, 112
hypothetical example, 55

identification with speaker, 37
idioms, 121
IEEE documentation system,
262
imagery, 118–19
images, digital, 151
immediacy, nonverbal, 136
impromptu speaking, 127–28
incitement ("fighting words"), 22
inclusivity, in public speaking, 6
indentation, of supporting
points, 82
individual debate format, 227
inductive reasoning, 179–80
information. *See also* sources
checking accuracy of, 63
definition of, 62
facts and statistics as, 56–59
new and interesting, 156–57
informative speech(es), 156–67
analogies in, 160–61
appeals to different learners
in, 161–62
in arts and humanities
courses, 240–43
audience involvement and,
156–57
communication strategies
in, 159–61
explaining complex infor-
mation in, 161
general purpose of, 48

increasing understanding
in, 157
organizational patterns in,
162–63
sample of, 163–67
subject matter of, 158
thesis statement in, 54
insider audience, 230, 231
inspiration, special occasion
speeches of, 196–97
Institute of Electrical and Electronics Engineers. *See* IEEE
documentation system
integrity, as foundation of ethical
speech, 23
internal previews, as transitions, 88
internal summaries, 88
Internet. *See also* websites
deep (invisible) Web
and, 61
sources and, 60–70
topic selection and, 48
interview(s). *See also* citations;
documentation systems
of audience members, 42
media, 266
oral citation for, 77
as source material, 64–66
intonation, 130–31
introduction, 11, 12, 80
motivating audience with,
157
preparing, 110–13
response to, 194
speeches of, 193
invective, 21
invention, as canon of rhetoric, 4

Jackson, Jesse, 123
jargon, 117
Jesus, 122
journal article review, 226

key-word outline, 96–97
King, Martin Luther Jr., 122,
132
Kluge, Holger, 115

language
abstract, 118
active and passive voice in,
120–21
alliterative, 122–23
for building credibility,
120–21
concrete, 118–20
culturally sensitive, 121

language *(cont.)*
> denotative *vs.* connotative
> > meaning and, 121
> figures of speech in, 119–20
> gender-neutral, 121
> imagery in, 118–19
> repetition and, 117–18
> rhetorical devices and,
> > 122–23
> simple, 117

language patterns, in dialects,
133–34
lavaliere microphone, 133
lay testimony, 56, 77
lazy speech, 132
LCD panels, 143
leadership styles, 211–12
> directive, 211
> supporting, 211
> achievement-oriented, 211
> participative, 212

leading questions, 65
learning styles, appealing to in
speeches, 161–62
lectures, 244
library portals, 60–61
licenses, for copyrighted works, 27
Lincoln, Abraham, 123
line graph, 140–41, 142
listeners. *See* audience
listening, 27–32
> active, 29, 30–31
> cultural barriers to, 29
> cultural difference in styles
> > of, 29
> defensive, 30
> definition of, 28
> distractions to, 29–30
> evaluation of evidence and
> > reasoning during, 31–32
> feedback loop and, 32
> learning by, 267–68
> obstacles to, 29–30
> responsible, 31
> selective, 28

literature review, in social sciences, 239
loaded questions, 65
logical fallacies, 179, 183–84
> begging the question fallacy,
> > 183
> either-or fallacy, 183
> in reasoning, 183–84
> non sequitur fallacy, 184
> red herring fallacy, 183
> slippery slope fallacy, 184

logos, as classical persuasive
appeal, 169

magazines
> citation of online, 73
> citation of print, 76

main points, 10–11
> as declarative sentences, 81
> identifying and retaining, 31
> organizing, 80–81
> in parallel form, 81
> preview of, 112–13
> restricting number of,
> > 80–81
> transitions between, 85

malapropisms, 120
Mandela, Nelson, eulogy of,
197–202
manuscript, speaking from,
126–27
maps, as presentation aids, 140
Maslow, Abraham, hierarchy of
needs by, 172–73
mass communication, 6
mathematics courses, presentations in, 231–35
Matthew (Bible), 123
McCabe, D. J., 163
McClellan, Mark B., 95
mean, statistical, 58
meaning
> denotative and connota-
> > tive, 121
> shared, 8

Mease, Paige, 16
media files, online, 150
> copyright for, 154

media interview, 266
median, statistical, 58
mediated communication,
265–66
meditation, for anxiety management, 18–19
medium (channel), 7
memory, speaking from, 4, 127
message, 7
metaphors, 119
methods/procedure presentation,
233–34
microphone, using, 133
Microsoft PowerPoint. *See*
PowerPoint design templates
mind (topic) mapping, 47–48, 49
misinformation, 62–63
mixed metaphors, 119
MLA documentation system,
256–59
mode, statistical, 58
models, 140
moderators, of panel discussions,
215–16

Modern Language Association. *See* MLA documentation system
monologue, 32
Monroe, Alan, motivated sequence pattern by, 186, 221
Morris, Lee, 14
motivated sequence pattern (Monroe), 186
    in sales presentation, 221
motivational warrants, 177
movement. *See also* body language
    for anxiety management, 19
multimedia, 141, 143
multitasking, while listening, 29
mumbling, 132
music files, digital, 150

narrative, sharing of, 55–56. *See also* story (narrative)
narrative pattern of arrangement, 94–95
National Issues Forum, 5
naturalness, in speech, 126
needs, Maslow's hierarchy of, 172–73
need step, in motivated sequence, 186
neutral questions, 65
noise, 8
non-native speakers of English, tips for, 267–70
nonverbal behavior, in team presentations, 217
nonverbal communication. *See* body language
nonverbal delivery, 13. *See also* body language
nonverbal immediacy, 136
Noonan, Peggy, 117
norms, cultural. *See* culture
nursing and allied health courses, presentations in, 245–47

Obama, Barack, 122, 195
    eulogy by, 197–202
offensive speech, avoiding, 22
Oliver, James, 111
one-sided message, 180
online-only publications. *See also* citations; documentation systems
    citations for, 73
online presentations, 204–10
    delivery modes for, 205–6

formats for, 206–9
planning checklist for, 209
unique demands of, 204–5
online sources, 60–70. *See also* Internet; websites
    evaluation of, 61–63, 68–69
    from library portal, 60–61
online video. *See also* citations; documentation systems
    citations for, 76
open-ended questions, 43
opinion polls, 43–44. *See also* surveys
oral citations, 24–26, 59, 70–72
    samples of, 72–73, 76–77
oral paraphrase, 25–26
oral scientific presentation, 233
oral style, 5–6, 117–18
oral summary, 25–26
oratory, 4, 127
organization of speech. *See also* outlines; patterns of organization
    of informative speeches, 162–63
    main points in, 80–81
    of persuasive speeches, 184–87
    supporting points in, 82
    transitions and, 85–88
    for unity, coherence, and balance, 84
outlines, 11–12, 95–108
    coordination and subordination in, 82, 83
    key-word, 96–97
    phrase, 96
    roman numeral, 83
    sentence, 95–96
    speaking, 13, 95, 104–5
        sample, 105–8
    working, 12–13, 95, 97
        sample, 97–104

panel discussions, 215–16
parallel form, 81
parallelism, 123
paraphrase, 25–26. *See also* citations; documentation systems
passive voice, 121
pathos, as classical persuasive appeal, 169–70
patterns of organization
    blending of, 91
    categorical, 93–94
    causal, 90–92
    comparative advantage, 186–87

patterns of organization (cont.)
motivated sequence, 186
narrative, 94–95
problem-solution, 185
refutation, 187
temporal, 89–90
topical, 93–94
pauses, in speaking, 131
percentages, statistical, 57
performance anxiety, 16. See also anxiety
personal communication, oral citation of, 77
personal knowledge and experiences, as form of supporting material, 45, 64, 176–77
personal pronouns, 118
persons with disabilities (PWD), 40
persuasive appeals
Aristotle's, 169–71
to needs and motivations, 171–74
persuasive speeches, 167–74
appeal to human psychology in, 168–69
appeal to needs and motivations in, 171–73
arguments in, 174–75
claims in, 175–76
classical appeals in, 169–71
counterarguments in, 180–82
credibility in, 170–71
culture and, 174
evidence in, 176–77
general purpose of, 49
logical fallacies and, 183–84
mental engagement in, 173–74
organization of, 184–87
reason and emotion in, 170
sample of, 188–91
thesis statement in, 54
warrants in, 175, 177–78
phrase outline, 96
phrases, 117
transitional, 88
pictograms, 141, 142
pictures, 140
pie graphs, 141, 142
pitch, vocal, 130
plagiarism, 24–26
podcast, 207–208
points. See main points; supporting points
policy, claims of, 176
policy proposal presentation, 240

political affiliation, of audience, 39
polls, opinion, 43–44. See also surveys
popping, 133
Porod, Wolfgang, 160
positive ethos, 20–21
poster presentation, 228–29
posters, 144
posture, 136
practice, of speech, 137, 215
preparation anxiety, 15
preparation outline. See working outline
pre-performance anxiety, 15–16
pre-preparation anxiety, 15
presentation(s). See also special occasion speeches; speech(es)
in arts and humanities courses, 240–43
business and professional, 218–23
compare and contrast, 242
debates as, 226–28, 242–43
in education courses, 243–45
group, 210–17
journal article review as, 226
in nursing and allied health courses, 245–47
online, 204–10
poster session as, 228–29
program evaluation as, 240
in science and mathematics courses, 231–35
service learning talk as, 229
in social science courses, 238–40
in technical courses, 235–38
vs. public speeches, 218
presentation aids, 13. See also software, presentation
crediting sources in, 76
design of, 144–48
display options for, 143–44
for group presentations, 215
media files as, 150
types of, 140–43
presentational speaking, 218
comparison to public speaking, 218
presentation (awards) speeches, 194
previews
of main points, 112–13
of topic and purpose, 112
as transitions, 85, 88
preview statement, 85, 88
primacy effect, 81
primary sources, 63, 64–67

print articles. *See also* citations; documentation systems
  oral citation of, 73
print sources, from library portal, 60–61
problem-cause-solution-feasibility pattern, 185
problem-cause-solution pattern, 185
problem-solution pattern, 92–93, 185
productive conflict, 211
professional presentations, 218–23
program evaluation presentation, 240
progress reports, 222
projectors, 143
pronouns
  gender and, 121
  personal, 118
pronunciation, 132–33
propaganda, 62
proposals
  in businesses, 218, 219–21
  policy, 240
  quality improvement, 246
props, 140
prototype, 236–37
Publication Manual of the American Psychological Association. See APA documentation system
public discourse, positive, 21
public domain, 27
public forum, 5, 217
public speaking. *See also* speech(es)
  advantages of learning, 2–4
  classical roots of, 4
  conversing, writing and, 4–5
  definition of, 6
  ethical, 20–27
  as interactive process, 7–8
  steps in process of, 8–13
public-speaking anxiety (PSA), 14. *See also* anxiety
purpose of speech
  in conclusion, 115
  general, 9, 48–49
  identification of, 48–49
  in introduction, 112
  specific, 10, 49–51

quality improvement proposal, 246
question-and-answer sessions, 263–64
questions
  in interviews, 65–66
  in introduction, 111–12
quotations. *See also* citations; documentation systems
  direct, 25, 26
  in introduction, 112

radio programs
  oral citations of, 76
  speaking on, 266
rate of speaking, 131
real-time presentations, 206
reason, appeals to in persuasive speech, 169
reasoning
  by analogy, 180
  causal, 180
  deductive and inductive, 178–80
  evaluation of, 31–32
  fallacies in, 183–84
receiver, 7
recency effect, 81
reckless disregard for truth, 22
recorded presentations, 206
reference works, oral citation of, 73
reflective thinking, Dewey's six-step method of, 213
refutation, as organizational pattern, 187
rehearsal, of group presentations, 215
relaxation response, 18–19
reliability. *See* credibility
religion, of audience, 39
repetition, 6, 117–18, 122
reports, 218–19, 220, 221–22
request for funding presentation, 237–38
request for proposal (RFP), 219
research, 238. *See also* sources
research presentation, 233
resolution, in debate, 227
respect, for audience, 23
responsibility (as ethical requirement)
  definition of, 20
  of listener, 31
  of speaker, 23
review-of-the-literature presentation, 239
rhetoric (oratory), 4, 127
rhetorical devices, 122–23
rhetorical questions, 111–12

rhythm, repetition for. *See* repetition
roast, as speech, 194–95
roles
in group presentations, 214
in groups, 210–11
roman numeral outline, 83
Roosevelt, Franklin D., 119
rough outline. *See* working outline
Runyon, Marvin, 112

Safire, William, 111
sales proposal (sales pitch), 220–21
Sandberg, Sheryl, 118
Sanford, Jenna, 19
sans serif typefaces, 146, 147
satisfaction step, in motivated sequence, 186
scale questions, 43
scanning, 135
schematic drawing, 140
science courses, presentation in, 231–35
scientific talk, 233
screencast, 206–7
scriptwriting, while listening, 30
secondary sources, 63, 67–70, 176
selective perception, 28
sender (source), 7
sentence fragments, 117
sentence outline, 95–96
serif typefaces, 146, 147
service learning presentation, 229
SES. *See* socioeconomic status
setting, of speech, 44
shared meaning, 8
shift report, in nursing and allied health courses, 247
simile, 119
six-by-six rule, of visual design, 145
skills, most desirable top ten, 2
slander, 22
small group communication, 6, 210–13
smiling, 134
social community (co-culture), 38
social news sites, 67, 70
social roles, in groups, 210–11
social science courses, presentation speeches in, 238–40
socioeconomic status (SES), of audience, 38–39

software, presentation
avoiding technical glitches with, 149
hiding behind, 149
planning with, 148–49
preparing to use, 152–53
source (sender), 7
source qualifier, 71–72
sources. *See also* citations; documentation systems; information; research; supporting material(s)
citing, 24–26, 70–77
credibility of, 21, 71–72, 74–75
on library portals, 60–61
in presentation aids, 76
primary, 63, 64–67
print and online, 60–70
qualifiers of, 71–72
secondary, 63, 67–70, 176
types of, 72–73, 76–77
spatial pattern of arrangement, 90
speaker
audience's feelings toward, 36–37
credibility of, 112, 170–71
expertise of, 45, 64, 176–77
speaking outline, 13, 95, 104–5
sample of, 105–8
steps in creating, 96
speaking rate, 131
special occasion speeches, 192–97
of acceptance, 193–94
after-dinner, 196
to celebrate, 192
to commemorate, 192
to entertain, 192
eulogies and other tributes as, 195
sample, 197–202
functions of, 192
general purpose of, 49
to inspire, 192, 196–97
of introduction, 193
of presentation, 194
roast as, 194–95
to set social agendas, 192
toast as, 194–95
specific speech purpose, 10, 49–50
vs. thesis statement, 50–51
speculative claim, 175
speech anxiety. *See* anxiety
speech points. *See* main points; supporting points

staff reports, 221–22

statistics, 56–59

stop-time technique, for anxiety control, 15–16

story (narrative). *See also* digital storytelling; narrative pattern
in introduction, 111
sharing of, 55–56

stress. *See* anxiety

stress-control breathing, 18–19

stretching, for anxiety management, 18

structured (closed-ended) questions, 42–43

style, 4, 5–6

subject matter, of informative speeches, 158

subject-specific databases, 48

subordinate points, 11–12

subordination, in outlines, 82–83

substantive warrants, 178

summary
oral, 25–26
as transition, 88

supporting material(s), 11. *See also* citations; sources
development of, 54–60
examples as, 54–55
facts and statistics as, 56–59
stories as, 55–56
testimony as, 56
variety of, 56

supporting points, 82

surveys
of audience members, 42–44
in primary research, 67

syllogism, 178–79

sympathetic audience, 182

symposium, 216–17

synchronous communication, 206

synonym, definition by, 159

tables, 141, 142

talking head, 136

target audience, 37

task roles, in groups, 210

team leader, 214

team presentations. *See* group presentations

technical presentations, 235–38

television programs
oral citations of, 76
speaking on, 265–66

temporal (chronological) pattern of arrangement, 89–90

testimony, 56, 77

thesis statement, 10, 50–51, 54

toast, as speech, 194–95

topical pattern of arrangement, 93–94

topic (mind) mapping, 47–48, 49

topic(s) of speech
in conclusion, 115
identifying possible, 44–48
in introduction, 112
listeners' feelings toward, 35–36
narrowing of, 49, 50, 52–53
selection of, 9

town hall meeting, 217

transition(s), 85–88
to signal end of speech, 114
between team speakers, 214–15

treatment plan reports, in nursing and allied health courses, 246–47

tributes, speeches as, 195

trustworthiness, of speaker, 23. *See also* credibility

truth, reckless disregard for, 22

Tufte, Edward, 146

two-sided message, 180–81

typefaces, for presentation aids, 146–47

underlining, in presentation aids, 147

uninformed audience, 182

unity, of organization, 84

unstructured (open-ended) questions, 43

vague questions, 65

value(s)
of audience, 21, 34, 41–42
claims of, 175–76
cross-cultural, 41–42
universal, 42

venues, 5

verbs, active (strong) and passive, 119, 121

Verdery, Morgan, 17

video(s), 141, 143. *See also* citations; documentation systems
online, 76, 150, 206–7

video capture software, 206

videorecording of speech practice, 137

Villarreal, Elpidio, 115

virtual presentations. *See* online presentations

visual aids. *See* presentation aids

visualization, for anxiety management, 17–18

visualization step, in motivated sequence, 186

vocal fillers, 131

vocal variety, 132

 for non-native English speakers, 269

 in online presentations, 205

vodcast, 207

voice, active and passive, 120–21

voice control

 in speaking, 129–34

 on television, 265

voice projection, 130

volume, of speaking, 130

voluntary audience, 37

warrant (in arguments), 175

 authoritative, 177–78

 motivational, 177

 substantive, 178

  by analogy, 178

  by cause, 178

watchdog Web sites, 63

Webinars, 208–9

Weblog. *See* blogs

websites. *See also* citations; documentation systems; Internet

 for digital media, 150

 evaluation of, 61–63, 68–69

 oral citation of, 76

 watchdog, 63

whiteboards, 143

Wikipedia, 67

Wilson, Phil, 119–20

word(s). *See also* language

 pronunciation and articulation of, 132–33, 269

 transitional, 88

word association, for brainstorming, 47–48

word origin, definition by, 159

working outline, 12–13, 95, 97

 sample of, 97–104

workplace, audience types in, colleagues within the field, 230–31

 expert or insider, 230–31

 lay, 230–31

 mixed, 230–31

works cited. *See* citations

QUICK TIPS

Voice Your Ideas in a Public Forum *5*
Speak with Purpose *10*
Be Aware of Your Nonverbal Delivery *13*
Envision Your Speech as a Conversation *17*
Stretch Away Stress *18*
Enjoy the Occasion *19*
Beware the Heckler's Veto *22*
Get Ahead by Listening *28*
Listening Styles and Cultural Differences *29*
Listen Responsibly *31*
Be Sensitive to Disability When Analyzing an Audience *40*
Explore Topics on *CQ Researcher* *45*
Use a Variety of Supporting Materials *56*
Use Statistics Selectively—and Memorably *58*
Avoid Cherry-Picking *59*
Dazzle Them with Digital Collection Materials *64*
Consider Audience Perception of Sources *72*
Credit Sources in Presentation Aids *76*
Save the Best for Last—or First *81*
Spend Time Organizing Speech Points *84*
Blend Organizational Patterns *91*
Find Freedom with the Topical Pattern *94*
Show Them the Transformation *111*
Bring Your Speech Full Circle *116*
Experiment with Phrases and Sentence Fragments *117*
Avoid Clichés and Mixed Metaphors *119*
Denotative versus Connotative Meaning *121*
Breathe from Your Diaphragm *130*
Control Your Rate of Speaking *131*
Use Movement to Connect *136*
Record Two Practice Sessions *137*
Hold the Handouts *144*
Beware of "Chartjunk" *146*
Using Serif and Sans Serif Type *147*
Enlighten Rather Than Advocate *156*
Don't Overwhelm the Audience *157*
Make the Introduction Motivating *157*
Use Analogies Accurately *161*
Reap the Rewards *168*
Respond to the Introduction *194*
Commemorate Life—Not Death *195*
Sounding Enthusiastic and Natural Online *205*
Put a Face to the Speaker(s) *210*
Optimize Decision Making in Groups *212*
Be Mindful of Your Nonverbal Behavior *215*
Adapt the Motivated Sequence to the Selling Situation *221*
Speak Ethically at Work *223*
Build Career Skills *223*
Flowing the Debate *227*
What Do Science-Related Courses Include? *232*
Clue the Audience in Quickly *234*
What Are the Technical Disciplines? *235*
Avoid These Technical Presentation Pitfalls *237*
Narrow Your Topic *239*
Disciplines in the Arts and Humanities *241*
Be Prepared to Lead a Discussion *242*
Focus on Interactive Learning *244*
Check for Quick Articulation *269*

SAMPLE SPEECHES

Informative Speech
◉ *Freeganism: More than a Free Lunch,* DJ McCabe   *163*

Student DJ McCabe educates his audience about the anti-consumerist movement known as freeganism.

Persuasive Speech
◉ *Becoming a Socially Conscious Consumer,* Jacob Hahn   *188*

Organizing his speech using Monroe's motivated sequence pattern, student Jacob Hahn argues that consumers share a responsibility to ensure safer conditions for workers.

Special Occasion Speech
*President Obama Speaks at a Memorial Service
    for Nelson Mandela   197*

U.S. President Barack Obama delivers a powerful eulogy for South African President Nelson Mandela to an audience over over 70,000 people in Johannesburg, South Africa.

VISUAL GUIDES

Selecting a Topic
*From Source to Speech: Narrowing Your Topic to Fit Your
    Audience   52*

Finding Credible Sources on the Internet
From Source to Speech: Evaluating Web Sources   68

Citing Sources in Your Speech
*From Source to Speech: Demonstrating Your Sources' Credibility
    and Accuracy   74*

Organizing the Speech
From Point to Point: Using Transitions to Guide Your Listeners   86

A Brief Guide to Presentation Software
*From Slide Show to Presentation: Getting Ready to Deliver a
    PowerPoint, Keynote, or Prezi Presentation   152*

CHECKLISTS

Getting Started
Steps in Gaining Confidence   *20*
An Ethical Inventory   *23*
Correctly Quote, Paraphrase, and Summarize Information   *26*
Dealing with Distractions While Delivering a Speech   *30*

Development
Appeal to Audience Attitudes, Beliefs, and Values   *36*
Reviewing Your Speech in the Light of Audience Demographics   *41*
Narrowing Your Topic   *50*
Identifying the Speech Topic, Purpose, and Thesis   *51*
Evaluating Your Research Needs   *60*
Finding Speeches Online   *65*
Preparing for the Interview   *66*
Offering Key Source Information   *77*

Organization
Reviewing Main and Supporting Points   *82*
Determining an Organizational Pattern   *94*
Steps in Creating a Speaking Outline   *108*

Starting, Finishing, and Styling

Guidelines for Preparing the Introduction *110*
Craft an Effective Introduction *113*
Guidelines for Preparing the Conclusion *114*
Craft an Effective Conclusion *116*
Using Effective Oral Style *123*

Delivery

Successful Delivery *129*
Practice Check for Vocal Effectiveness *132*
Tips on Using a Microphone *133*
Tips for Using Effective Facial Expressions *135*
Using Gestures Effectively *136*

Presentation Aids

Create Effective Line, Bar, and Pie Graphs *141*
Incorporating Presentation Aids into Your Speech *144*
Apply the Principles of Simplicity and Continuity *148*
Tips for Successfully Using Presentation Software in Your Speech *154*

Types of Speeches

Strategies for Explaining Complex Information *161*
🄴 Be a Culturally Sensitive Persuader
Identify the Nature of Your Claim *176*
Strategies for Addressing Counterarguments *182*

Online, Group, and Business Contexts

Guidelines for Introducing Other Speakers *193*
Creating a Podcast *207*
Online Presentation Planning *209*
Group Presentation Tips *216*
Using Monroe's Motivated Sequence in a Sales Presentation *221*

Speaking in Other College Courses

Tips on Presenting to a Mixed Audience *231*
Focusing Your Scientific Talk *233*
Steps in Preparing a Focused Scientific Presentation *235*

Sample Speech Videos ●●●●

LaunchPadSolo Go to LaunchPad: macmillanhighered .com/pocketspeak5e to find over 220 videos, including model speech clips and "needs improvement" clips, on a variety of speech topics that show you how to improve your technique and deliver a strong, effective speech.

Here's a list of topics and the number of videos available for each one noted:

- ▶ Ethics (4)
- ▶ Audience Interaction (4)
- ▶ Supporting Material (23)
- ▶ Choosing a Topic (7)
- ▶ Organization (24)

- ▶ Thesis Statement (8)
- ▶ Introductions (15)
- ▶ Conclusions (15)
- ▶ Language (21)
- ▶ Methods of Delivery (7)

- ▶ Body in Delivery (7)
- ▶ Vocal Delivery (8)
- ▶ Speeches of Introduction (3)
- ▶ Informative Speaking (23)
- ▶ Persuasive Speaking (27)

- ▶ Special Occasion Speaking (4)
- ▶ Argument (11)
- ▶ Presentation Aids (11)

Contents ●●●●

Part 1 • Getting Started   1

1. Becoming a Public Speaker   2
A Vital Life Skill
Classical Roots
Learning to Speak
Speech as Communication
An Interactive Process

2. Speech Overview   8
Analyze the Audience
Select a Topic
Speech Purpose
Thesis Statement
Main Points
Supporting Materials
Separate Speech Parts
Outline
Presentation Aids
Delivery

3. Speech Anxiety   13
Causes of Anxiety
Onset of Anxiety
Boosting Confidence
Relaxation Techniques
Using Movement
Learning from Feedback

4. Ethics   20
Character
Audience Values
Positive Public Discourse
Free Speech and Responsibility
Ethical Ground Rules
Avoid Plagiarism
Fair Use, Copyright, and Ethics

5. Listening   27
Selective Listening
Listening Obstacles
Active Listening
Evaluating Evidence
Exchanging Ideas
Feedback

Part 2 • Development   33

6. Audience Analysis   34
Psychology
Demographics
Culture
Seeking Information
Setting and Context

7. Topic and Purpose   44
Where to Begin
General Speech Purpose
Narrowed Topic
From Source to Speech:
  Narrowing Your Topic to Fit
  Your Audience

8. Developing Support   54
Examples

Stories
Testimony
Facts and Statistics
Oral References

9. Finding Credible Sources in Print and Online   60
Using a Library Portal
Evaluate Sources
Mix Primary and Secondary Sources
Primary Sources
Secondary Sources
From Source to Speech:
  Evaluating Web Sources

10. Citing Sources   70
Source Information
Delivery
Sample Oral Citations
From Source to Speech:
  Demonstrating Source Credibility

Part 3 • Organization   79

11. Organizing the Body of the Speech   80
Main Points
Supporting Points
Coordination and Subordination
Organization
Transitions
From Point to Point:
  Using Transitions

12. Organizational Patterns   89
Chronological
Spatial
Causal (Cause-Effect)
Problem-Solution
Topical
Narrative

13. Outlining the Speech   95
Create Two Outlines
Working Outlines
Speaking Outlines

Part 4 • Starting, Finishing, and Styling   109

14. Introductions and Conclusions   110

15. Language   117
Writing for the Ear
Concrete Words, Vivid Imagery
Building Credibility
Creating an Impression

Part 5 • Delivery   125

16. Methods of Delivery   126

17. The Voice   129
Volume